Project Management Institute

SOFTWARE EXTENSION TO THE PMBOK® GUIDE FIFTH EDITION

Library of Congress Cataloging-in-Publication Data

Software Extension to the PMBOK® Guide Fifth Edition.
    pages cm
 Includes bibliographical references and index.
 ISBN-13: 978-1-62825-013-8 (alk. paper)
 ISBN-10: 1-62825-013-5 (alk. paper)
 1. Project management--Data processing. I. Project Management Institute. II. Guide to the project management body of
knowledge (PMBOK guide)
 HD69.P75S63 2013
 658.4'0402855--dc23

                                        2013023767

ISBN: 978-1-62825-013-8

Published by:
    Project Management Institute, Inc.
    14 Campus Boulevard
    Newtown Square, Pennsylvania 19073-3299 USA
    Phone: +610-356-4600
    Fax: +610-356-4647
    Email: customercare@pmi.org
    Internet: www.PMI.org

NOTICE

The Project Management Institute, Inc. (PMI) standards and guideline publications, of which the document contained herein is one, are developed through a voluntary consensus standards development process. This process brings together volunteers and/or seeks out the views of persons who have an interest in the topic covered by this publication. While PMI administers the process and establishes rules to promote fairness in the development of consensus, it does not write the document and it does not independently test, evaluate, or verify the accuracy or completeness of any information or the soundness of any judgments contained in its standards and guideline publications.

PMI disclaims liability for any personal injury, property or other damages of any nature whatsoever, whether special, indirect, consequential or compensatory, directly or indirectly resulting from the publication, use of application, or reliance on this document. PMI disclaims and makes no guaranty or warranty, expressed or implied, as to the accuracy or completeness of any information published herein, and disclaims and makes no warranty that the information in this document will fulfill any particular purposes or needs. PMI does not undertake to guarantee the performance of any individual manufacturer or seller's products or services by virtue of this standard or guide.

In publishing and making this document available, PMI is not undertaking to render professional or other services for or on behalf of any person or entity, nor is PMI undertaking to perform any duty owed by any person or entity to someone else. Anyone using this document should rely on his or her own independent judgment or, as appropriate, seek the advice of a competent professional in determining the exercise of reasonable care in any given circumstances. Information and other standards on the topic covered by this publication may be available from other sources, which the user may wish to consult for additional views or information not covered by this publication.

PMI has no power, nor does it undertake to police or enforce compliance with the contents of this document. PMI does not certify, test, or inspect products, designs, or installations for safety or health purposes. Any certification or other statement of compliance with any health or safety-related information in this document shall not be attributable to PMI and is solely the responsibility of the certifier or maker of the statement.

TABLE OF CONTENTS

LIST OF TABLES AND FIGURES

©2013 Project Management Institute. *Software Extension to the PMBOK® Guide Fifth Edition*

FOREWORD

Professional project managers understand that not every project can or should be managed exactly the same as every other. The nature of the industry, the organization, the project itself, or requirements of the project sponsors combine in unique ways for every project. Project managers are expected to know how to customize their approach to suit the specific requirements of the project and its sponsor.

The Project Management Institute (PMI) and the IEEE Computer Society have joined together to develop specific guidance for managers of software development projects. A committee of volunteers from both organizations, all experts in project management and in software development, have developed this *Software Extension to the PMBOK® Guide Fifth Edition*.

A Guide to the Project Management Body of Knowledge (PMBOK® Guide) – Fifth Edition is the latest in the seminal series of standards for the profession that identifies the most effective global practices in project management. The *PMBOK® Guide* provides a foundation that is fundamental for the universal standard practice of project management across industries, geographies, and project types. This *Software Extension* serves as an essential companion to the *PMBOK® Guide* written specifically to provide guidance for those who lead software development projects.

Both PMI and the IEEE Computer Society have approved this *Software Extension*, which is published under the logos of both organizations. We enthusiastically recommend this *Software Extension to the PMBOK® Guide Fifth Edition* to project managers worldwide.

Mark A. Langley, President & CEO
Project Management Institute

Angela Burgess, Executive Director
IEEE Computer Society

PREFACE

A Guide to the Project Management Body of Knowledge (*PMBOK® Guide*) is the globally recognized standard for the project management profession. The knowledge contained in the *PMBOK® Guide* has evolved from the good practices of the project management practitioners who contributed to the development of the standard. In a similar manner, the knowledge contained in this *Software Extension to the PMBOK® Guide* – Fifth Edition includes good practices of software project management contributed by the PMI – IEEE Computer Society *Software Extension* committee, the subject matter experts, and the public reviewers, all of whom provided insightful comments and recommendations. This *Software Extension*, like the *PMBOK® Guide*, does not cover every conceivable situation but rather presents generally recognized good practices.

Many of the 47 processes in the *PMBOK® Guide* are applicable to the management of software projects. This extension builds upon the *PMBOK® Guide* by describing additional knowledge and practices and by modifying some of them. It is intended to be consistent with the *PMBOK® Guide*. The primary contribution of this extension to the *PMBOK® Guide* is description of processes that are applicable for managing adaptive life cycle software projects. Adaptive development methods and life cycles are well suited for development of software and management of software projects because they take advantage of the intangible nature of software. Used together, the *PMBOK® Guide* and this extension provide a balanced view of methods, tools, and techniques for managing software projects across the life cycle continuum from highly predictive life cycles to highly adaptive life cycles.

This *Software Extension* is written in the style of, and follows the structure of the *PMBOK® Guide*. For consistency and ease of reference, the paragraph naming and numbering coincides with the *PMBOK® Guide*. This extension is also based on the relevant ISO/IEC and IEEE standards for software engineering. These standards are cited, as appropriate, throughout this extension.

1

INTRODUCTION

This *Software Extension to the PMBOK® Guide Fifth Edition* describes commonly accepted practices for managing software projects; it addresses those practices applicable for managing projects to develop new software and to modify existing software. The objective of this *Software Extension* is to expand and elaborate on the project management processes, tools, and techniques and the vocabulary found in *A Guide to the Project Management Body of Knowledge (PMBOK® Guide) –* Fifth Edition [1],[1] and to provide more specific and precise terms, processes, and methods for managing software projects.

Many project managers, including those certified by PMI, can improve their ability to manage projects that involve development or modification of software by increasing their knowledge and skills concerning the processes, methods, tools, and techniques used to manage software projects, as covered in this extension to the *PMBOK® Guide*. Conversely, software project managers can improve their knowledge and skills to manage their projects by understanding the practices that are documented in the *PMBOK® Guide*.

Software project managers and their project teams develop and modify application software, system software, and the software elements of software-intensive systems. Application software is constructed using interfaces to system software, communication protocols, and software development tools. Application software provides capabilities for computer users, such as word processing, spreadsheets, accounting software, and multimedia players.

System software is the infrastructure software that provides the platform on which application software is developed and executed. It includes operating system components such as a scheduler, memory manager, and input/output software.

A software-intensive system is a collection of hardware, software, and, in some cases, manual procedures performed by operational personnel who are elements of the total system. In these systems, software is the primary component that integrates and coordinates the operation of the system. Software-intensive systems sometimes incorporate special purpose hardware and may require tailoring of the operating system, communication protocols, and other infrastructure components. The scope of the product to be developed for a software-intensive system includes components to be developed or modified in addition to the software, which is not the case for application software.

Application software, system software, and software-intensive systems support all aspects of modern society, ranging from information technology support for organizations, to large ERP (enterprise resource planning) systems for running business operations, to network communication protocols, to operating systems, to embedded software in home appliances, automobiles, mobile phones, spacecraft, consumer products, and aviation; as well as software for fields such as defense, life sciences, transportation, energy sector, finance, banking and insurance, research and development, simulation and training, recreational games, and software tools used to develop software (software

---

[1] The numbers in brackets refer to the list of references at the end of this *Software Extension*.

editors, language compilers, database tools, etc.). Development and modification of software often affect and are affected by operational policies and business practices.

Managers of software projects face increasing challenges as software projects grow larger and more complex at an increasing rate, with increasing expectations of customers and users; with the need for compliance with government, industry, and organizational policies; with the technological challenges of frequently updated hardware and software platforms; with increasing interplay between hardware development, firmware development, and software development; and the considerations related to the ergonomics of the human elements of these systems. In addition, software projects often involve issues of safety, security, reliability, and other quality requirements. Expanding global markets provide software products to a wider variety of cultures, languages, and ways of life, thus increasing the scope and complexity of software to be developed and modified.

1.1 Purpose of the *Software Extension to the PMBOK® Guide*

The primary purpose of the *PMBOK® Guide* is to identify and document that subset of the Project Management Body of Knowledge generally recognized as good practice on most projects, most of the time. The purpose of this *Software Extension to the PMBOK® Guide Fifth Edition* is to supplement the *PMBOK® Guide* with knowledge and practices that can improve the efficiency and effectiveness of software project managers, their management teams, and their project members.

As stated in Section 1.1 of the *PMBOK® Guide* "good practice for most projects, most of the time" does not mean the knowledge described should always be applied uniformly to all projects; the organization and/or project management team is responsible for determining what is appropriate for any given project or situation. A similar statement applies to this *Software Extension*.

While this extension focuses on management of software development projects, it will also be useful to organizations that engage in IT projects. First, these organizations need to manage solutions that involve development or modification of IT software. These projects may require in-house development of application software or software-intensive systems; this extension applies directly to those projects. Second, organizations may outsource IT software development to external third-party organizations. In these cases, this extension provides helpful information to those responsible for monitoring the external effort. The information can be used to review a third-party's project plans, analyze project status, identify and confront risks, and understand issues that may arise during the course of the contract. Third, most of the organizational and team considerations explained in this document apply equally to IT technology development. Similar considerations apply to engineering projects.

The *PMBOK® Guide* also provides and promotes a common vocabulary within the project management profession for discussing, writing about, and applying project management terminology and concepts. Like all professional disciplines, the software domain has a specialized vocabulary for discussing, writing about, and applying software terminology and concepts. Software project terminology is documented in the glossary to this *Software Extension* and in ISO/IEC/IEEE Standard 24765 (SEVOCAB) [2], which provides terminology for software, hardware, and systems. In cases of conflicting terminology for project management, the Glossary in the *PMBOK® Guide* and the *PMI Lexicon of Project Management Terms* [3] shall prevail.

The *PMBOK® Guide* also references and explains the purpose of the *Project Management Institute Code of Ethics and Professional Conduct* [4] (see www.PMI.org). For information on software engineering ethics, consult the *IEEE Software Engineering Code of Ethics and Professional Practice* [5], which was developed as a resource for teaching and practicing software engineering and was adopted by the IEEE Computer Society and the Association for Computing Machinery. In addition, the Association of Information Technology Professionals (AITP) has developed a code of ethics [6]. See also the American Society for Information Science and Technology (AIS&T) *Professional Guidelines* [7].

1.1.1 Audience for the *Software Extension* to the *PMBOK® Guide*

The audience for this *Software Extension* includes, but is not limited to:

- Project managers;
- Software project managers;
- Functional managers;
- System analysts;
- System designers;
- Software architects;
- Software team leaders;
- Software systems engineers;
- System software developers;
- Application software developers;
- Test engineers;
- Verification and validation (V&V) personnel;
- Information systems and software security specialists;
- Project infrastructure personnel;
- IT infrastructure personnel;
- Web developers;
- IT project managers;
- Software process engineers;
- Business analysts, enterprise architects, business continuity planners, and those in related disciplines;
- IT CIOs, strategists, directors, analysts, solution designers, solution providers, IT security engineers, and service personnel;
- Program managers;
- Portfolio managers;

- Product managers;
- Customers;
- Acquirers;
- System integrators; and
- Other stakeholders who affect, or are affected by, a software project.

1.2 What is a Project?

According to Section 1.2 of the *PMBOK® Guide*, a project is a temporary endeavor undertaken to create a unique product, service, or result. Attributes of projects, including software projects, are described in Section 1.2 of the *PMBOK® Guide*. Software projects, like all projects, are undertaken to achieve a specific objective. In addition to creating new products, software projects are often undertaken to modify an existing software product, to integrate a set of existing software components, to extend the capabilities of software products, or to modify the software infrastructure of an organization.

Software projects may also be undertaken to satisfy service requests, maintenance needs, or to provide operations support. These activities may occur as level-of-effort (LOE) activities; they are considered projects when they are specified as temporary endeavors to provide deliverables and outcomes. Software product life cycles, in contrast to project life cycles, typically involve maintenance and support activities that include both projects and level of effort activities. IT projects, such as design of an enterprise information system, IT service transition to another vendor, or deploying a solution to end users are not software projects in the traditional sense, but many of the concepts and practices described in this extension can prove useful in IT organizations. Similarly, projects in the traditional engineering disciplines and knowledge-based projects will find this *Software Extension* to be useful.

1.2.1 The Relationships Among Portfolios, Programs, and Projects

Section 1.2.1 of the *PMBOK® Guide* describes the relationships that exist among portfolios, programs, and projects; see also Figure 1-1 of the *PMBOK® Guide*. Specifics that apply to management of portfolios, programs, and software projects are illustrated in Figure 1-1 and discussed in Section 1.4 of this *Software Extension*.

1.3 What is Project Management?

According to Section 1.3 of the *PMBOK® Guide*, project management is the application of knowledge, skills, tools, and techniques for project activities to meet the project requirements. Project management is accomplished through the appropriate application and integration of the 47 logically grouped project management processes comprising five Process Groups. These five Process Groups are:

- Initiating,
- Planning,

- Executing,
- Monitoring and Controlling, and
- Closing.

The unique nature of software, as described in Section 1.2.1 of this extension, allows the elements of the 47 processes within the 5 Process Groups of the *PMBOK® Guide* to be overlapped, interleaved, and iterated in various ways, which results in modifications of and extension to the methods, tools, and techniques in the *PMBOK® Guide* that are used to manage software projects.

According to Section 1.3 of the *PMBOK® Guide*, project management involves balancing competing constraints, which include but are not limited to:

- Scope,
- Quality,
- Schedule,
- Budget,
- Resources, and
- Risk.

Technological factors that can place constraints on software projects and software products include:

- State of hardware and software technology;
- Hardware platforms, software platforms, operating systems, and communication protocols;
- IT architecture integrity, limitations, and protocols;
- Software development tools;
- Software architecture;
- Backward and forward compatibility requirements;
- Reuse of software components from a library;
- Use of open source versus closed source software components;
- Use of customer-supplied software components;
- Interfaces to hardware and other software; and
- Creation and use of intellectual property.

Other factors that can place constraints on software projects include but are not limited to requirements for system safety, security compliance, reliability, availability, scalability, performance, testability, information assurance, localization, maintainability, supportability, regulations, customers' policies, infrastructure support, team member availability and skills, software development environment and methods, and organizational maturity and capability.

1.3.1 Why Software Project Management Is Challenging

Every discipline has unique aspects that differentiate it from other disciplines. Within those disciplines, the general principles of project management are adapted to account for the special aspects of the projects in those disciplines. Many factors make software projects and management of software projects challenging. Some of those factors are:

- Software projects are challenging because software is an intangible and malleable product; source code for software is written text. In most cases, teams of software developers generate and revise shared documents (e.g., requirements, design specifications, code, and test plans). Software development is often characterized as a learning process in which knowledge is gained and information is generated during the project.

- Key attributes that make software projects challenging are complexity of the project and the product, nonlinear scaling of resources, measurement of project and product, initial uncertainty in project and product scope, and knowledge gained as a project evolves.

- Software requirements often change during a software project as knowledge is gained and the scope of the project and the product emerge.

- Requirements for new and modified software often influence, and are influenced by, an organization's business processes and the workflow processes of employees.

- Intellectual capital of software personnel is the primary capital asset for software projects and software development organizations because software is a direct product of human cognitive processes.

- Communication and coordination within software teams and with project stakeholders often lack clarity. Many of the tools and techniques used in software engineering are intended to improve communication and coordination.

- Creation of software requires innovative problem solving to create unique solutions. Most software projects develop unique products because replication of existing software is a simple process, as compared to replication of physical artifacts. Software projects are more akin to research and development projects than to construction or manufacturing projects.

- Software projects involve risk and uncertainty because they require innovation, the product is intangible, and stakeholders may not effectively articulate or agree upon the needs to be satisfied by the software product.

- Initial planning and estimation for software projects is challenging because these activities depend on requirements, which are often imprecise or part of historical data that is often missing or inapplicable. Preparation of accurate estimates is also challenging because the efficiency and effectiveness of software developers is widely variable.

- Product complexity makes development and modification of software challenging because of the enormous number of logical paths within program modules combined with data values that exercise the paths, and the combinations of interface details among program modules.

- Exhaustive testing of software is impractical because of the time that would be required to test all logical paths and interfaces under all combinations of input data and other input stimuli.

- Software development often involves inclusion of different vendor products and development of interfaces to other software; this may result in integration and performance issues.

- Because most software is interconnected, information security techniques are necessary. Software security is a large and growing challenge.

- Objective quantification and measurement of software quality is difficult because of the intangible nature of software.

- Software developers use processes, methods, and tools that are constantly evolving and are frequently updated.

- Software is often the element of a system that is changed when functionality, behavior, or quality attributes are to be changed.

- A software product may be required to operate on a variety of hardware platforms and infrastructure software.

- Executable software is not a stand-alone product. It is executed on computing hardware and is often an element of a system consisting of diverse hardware, other software, and manual procedures.

- Platform technologies, infrastructure software, and vendor-supplied software are frequently changed or updated, which can necessitate changes to the software being developed.

Like many products of knowledge work, software is intangible; it is not a physical entity that can be evaluated by traditional measures (mass, volume, conductivity, specific gravity). It is, however, constrained by factors such as the processing hardware, available memory, and communication bandwidth.

The intangible nature of software creates challenges in measuring the current state of the product, which in turn complicates monitoring and controlling a software project. Traditional approaches, such as work breakdown structures, schedule networks, and earned value reporting, are tailored to fit the needs of software projects. These traditional techniques are augmented with techniques such as iterative and/or incremental development with frequent demonstrations of partially completed software.

The malleable nature of software has both positive and negative connotations for managing software projects. On the positive side, the malleability of software makes it possible to sometimes (but not always) respond rapidly to changing user needs and other environmental factors, as compared to changing the elements of computer hardware or other physical artifacts. On the negative side, interrupting ongoing work to responding to requested changes may overwhelm schedule and budget constraints.

Every software project is a unique endeavor because replication (i.e., copying) of existing software is a straightforward process—unlike replication of the physical artifacts of manufacturing and construction projects. Every software project is thus an undertaking that produces a unique product. The goal of manufacturing is to repeatedly produce artifacts that are as nearly identical as possible, given the constraints of material science and practicalities of manufacturing technology and market acceptability; whereas the goal of a software project is to produce one perfect copy of a software product, within the constraints of schedule, budget, resources, and software and hardware technology.

Software is a direct product of the cognitive processes of individuals engaged in intellect-intensive, innovative teamwork. While it is true that all engineers engage in intellect-intensive teamwork, the fact that software is developed and modified without the intervening constraints of physical media or manufacturing processes makes software teamwork different in kind from teamwork in other engineering disciplines. As a result, many of the procedures and techniques used in software project management are designed to facilitate communication and coordination among team members engaged in closely coordinated, intellect-intensive work.

Accurate planning and estimation of cost and schedule is difficult for all kinds of projects, but it is particularly difficult for software projects because: (1) software is developed and modified by the cognitive work activities of the developers, (2) productivity among individual software developers varies widely (in both quantity and quality of work), (3) requirements upon which estimates are based are often poorly defined, and (4) continuing evolution of technology may make historical data inaccurate for new projects. For these reasons, current software development methods tend to focus on developing an expanding set of product increments so that tradeoffs among schedule, budget, resources, functionality, and quality attributes can be continually adjusted.

Productivity in software projects includes both quantity and quality of work. The amount of software written (i.e., number of lines of code) is not a good measure of programmer productivity; a programmer who writes a small, efficient program is more productive in contributing to a successful outcome than a programmer who writes a large, inefficient program. Similarly, a programmer who rushes through a task but makes many mistakes that will require corrective rework is less productive than a programmer who proceeds more slowly but produces a program that has fewer defects. Productivity of programmers with similar backgrounds and experience, as measured by quantity and quality of the resulting software, has been repeatedly demonstrated to vary by factors of 10 and more [8, 9].

With the advent of widespread interconnectivity, software security has become a major consideration when building or modifying a software product. Like other quality attributes, security attributes need to be planned, designed, constructed, verified, and validated. Like other quality attributes, software security cannot be "tested in."

Software projects are also difficult because software is always part of a system. Software as a stand-alone entity is useless; to be of use, software is executed on digital hardware. In some cases, a software project is one element of a development program that involves the accompanying development of hardware components or development of related software by other projects. In other cases, development of software may be limited to developing application software for a population of known users. In these cases, the system includes specified computer, operating system, and programming language or languages to provide the needed capabilities.

1.4 Relationships with Program and Portfolio Management

The information in Section 1.4 of the *PMBOK® Guide* is equally applicable to software projects and their relationships with program and portfolio management.

The relationships among projects, programs, and portfolios are illustrated in Figure 1-1.

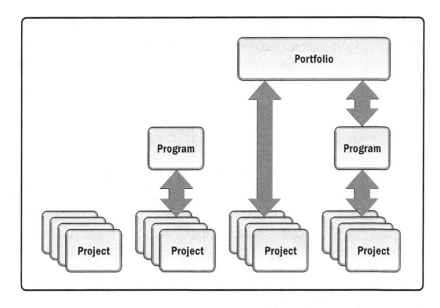

Figure 1-1. Relationships Among Portfolios, Programs, and Projects

Many software projects are not parts of programs and not all organizations manage software projects on a portfolio basis. In these cases, each software project exists as an independent entity. Some software projects may be part of programs and some programs may be included in portfolios.

Software product lines are similar to programs. A product line consists of a base component that supports additions and extensions, which result in specific products within the product line. For example, a product line could consist of a base component for financial accounting to which different user interfaces are added to accommodate different languages and cultures. A product baseline may evolve over time. Product lines are sometimes included in portfolios.

While software has a strong impact on organizations and their operations (both infrastructure software and application software), there are different ways in which software can generate value, for example, financial value, social value, public welfare, and impact on work places and recreational environments. Therefore, establishing prioritization criteria for programs and projects within a portfolio may be a difficult balancing act among different value criteria.

1.4.1 Portfolio Management

As stated in the *PMBOK® Guide,* a portfolio refers to a collection of projects or programs and other work that are grouped together to facilitate effective management of that work to meet strategic business objectives.

Organizations whose primary mission is the development and modification of software sometimes treat software projects as elements of a portfolio in order to increase efficiency and effectiveness of their work activities and to engage in process improvement initiatives that will be of benefit to all projects within the organization's portfolio. Within a portfolio, software projects are prioritized for execution based on parameters such as: complexity, degree of uncertainty, business value, return on investment, and so forth. Standardized life cycle frameworks that can be tailored for each project are important elements of portfolio management for software organizations.

1.4.2 Program Management

Software is sometimes regarded as a secondary system component in programs that involve development of diverse components; as a result, there may be no explicitly designated software project manager. Given the central role of software in current systems and the impact software has on system characteristics (as well as software being a primary component that can impact completion of a system on a predetermined schedule), a designated software project manager should be a member of the program management team.

1.4.3 Projects and Strategic Planning

In addition to the strategic considerations for authorizing projects, as mentioned in the *PMBOK® Guide*, software projects are sometimes undertaken to explore the feasibility of using a new development process within a specific context (such as an adaptive project life cycle model), to explore and learn a new technology (such as cloud computing), to develop a prototype of a new style of user interface (such as a holographic or 3-dimensional display), or to exploit a software-based innovation (such as including a multimedia interface to a software application). In these cases, the business value of the software project is not the output product but the institutional knowledge gained from the project.

1.4.4 Project Management Office

In addition to the functions and objectives cited in the *PMBOK® Guide,* a project management office (PMO) that manages a collection of software projects (perhaps in addition to managing other kinds of projects) may also:

- Provide a common repository for data relating to effort, cost, schedule, defects, stakeholders, and risk factors collected from software projects within an organization;
- Use the data repository to develop one or more cost models;
- Use the data repository to analyze strengths and weaknesses among software projects as a basis for process improvement initiatives and for analyzing the results of process improvement activities;
- Assist project managers in making cost and schedule estimates and preparing project plans;
- Provide templates, forms, and automated data collection;
- Acquire and harmonize the use of new tools and platforms for software development, program management, and portfolio management throughout the organization;
- Maintain a library of reusable code modules;

- Manage shared resources;
- Ensure the business value of each software project;
- Disseminate trends in factors such as methods, tools and techniques, life cycle management, and usability patterns and techniques throughout the organization; and
- Provide training for project managers and project teams.

In some organizations, a PMO may also be involved in project management process compliance audits, project management maturity assessment, and process improvement initiatives. Project management offices, like software projects, may be subject to organizational constraints. A PMO for software projects may be a stand-alone entity or an element of a larger organizational PMO. Some IT organizations have an information technology project management office that handles multiple projects (e.g., infrastructure, telecom, networking, etc.).

1.5 The Relationship Between Project Management, Operations Management, and Organizational Strategy

As stated in the *PMBOK® Guide*, operations are an organizational function performing the ongoing execution of activities that produce the same product or provide a repetitive service. Operations evolve to support the day-to-day business, and are necessary to achieve strategic and tactical goals of the business. An example of operations management is software and IT infrastructure support and maintenance.

Software production support may include supporting processes for elements such as software component integration, software configuration management, software quality assurance, software release management, and software system testing. Some or all of these supporting processes may be under the control of the software project manager; however, separate organizational units may provide some or perhaps all of them. When these supporting processes are provided by separate organizational units, the software project manager provides coordination across organizational boundaries to ensure the project achieves its goals.

1.5.1 Operational Issues and Project Management

Software project managers are sometimes responsible for sustaining the operation of one or more software systems while simultaneously developing a new system or a new version of an existing system. Operations personnel may report defects to be fixed in an existing system or request enhancements to an existing system. Updates in vendor-supplied software may need to be installed. Fixing defects, providing enhancements, and installing updates may divert resources from the project at hand and thus disrupt schedules and budgets.

1.5.1.1 Operations Management

As stated in Section 1.5.1.1 of the *PMBOK® Guide*, operations management is a subject area that is outside the scope of formal project management. However, estimates of product life cycle sustainment costs may be made during the initiation and planning phases of a software project.

1.5.1.2 Operational Stakeholders in Software Project Management

The *PMBOK® Guide* distinguishes between operational personnel and product users. While operations management is different from project management (see Section 1.5.1.1 of the *PMBOK® Guide*), the needs of the stakeholders who perform and conduct business operations are important considerations in managing software projects. The software supported by and used by operational personnel exerts a strong influence on the efficiency and effectiveness of their work processes and procedures; therefore the inputs of operational stakeholders are important sources of requirements that software projects strive to satisfy. It is important to address requirements that will improve the efficiency and effectiveness of sustainment; software project managers may also consider issues related to deployment, replacement, and retirement/disposal (end of life) of the software product.

1.5.2 Organizational Issues and Software Project Management

As stated in the *PMBOK® Guide,* governance usually sets high-level strategic direction and performance parameters. The strategy provides the purpose, expectations, goals, and actions necessary to guide business pursuit, and is aligned with business objectives.

IEEE Standards 15528 [10] and 12207 [11], the constellation of CMMI capability maturity models (for acquisition, development, services, people) [12, 13, 14, 15], and various safety and security standards are used by many software and IT organizations as frameworks for specifying strategic directions and performance parameters. They also serve as models for process and product improvement initiatives.

1.5.2.1 Project-Based Organizations

Many software organizations are project-based. As stated in the *PMBOK® Guide*, project-based organizations weaken the hierarchy and bureaucracy inside the organizations as the success of the work is measured by the final result rather than position or politics. A project-based organization is desirable for software projects, which are often comprised of self-enabling teams of creative individuals.

1.5.2.2 Link Between Project Management and Organizational Governance

As stated in the *PMBOK® Guide,* projects (and programs) are undertaken to achieve strategic business outcomes, for which many organizations now adopt formal organizational governance processes and procedures. Some IT projects are undertaken to develop and modify information systems that are crucial to organizational governance, including those that provide data warehousing, data mining, trend analysis, and other business intelligence. In addition to developing software to support organizational governance, software and IT projects are also constrained by governance policies.

In addition, software projects are conducted for external customers who may require that certain processes and procedures be followed when developing software that may place at risk the health, safety, or welfare of the public. There may also be compliance requirements, such as Sarbanes-Oxley in the United States or the policies governing development of medical devices that contain software. Many IT organizations use COBIT 5 for the governance of

Enterprise IT.[2] The type of contract with an external customer may also affect the way in which a software project is governed.

1.5.2.3 The Relationship Between Project Management and Organizational Strategy

The statements in Section 1.5.2.3 of the *PMBOK® Guide* apply equally to software projects, which should be undertaken to support the strategies and goals of the organization. Successful software organizations align their projects with the organization's strategic goals to ensure that organizational assets are best utilized towards the attainment of those goals.

1.6 Business Value

According to Section 1.6 of the *PMBOK® Guide,* business value is defined as the entire value of the business; the total sum of all tangible and intangible elements. A software product may be a proprietary product of the business and provide a major revenue stream for that business or business unit. In some cases, infrastructure and customer support software may be capitalized and depreciated over time. Software products are sometimes developed for use across multiple systems, thus increasing the business value of those products.

Because software is the product of closely coordinated teamwork that is often innovative, the intellectual capital of a software organization (the software developers, maintainers, and other software personnel) is an especially important element of business value. Another important element of business value for software organizations is the set of processes, procedures, and techniques that enable software project managers and product developers to be efficient and effective by enhancing communication and coordination among individuals, teams, projects, programs, clients, users, customers, customer bases, and other external stakeholders. Proprietary and unique processes, procedures, and techniques that provide business also add business value.

1.7 The Role of a Project Manager

As stated in Section 1.7 of the *PMBOK® Guide*, the role of a project manager is distinct from that of a functional manager or an operations manager. However, software project work may be organized by product component (e.g., user interface, database, computation, and communication software), functionally by process component (e.g., analysis, design, construction, testing, and installation/training processes), or by subsystem (e.g., weather, radar, air traffic display). The project team may be organized in a functional manner, for example, and the software project manager may be the manager of the project's functional units during planning and execution of that project. Furthermore, a large software project may be treated as a software program that is decomposed into multiple projects; each having a project manager whose work products are merged into a product stream.

In addition to the characteristics of project managers listed in the *PMBOK® Guide* (knowledge, performance, and personal), software project managers provide leadership in:

- Initiating, planning, and developing estimates and plans both initially and on an ongoing basis as conditions change;

---

[2] COBIT 5 is a series of products available from ISACA.

- Monitoring and controlling schedule milestones, budget expenditures, requirements stability, staff performance, resource utilization, and identified risk factors using a systematic version control process;

- Leading and directing by defining the project vision and maintaining it as requirements and other constraints change and by providing hands on, day-to-day leadership of team leaders, software developers, and supporting personnel who are engaged in innovative teamwork;

- Maintaining compliance with organizational policies and contractual requirements;

- Managing risk by identifying, analyzing, prioritizing, and responding to risk factors on an ongoing, continuous manner;

- Facilitating, coaching, monitoring, inspiring, and working with the software engineering knowledge workers to obtain desired results; and

- Communicating with stakeholders to bridge the "technology gap" by using terms and concepts that are familiar to stakeholders [16].

On a small project (e.g., fewer than ten people) the project manager may have additional roles such as team leader and/or software designer, software architect, business analyst, or other contributing roles. Alternatively, the manager of a small software project may simultaneously manage one or more other small projects; however, care should be taken to not overload the manager of a small manager with other duties.

1.7.1 Interpersonal Skills of a Project Manager

A software project manager needs to ensure that effective communication and coordination occurs within the project team and with stakeholders external to the project.

Interpersonal skills that are particularly important for software project managers, some of which are in Section 1.1.1 of the *PMBOK® Guide,* include but are not limited to:

- Leadership,

- Humility,

- Effective listening,

- Team building,

- Motivation,

- Communication,

- Collaboration and knowledge sharing,

- Influencing,

- Managing conflict,

- Decision making,

- Political and cultural awareness, and

- Negotiation.

1.8 Project Management Body of Knowledge

As stated in Section 1.8 of the *PMBOK® Guide,* "project management standards do not address all details of every topic. This standard is limited to single projects and the project management processes that are generally recognized as good practice. Other standards may be consulted for additional information on the broader context in which projects are accomplished."

In a similar manner, this *Software Extension* is limited to individual software projects and the software project management processes that are generally recognized as good practice. Good practices in this *Software Extension* are generally applicable to most software projects, most of the time. In addition, this *Software Extension* provides information about ISO/IEC/IEEE standards for software and systems development that reflects good practices in the software industry. These standards are cited throughout this *Software Extension*.

The following observations summarize some of the key points made in this section and provide pointers to the following sections of this *Software Extension*.

- Because software is an intangible product, there are many possibilities for software project life cycles and many different approaches to applying the techniques of software project management to those life cycles. Section 2.4.2 of this *Software Extension* describes the continuum of software project life cycles that vary from highly predictive to highly adaptive.

- The principle of "most projects, most of the time" is modified to accommodate variations within the continuum of life cycles for developing software; software project managers adapt the methods, tools, and techniques for project management to the particular aspects of various software project life cycles.

- Software project managers are not expected to have the in-depth knowledge and skills of their team members, but they should understand the issues and concerns their team members deal with and should be familiar with the terminology used by the team members. Software project managers should also understand various approaches to managing software projects within the continuum of software project life cycles.

- Software project managers may have technical backgrounds, but not always in software. Those project managers who do not have strong software skills may need to work closely with a technical leader on their software projects. Those with strong software skills may need to focus on developing their business, project management, and interpersonal skills.

- Two important aspects for software project managers are interpersonal skills and management of software quality. Section 1.7.1 of this *Software Extension* lists interpersonal skills that are particularly important for software project managers. Quality considerations are introduced in Section 1.9 of this *Software Extension* and presented in detail in Section 8 of this extension.

1.9 Quality Management

Management of software quality is increasingly important because the safety, security, and welfare of the general public are increasingly dependent on software.

Each of the deliverable work products should have acceptable quality, as determined by the needs of the users and other stakeholders. Management of quality assurance, quality control, verification, and validation are important elements of managing software projects.

Software quality attributes that are important to users and other stakeholders include, but are not limited to attributes such as:

- Safety,
- Security,
- Reliability,
- Resilience,
- Dependability,
- Scalability,
- Performance,
- Ease of learning,
- Ease of use (usability),
- Interpretation of error messages,
- Availability,
- Accessibility,
- Efficiency,
- Flexibility,
- Interoperability, and
- Robustness.

Software quality attributes that are important to software developers include, but are not limited to:

- Testability,
- Maintainability,
- Portability,
- Extensibility, and
- Reusability.

1

While these quality attributes are not unique to software, it is important that a software project manager understand the priorities among the required and desired quality attributes of the software work products and the influence that quality attributes on the methods, tools, and techniques used to manage and conduct software projects. These topics are addressed in Section 8 of this *Software Extension*.

1.10 Project Life Cycles and Agile Methods

Software project managers are responsible for selecting the development methods for their projects (in consultation with others) and therefore should be aware of different software development methods, as well as the relative pros and cons of those methods. Agile methods for developing software have become sufficiently widespread to merit discussion in this *Software Extension* to the *PMBOK® Guide*. However, this extension does not provide definitions of "agile" and "agile methods" because those terms are widely used with differing meanings. Instead, elements of agility found in various adaptive software project life cycles are addressed as follows:

- Collaboration teams are described in Section 2.3.2.

- Adaptive life cycles are described in Section 2.4.

- Other aspects of agility for software projects that use adaptive life cycles are described in the appropriate sections of this *Software Extension*.

It should be noted that agile methods are not project life cycles; they are development methods that can be embedded in adaptive software project life cycles. Aspects of agility are presented in Section 2.4.2.4 of this *Software Extension*, but the specifics of various agile methods as they relate to software engineering practice are not presented in this extension.

1.11 Explanation of *Software Extension* Processes: Inputs, Tools and Techniques, and Outputs

This *Software Extension* follows closely the structure and organization of the *PMBOK® Guide* – Fifth Edition. This enables easier cross-referencing between equivalent sections of this *Software Extension* and the *PMBOK® Guide*.

The *PMBOK® Guide* describes the inputs, tools and techniques, and outputs for each project management process. For each process, it includes a table that lists three types of elements. This *Software Extension* includes overview tables that incorporate the following format:

- Elements that remain unchanged from the *PMBOK® Guide* – Fifth Edition are shown in plain text.

- New items are shown in ***bold italics***

- Changed elements are shown in *italics*.

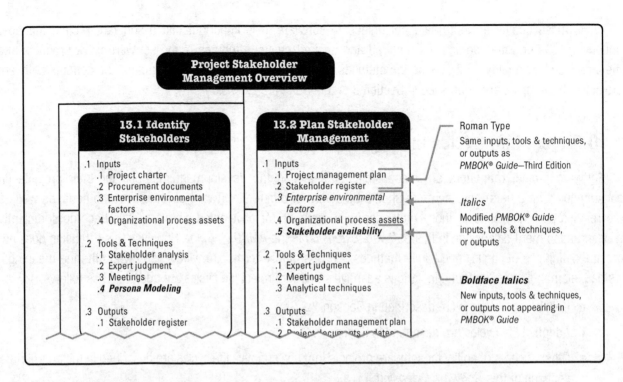

Figure 1-2. Identification of Revised Inputs, Tools & Techniques, and Outputs

2

2

PROJECT LIFE CYCLE AND ORGANIZATION

This section of the *Software Extension to the PMBOK® Guide – Fifth Edition* describes software project life cycles; how software projects interact with ongoing operational work and other elements of an organization; the influence of stakeholders beyond the software development team; and how organizational structure affects the way a project is initiated, planned, executed, monitored and controlled, and closed. Emphasis is placed on tools and techniques that have been developed to accommodate the special and unique aspects of software projects and management of software projects.

2.1 Organizational Influences on Project Management

Organizational culture, structure, and leadership style have a strong influence on how software projects are managed and conducted because software engineers are knowledge workers who develop and modify software by engaging in closely coordinated teamwork.

2.1.1 Organizational Cultures and Styles

There is a wide range of organizational cultures, structures, and leadership styles within organizations that develop and modify software. Culture, structure, and leadership style for software projects are shaped and influenced by factors such as the organization's mission, vision, and values; organizational norms of behavior; the product domain; interactions with other functional units of the organization and the larger enterprise; and relationships with customers and other project stakeholders.

In addition, because of the unique nature of software projects (intangible product and closely coordinated teamwork), the organizational factors that influence the morale and motivation of software workers are somewhat different than for others who work in organizations.

Organizational factors that tend to increase motivation, engagement, and productivity of software personnel include factors such as:

- Workplace free of external disruptions,
- Challenging technical problems,
- Autonomy to solve problems,
- Ability to control one's work schedule,

- Learning new things,
- Competent technical leaders,
- Opportunities to experiment with new ideas,
- Compelling vision or end-state,
- Adequate training and mentoring, and
- Adequate software tools and computing technology.

Software development tends to be a learning and knowledge-sharing experience. In addition to the factors identified in the *PMBOK® Guide*, organizational factors that increase learning and sharing among project team members and that therefore increase product quality and project performance include:

- Collaborative culture and work environment,
- Easy access to cross-functional team members,
- Opportunities to discuss issues in a timely fashion,
- Access to needed information,
- Well-defined and effective organizational interfaces,
- Colocation or electronic connectivity that results in easy communication among the team members, and
- High level of trust among the team members and among the project team and the project manager, other managers, and the customer that provides for open discussion of challenges and options.

Conversely, the absence of these factors can result in decreased motivation and morale at both the individual and team level. These factors are important for all knowledge workers; they are very important for software developers.

2.1.2 Organizational Communications

Software organizations, like other modern organizations, utilize the communication mechanism noted in Section 2.1.2 of the *PMBOK® Guide*. In particular, the representation of software work products in electronic media and the growth of the Internet and web infrastructure have made possible the globalization of software development. Software project managers increasingly manage geographically dispersed projects.

2.1.3 Organizational Structures

Software enterprises can organize projects as individual entities, project-by-project (projectized organization); by coordination among functional units (functional organization); or as a matrix organization that combines projectized and functional structures. Various kinds of organizational structures are presented in Section 2.1.3 of the *PMBOK® Guide*.

Internally a software project is typically organized into one or more small teams (i.e., ten or fewer members per team) where the number of teams depends on the scope of the project. Small, coordinated teams minimize the problems of communication within and among teams because the number of communication paths within a closely coordinated team increases exponentially with the number of team members. Several small teams have fewer overall communication paths than one large team when each team has a single point of contact with other teams (see Section 5 of this *Software Extension*). Other functional elements of a software organization may provide supporting services such as configuration management, infrastructure tools and support, and separate verification and validation capabilities.

Alignment of a software project's organizational structure with the desired structure of the software product is another consideration. Melvin Conway, in a statement that became known as Conway's Law, made the following observation:

> *"Any organization that designs a system (defined more broadly here than just information systems) will inevitably produce a design whose structure is a copy of the organization's communication structure."* [17]

According to Conway's Law, a project that is organized using three software development teams (or a single team of 3 members) will tend to develop a software product having three components; when a project of four teams (or a single team of 4 team members) develops the same product it will likely have four components, because software is a product of the closely coordinated effort of teams and team members who allocate among themselves the features and interfaces to be implemented.

Like all "software laws," Conway's Law is a guideline rather than a law of physics or chemistry.

2.1.4 Organizational Process Assets

According to Section 2.1.4 of the *PMBOK® Guide*, organizational process assets include any and all process-related assets that can be used to influence the project's success, from any or all of the organizations involved in the project. In the *PMBOK® Guide,* organizational project assets are grouped as processes and procedures, and the corporate knowledge base. The *PMBOK® Guide* provides examples of project assets; they are applicable to software projects. Additional considerations for software projects include the following.

2.1.4.1 Processes and Procedures

The processes and procedures of many software development and service organizations are based on ISO/IEC and IEEE standards for software engineering, and on the Capability Maturity Models and the process asset library of the Software Engineering Institute.

Some ISO/IEC and IEEE standards that have been harmonized and issued as joint standards (ISO/IEC/IEEE) include:

- ISO/IEC/IEEE 12207: Systems and software engineering—Software project life cycle processes, and
- ISO/IEC/IEEE 16326: Systems and software engineering—Life cycle processes—Project management [18].

The Capability Maturity Models Integrated (CMMI), developed and maintained by the Software Engineering Institute, include:

- CMMI for Development (CMMI-DEV),
- CMMI for Services (CMMI-SVC, and
- CMMI for Acquisition (CMMI-ACQ).

CMMI for Development is a collection of best practices for system and software engineering. CMMI-DEV, V1.3 contains 22 process areas. The process areas are grouped into 4 categories; one of the categories is project management, which has 7 process areas; they are listed here, along with the corresponding Process Groups and Knowledge Areas in the *PMBOK® Guide* and this *Software Extension*.

- Project Planning [Planning Process Group],
- Project Monitoring and Control [Monitoring and Controlling Process Group],
- Supplier Agreement Management [Project Procurement Management Knowledge Area],
- Integrated Project Management [Project Integration Management Knowledge Area],
- Requirements Management [Project Scope Management Knowledge Area],
- Risk Management [Project Risk Management Knowledge Area], and
- Quantitative Project Management [Project Quality Management Knowledge Area].

2.1.4.2 Corporate Knowledge Base

Section 2.1.4.2 of the *PMBOK® Guide* provides examples of information that is typically contained in a corporate knowledge base. Many software organizations maintain corporate knowledge bases that contain information similar to that in Section 2.1.4.2 of the *PMBOK® Guide*.

CMMI-DEV includes the process area, Organizational Process Definition, the purpose of which is to establish and maintain a usable set of organizational process assets and work environment standards. Also, generic practice GP3.2 in CMMI-DEV (Collect Improvement Information) states: "information and artifacts are stored in the organization's measurement repository and the organization's process asset library."

Many software organizations maintain a corporate knowledge base for software engineering and software project management.

2.1.5 Enterprise Environmental Factors

The factors cited in Section of 2.1.5 of the *PMBOK® Guide* apply equally to software projects. They include, but are not limited to:

- Organizational culture, structure, and processes;
- Government or industry standards;

- Laws, regulations, and policies;
- Infrastructure (e.g., facilities and capital equipment);
- Human resources;
- Personnel administration;
- Political climate; and
- Project management information systems.

2.2 Project Stakeholders and Governance

2.2.1 Project Stakeholders

A software project stakeholder is any individual or organizational entity that affects or is affected by a software project or the resulting software product. Stakeholders include both internal and external stakeholders. Internal stakeholders include the project team and other organizational entities such as a marketing or contract administration department. External stakeholders include acquirers, integrators, customers, and users and may include policy makers and regulatory agencies.

Because of software's abstract nature, software project deliverables are subject to broader and more variable interpretations by project stakeholders than are physical entities. It is important to engage, coordinate, integrate, and proactively manage the appropriate stakeholders in issues of relevance to them as often as is appropriate in order to manage expectations for the project deliverables and project governance. Some stakeholders may be designated at key stakeholders for different aspects of a software projects and at different times during a project. Stakeholder satisfaction is cited as a project deliverable in the *PMBOK® Guide*. This topic is explored in depth in Section 13 of this *Software Extension*.

2.2.2 Project Governance

According to the *PMBOK® Guide*, "project governance is the alignment of project objectives with the strategy of the larger organization by the project sponsor and project team." Governance is concerned with issues such as decision making, prioritization, and alignment of vision and strategy with an organization's work. Organizational governance for software projects may include elements such as a project management office, project portfolio management, or an IT strategy group. The intangible nature of software may result in a high level of formality in the governance model, in an attempt to bring visibility to an inherently invisible product. Software projects typically involve discovery of requirements and constraints within a learning environment as the projects evolve. Formal governance models that treat software development as a linear, predictive process may exert a detrimental impact on the software projects conducted by the organization. While different types of projects call for different levels of governance formality, it is important that governance models are suited to the nonlinear, adaptive learning environment of software development.

2.3 The Project Team

2.3.1 Composition of Project Teams

The composition of a software project team is often a balance between ideal considerations and practical constraints. Ideal considerations for composing software development teams include:

- **Dedicated vs. non-dedicated team members.** In the world of knowledge work, switching context between multiple assignments incurs intellectual overhead. Therefore, software projects benefit from dedicated resources. Assigning team members to one project at a time can limit switching of contexts among multiple, part-time tasks and improve the productivity of software teams. However, some projects do not have enough work for the various specialized skill sets required nor the budget to support dedicated resources for those specialized skills. As a result, many software project managers strike a balance between dedicated and non-dedicated resources.

- **Collaborative team vs. functional division**. In some organizations, collaborative dedicated team members possess all of the skills required to deliver tested working software rather than allocating software to be developed among separate functional units. The latter approach may involve assigning development of user interface components to the user interface group and database components to the database group, etc. In contrast, a collaborative team may include expertise in user interfaces, databases, and other needed specialties. Aligning teams in a collaborative manner increases feedback among team members and reduces feedback time. It also allows learning to occur throughout the course of the project, which is reflected in the work products and interactions among the team members. Some software organizations maintain functional groups in the interest of maximizing utilization of specialty resources. As indicated previously, striking a balance between dedicated and non-dedicated resources, which may be reflected as a collaborative team versus functional divisions, is a challenging economic dilemma in software development. Managers of collaborative teams sometimes alleviate the collaborative versus functional dilemma by assigning functional specialists for varying periods of time, as needed.

- **Virtual vs. colocated.** The complex and abstract nature of software makes it difficult for software engineers to communicate detailed technical issues in written form. In order to convey abstract ideas and achieve the collaboration needed for innovation, many teams benefit from face-to-face discussions. An additional benefit is the tacit knowledge that is gained and used when project team discussions are held in common meeting areas. However, some organizations control costs and utilize specialized resources by outsourcing to low-cost providers. As a result, a software project manager may choose to strike a balance between face-to-face communication for activities such as project initiation and planning, orientation, and training with day-to-day work performed in a virtual environment.

- **Specialists vs. generalists**. Software projects often require specialized skills that incur high labor costs. Many project managers staff their software projects with project members who have generalist skills and rely on them to perform the majority of the work. Periodically, an expert will be called upon to mentor and assist the generalists in specialized areas. Another benefit of this approach is that generalists may offer broader perspectives than specialists and may develop more solution options.

- **Stable vs. interim**. Many organizations create a new project team for each software project and disband the team when the product is delivered. For ongoing maintenance, enhancement, and support of software products, it is beneficial to keep cross-functional teams together over time so that knowledge is retained, team interactions and learning are maintained and improved, and teams maintain high levels of performance. Another benefit of stable teams is that project performance throughout the organization typically becomes more predictable.

In practice, organizations may have to make trade-offs among these considerations. A detailed exploration of software project teams is included in Section 9 of this *Software Extension*.

2.3.2 Collaborative Teams

Software projects benefit from project team structures that improve collaboration within and among the teams. As presented in Table 2-1, collaborations are intended to boost productivity and facilitate innovative problem solving. Formation of a collaborative team sometimes incurs initial costs, which are recovered over the duration of the project.

Although the benefits of collaboration also apply to predictive life cycle teams, collaborative teams are often critical to the success of adaptive life cycle projects because adaptive teams require a collaborative work environment to accommodate dynamically evolving project work.

2.4 Project Life Cycle

Software project life cycles and *software product life cycles* are distinct concepts. A software product life cycle includes an initial software project life cycle but also includes the processes for deployment, support, maintenance,

Table 2-1. Attributes of Collaborative Teams

Attribute	Goal
Dedicated Resources	• Increased focus and productivity
Multi-Skilled Teams	• Accelerated integration of distinct work activities • Incorporation of frequent wide-band feedback
Colocation	• Better communication • Improved team dynamics • Knowledge sharing • Reduced cost of learning
Generalists and Specialists	• Dedicated expertise and flexibility of work assignments
Stable Work Environment	• Simplified human resource planning • Preservation and expansion of intellectual capital

evolution, replacement, and retirement of a software product. Enhancement and adaption of the initially delivered software may involve several project life cycles beyond the initial one. This *Software Extension* to the *PMBOK® Guide* covers software project life cycles.

According to Section 2.4 of the *PMBOK® Guide*, "A project life cycle is the series of phases that a project passes through from its initiation to its closure. The phases are generally sequential." Section 2.4 of this *Software Extension* describes the ways in which software project life cycles are similar to and different from the project life cycles presented in the *PMBOK® Guide*.

Section 2.4 of the *PMBOK® Guide* also states that project life cycles occupy a continuum from predictive to adaptive. Factors that characterize the positions of life cycles for software projects within the continuum include (but are not limited to) the various ways requirements and plans are handled, how risk and cost are managed, and the involvement of key stakeholders. The continuum of life cycles for software projects is illustrated in Figure 2-1.

Highly predictive software project life cycles are characterized by emphasis on specification of requirements and detailed planning during the initiation and planning phases of a software project. Detailed plans based on known requirements and constraints reduce risk and cost. Milestones for key stakeholder involvement are also planned.

Highly adaptive life cycles for software projects are characterized by progressive specification of requirements based on short iterative development cycles. Risk and cost are reduced by progressive evolution of initial plans; key stakeholders are continuously involved.

The following considerations apply to the middle area of the predictive-adaptive continuum: (a) risk and cost are reduced by iterative evolution of initial plans; and (b) key stakeholders have more opportunities to be involved in predictive-adaptive iteration cycles than stakeholders at the typically infrequent project milestones of highly predictive life cycles. However, stakeholders in predictive-adaptive projects have fewer opportunities to be involved than key stakeholders who are continuously involved in highly adaptive life cycles.

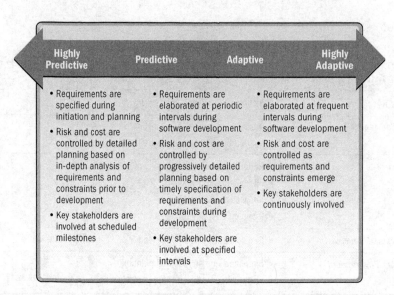

Figure 2-1. The Continuum of Software Project Life Cycles

Software project life cycles in the middle region of the life cycle continuum tend to align more closely with the predictive side or the adaptive side of the continuum depending on the way requirements are specified, how risk and cost are handled, and the nature of key stakeholder involvement.

Key stakeholders are those individuals and groups whose involvement is essential for a successful outcome. Key stakeholders may include but are not limited to potential users, customers, system engineers, system integrators, acquirers, operators, and maintainers. Different key stakeholders may need to be involved at different times during software development.

Also, it should be emphasized that software project life cycles are complex and multidimensional. They include processes for activities such as configuration management, process and product quality assurance, independent testing, and other activities as appropriate and needed. In addition, software projects may be elements of programs, and may include interfaces to other functional units of the software development organization or business enterprise, to affiliated projects, and/or to subcontracted groups or projects.

There is a distinction between planning and conducting a software project and preparing for and delivering the resulting product. The customer and other key stakeholders for a predictive software life cycle project could choose (a) to accept a single product delivery at the end of the project; (b) to accept delivery of preplanned increments of functionality at specified milestones during product development; (c) to accept delivery at the end of the project but with periodic demonstrations of product increments during product development; or (d) to have no involvement between initial requirements specification and delivery of the product. Similarly, a customer and other key stakeholders for an adaptive life cycle software project could choose to witness demonstrations of evolving capabilities at the ends of iteration cycles with a single delivery of the product at the end of the project, or to accept delivery of product increments at planned or emerging intervals.

Other variations are possible: (a) a software project manager could initially prepare detailed plans and requirements (in a predictive manner) with frequent iteration cycles during software construction (in an adaptive manner); (b) a software project could be conducted iteratively during analysis and design with the product constructed as a single product increment; (c) a software product could be developed incrementally with no iterations during development of the increments; or (d) a software product could be developed with no iterations and a single product increment.

Project execution and product delivery are distinct activities. The life cycle model for project execution and product delivery should be designed as carefully as the software product, based on factors such as those in listed in Figure 2-1.

2.4.1 Characteristics of Project Life Cycles

Creation of software deliverables typically requires a variety of project life cycle processes. According to ISO/IEC/IEEE Standard 12207, development of software includes the following processes (see also Figure 1 of 12207):

- **Analyze**: Software Requirements Analysis Process,
- **Architect**: Software Architectural Design Process,
- **Design**: Software Detailed Design Process,

- **Construct**: Software Construction Process,
- **Integrate**: Software Integration Process, and
- **Test**: Software Qualification Testing.

For purposes of exposition, this *Software Extension* will use these six processes (analyze, architect, design, construct, integrate, and test) to describe the software project life cycle variations found in the software industry.

Figure 2-9 of the *PMBOK® Guide* illustrates cost and staffing levels across the project life cycle. The figure depicts a profile that rises during initiation and planning, peaks during execution and monitoring and controlling, and decreases during project closure. This profile is typical for predictive software project life cycles. Adaptive software life cycles tend to lower the peak of cost and staffing level during the execution and monitoring-and-controlling phases and shift the entire profile to earlier stages. This is possible because adaptive life cycles validate increments of working software on a continuing basis to minimize the impact and cost of subsequent changes. In addition, adaptive life cycles that maintain a constant staffing level during execution and monitoring and controlling tend to flatten the profile during those elements of software project life cycles.

2.4.2 Project Phases

2.4.2.1 Phase-to-Phase Relationships

According to the *PMBOK® Guide,* there are two basic types of phase-to-phase relationships: sequential and overlapped. The nature of software allows for significant flexibility in overlapping, interleaving, and iterating software development phases. ISO/IEC/IEEE Standards 15288 and 12207 use the term *stages* rather than *phases* to indicate that these stages are to be used throughout a project whenever they are needed to achieve project objectives. Highly adaptive software project life cycle models, for example, execute many of the stages during each iterative cycle, as explained in Section 2.4.2.4 of this *Software Extension*.

2.4.2.2 Predictive Life Cycles

Section 2.4.2.2 of the *PMBOK® Guide* defines predictive life cycles as those for which the project scope, and the time and cost required to deliver that scope, are determined as early as practically possible in the project life cycle.

A predictive life cycle model for software projects, as illustrated in Figure 2-2, is characterized by a sequence of overlapping development phases with feedback to and repetition of previous phases as needed.

Each of the overlapping circles in Figure 2-2 includes the five Process Groups of the *PMBOK® Guide*: Initiating, Planning, Executing, Monitoring and Controlling, and Closing processes (see also Figure 3-1 of the *PMBOK® Guide*). The processes in each Process Group are conducted for the six phases in a sequential or overlapping manner. Some processes in earlier phases may be repeated, based on feedback from later phases. Phases may be overlapped in time, as indicated in Figure 2-2, or they may be executed sequentially.

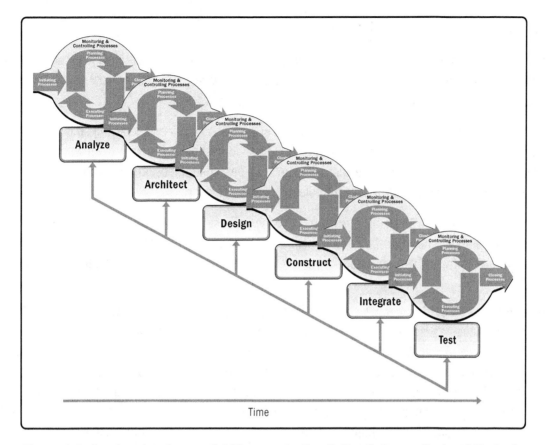

Figure 2-2. Overlapping Sequential Phases of a Predictive Software Project Life Cycle

Phases may be overlapped when the partially completed previous phase has provided sufficient work products to allow the following phase to proceed, and provided there are sufficient resources to permit two phases to proceed concurrently.

The need to repeat some processes of a previously completed project phase may occur because: (a) the requirements are emergent in nature; (b) new understandings arise around stakeholder expectations regarding product scope; (c) new insights into the technology are gained; or (d) errors in previous work need to be fixed.

Detailed, initial planning for a predictive software project life cycle does not equate to a single "big bang" delivery of the resulting software product. A predictive software life cycle can include iterations that involve one or more of the six phases depicted in Figure 2-2. Some of the iterations can result in tested, deliverable software that may, when desired, be delivered into the users' environment.

Predictive life cycles are most successful for software projects that have well-defined requirements, a familiar problem domain, stable technology, and a familiar customer. These attributes allow the project scope, and the time and cost required to deliver that scope, to be determined early in the project life cycle.

2.4.2.3 Iterative and Incremental Life Cycles

According to Section 2.4.2.3 of the *PMBOK® Guide,* iterative and incremental life cycles are those in which the project scope is generally determined early in the project life cycle, but time and cost estimates are routinely modified as the project team's understanding of the product increases.

For software projects, requirements are often modified in addition to routinely modifying time and cost estimates, thus making trade-offs possible among requirements, time, and cost as the project team's understanding of the product increases. One or more of these three factors may be constrained, thus limiting the trade-off options. Constraining all three factors usually results in project and product failure.

As described in Section 2.4.2.2 of this *Software Extension*, process iterations and product increments are distinct concepts. Iterations are elements of the development process while increments are elements of the product. The intangible nature of software permits interleaving, overlapping, and intermixing of iterations and increments in various ways.

- **Iterative project life cycles.** Iterative life cycles for software projects repeat one or more of the software development stages; the number of stages included in one iteration may vary from iteration to iteration. Some iterations may involve only one development stage, whereas others may involve multiple stages. The software product is progressively elaborated; feedback is incorporated as new information is gained and understanding increases. New requirements may emerge, existing requirements may be modified, and derived requirements may be added. A life cycle is often beneficial when complexity is high, when the project incurs frequent changes, or when the scope is subject to differing stakeholders' views of the desired final software product. Figure 2-3 illustrates some elements of a software project life cycle for a single product delivery that iterates between two project phases and among three stages in each of the phases.

- **Incremental product development.** Each increment of incremental product development adds functionality that increases the product scope. This approach provides the opportunity for project managers and stakeholders to view intermediate demonstrations of working software and for the

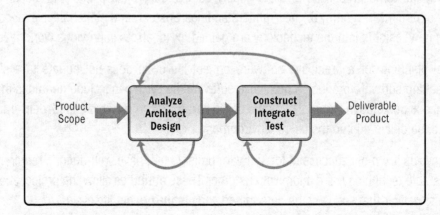

Figure 2-3. A Software Project Life Cycle with Two Iterative Phases, Each Having Three Iterative Stages

customer to receive early delivery of working product increments, when desired. The extent of product scope included in the increments may vary from increment to increment. The duration of incremental phases also varies widely among software projects. Some projects include plans for fewer increments, each to be completed over a longer time frame, while other projects plan more increments, each of a shorter duration.

An example of incremental product development is illustrated in Figure 2-4. The product features have been prioritized and partitioned into four feature sets that are to be built in successive increments. The features and feature sets were prioritized during preceding analysis and architect phases and are prioritized based on predetermined prioritization criteria (for example, construct foundation software first has the highest priority, followed by construct most critical software elements first, construct the user interface software first, etc.). Prioritization of features and features sets is determined in part by noting that the features implement first will be tested and demonstrated

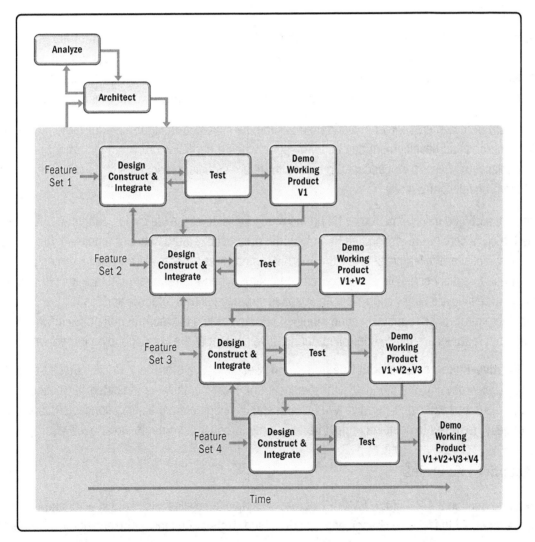

Figure 2-4. Incremental Software Product Development

most, in conjunction with features that are added subsequently. The analysis and architect phases may be revisited based on demonstrations of the deliverable product increments.

As illustrated in Figure 2-4, increments 2, 3, and 4 add features that build on previously built features in accordance with prioritization of the feature sets. Each increment of product capability is verified with respect to the requirements for that feature set during the Test stage and validated by demonstrating incremental capabilities for the appropriate stakeholders during the Demo Working Product stage. Verification techniques during the Test stage may include testing, analysis, inspection, and review.

Iteration may occur (or not) within the Design, Construct, and Iterate stages and within the Test stage, as well as between the two phases.

In Figure 2-4, the feedback arrows from development of an increment to a previous one indicates that adding new features may expose defects to be fixed in the previous increment or that refactoring of a previous increment may be needed to better accommodate the features being added.

The number of features included in a feature set, the time allocated for development of the features, and the resources to be applied provide a trade-off space of features, time, and resources. The duration of each incremental development phase is often limited to one month or less so that feedback is provided frequently and corrections can be made before defects are propagated to larger units of software, which would require more rework.

Development of increments may be overlapped in time, as indicated in Figure 2-4, or they may be developed sequentially. Incremental development can be overlapped when a partially completed increment provides a basis to allow the following phase to proceed, and provided there are sufficient resources to permit development of two increments to proceed concurrently.

Incremental software development may be on the predictive side of the life cycle continuum or on the adaptive side of the life cycle continuum, depending upon how the prioritized feature sets are managed. Predictive product development establishes the feature sets and the priorities among them prior to starting the incremental development phases, perhaps to satisfy schedule and resource constraints when the requirements are known and are stable; changes to feature sets are tightly controlled. An adaptive approach allows features and feature sets designated for subsequent increments to be reprioritized and modified prior to starting the incremental phase in which they will be implemented but features are tightly controlled during development of the corresponding increment.

- **Iterative-incremental product development.** Section 2.4.2.3 of the *PMBOK® Guide* states that most life cycles develop the product both iteratively and incrementally. As indicated in Sections 2.4.2.2 and 2.4.2.3 of this extension, iterative and incremental development are distinct concepts that allow software project life cycles to combine project iterations and product increments in various ways.

2.4.2.4 Adaptive Life Cycles

According to Section 2.4.2.4 of the *PMBOK® Guide*: "Adaptive life cycles (also known as change-driven or agile methods) are intended to facilitate change and require a high degree of ongoing stakeholder involvement."

As stated in Section 1.10 of this *Software Extension*, "agile" is not a project life cycle; it is a term used to characterize certain attributes that adaptive life cycles share to varying degrees. Adaptive life cycles for software projects are illustrated on the right side of the life cycle continuum in Figure 2-1 of this *Software Extension*. Attributes of agility for adaptive life cycle software projects include, but are not limited to:

- Increments of working deliverable software are produced on a periodic basis.

- Durations of adaptive iteration cycles vary from daily to weekly to monthly, but usually not more than monthly.

- Adaptive iteration cycles are often of the same duration (i.e., are "time boxed") but some cycles may be of longer or shorter duration by exception.

- Increments of working deliverable software are not necessarily produced by each iteration cycle—increments and iterations are distinct.

- Requirements, design, and the software product emerge as the project evolves.

- A representative customer, customer's representative, and/or knowledgeable user is involved on a continuing basis; involvement includes observation of periodic demonstrations of working, deliverable software at the ends of iterative development cycles that produce increments of working deliverable software (i.e., on a daily, weekly, bi-weekly, or monthly basis). In addition, a representative customer, customer's representative, or knowledgeable user provides guidance for further product development based on demonstrations of working deliverable software and the constraints on project scope (schedule, budget, and resources).

- Adaptive software development teams are small (i.e., 10 or fewer members) and are self-organizing; large projects include multiple small teams.

- All members of each software development team are assigned to one project at a time.

- Each software development team includes the generalists and specialists needed to accomplish the work activities; functional experts may be involved periodically or as needed.

Some additional attributes of iterative software development that may be incorporated into an adaptive software project life cycle are presented in Table 2-2.

The short duration of iterations allows rework to be integrated within the iterations rather than accumulated as a large rework effort that should be accomplished at the end of software development. Performing rework in small increments is more cost effective than the large amount of rework that typically occurs during the integration and testing phases of a predictive life cycle for a software project because the software developers have all of the details in mind and the amount of rework to be accomplished is small.

Adaptive project life cycles are particularly appropriate when a precise, early definition of customer needs is difficult or when the technology is used in a way that is different than has historically been applied. Although adaptive practices tend to improve overall quality and reduce total cost of ownership of software over its product life cycle, the cost-of-quality curve differs from that of predictive software project life cycles. This point is discussed further in Section 8 on Quality Management of this *Software Extension*.

Table 2-2 Attributes of Iterations in Adaptive Software Project Life Cycles

Attribute	Goal
Multi-Stage Iterations: Iterations incorporate as many software engineering stages as desired (from analyze to test).	Systematic elaboration of product scope Reduction of technical risk using iterations of construction, integration, and testing followed by demonstration
Vertical Slices: Iterations can deliver increments of functionality that include as many architecture components as desired.	Detection and correction of integration issues and interface defects on a continuing basis Increased understanding for software developers, customers, users, and other stakeholders based on intermediate software deliverables
Short Durations: Iterations typically range in duration from daily to monthly.	Timely oversight and corrective action based on frequent demonstrations and reviews of evolving, working software
Time Boxes: All iterations are planned to have the same duration.	Simplified project planning Improved estimates, based on accumulated data such as velocity and burndown rate

Another important aspect of adaptive software project life cycles is the relationship among product scope, size, cost, and schedule. For many adaptive life cycle projects, the cost and schedule for each iterative cycle are fixed because the number of personnel and the time box are fixed for each iteration. The scope of work, and therefore the product features that can be implemented on each iteration are adjusted to fit the constraints of fixed cost and fixed schedule per iteration.

For adaptive software projects, the software to be developed is often characterized by stories, use cases, or features implemented rather than modules or lines of code implemented. An adaptive project team quickly learns how much work can be accomplished during each iterative cycle. Accumulated experience also allows teams to accurately forecast how much time it will take to complete the implementation of a set of features. A measure of productivity derived from the production rate, called *velocity*, is the ratio of work products produced to the amount of effort expended by the team during an iteration cycle. Velocity measurements can be accumulated during development iterations and used to track planned versus actual progress and to forecast final cost and completion date, which is similar to the way earned value is used to track the construction phase of predictive life cycle projects.

A generic example of a software development method for an adaptive software project life cycle is illustrated in Figure 2-5. This is a common software development pattern, often used as a basis for agile development methods. Examples that use variations of this pattern include Scrum, eXtreme Programming, Feature-Driven Development, Test-Driven Development, and the Dynamic System Development Method.

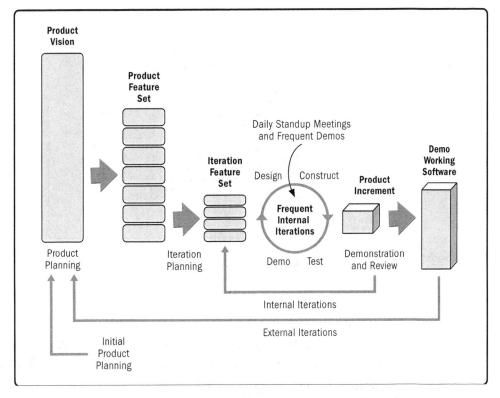

Figure 2-5. An Adaptive Software Development Method

Key elements of the adaptive software development method illustrated in Figure 2-5 include the product vision, the product feature set, and the iteration feature set (referred to as the feature backlog and the iteration backlog in Scrum). A product feature set is the result of the product vision developed during initial product planning. Features in the product feature set can be added, deleted, and reprioritized as a result of ongoing product planning, which may be influenced by external demonstrations of working software for the customer and other key stakeholders. Features in an iteration feature set are selected from the features in the product feature set. Development of features in an iteration feature set involves daily stand-up meetings and frequent internal development iterations. Development iterations may occur on a daily or weekly basis. The outer (external) iteration cycles produce increments of working, deliverable software for demonstration and review by customers and other stakeholders. The outer, external iteration cycles typically occur on cycles of 1, 2, or 4 weeks. Some instances of the adaptive method in Figure 2-5 do not allow changes to features in an iteration feature set during an external iteration cycle; other instances allow limited changes.

Figure 2-6 illustrates the internal iterations that typically occur in software development methods based on Figure 2-5. The internal iterations provide the developers with continuing demonstrations of progress. These internal iterations may occur hourly, daily, or weekly, as desired; different team members may proceed at different cadences with designated rendezvous points for integration, test, and demonstration. The daily stand-up meetings in Figure 2-5 are short-duration meetings in which the project team members review progress, problems, and issues, and agree on work tasks.

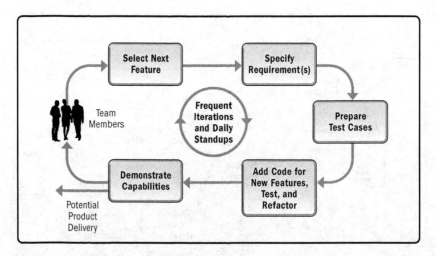

Figure 2-6. Internal Development Cycles for Adaptive Software Development

Figure 2-6 illustrates the internal details of the software development cycles in Figure 2-5. Note that features are translated into requirements and that test cases are written before the code for new features is added (i.e., test-driven development). Code is added and the software is tested (perhaps iteratively). The software is then refactored to improve the structure without altering the behavior. Some software developers alter the sequence "add code for new features, test, and refactor" to "test, add code for new features, test, and refactor." The latter sequence indicates an approach that iteratively applies the tests to the code, which will fail without the new features, the code is iteratively written and the test scenarios are applied until the new code passes the tests; the code is then refactored.

The next increment of tested, deliverable software is demonstrated to the customer, users, and other stakeholders when the features in the feature set are implemented. The demonstration may result in acceptance of the software or may result in requests for revisions. Corrections, additions, and adjustments to the software can usually be accommodated during the next iteration cycle without disrupting the cadence of iterations because the iteration cycles are short and the added functionality to be corrected is not large. The short-cycle feedback loop is efficient because the software developers have all of the details in mind. The team velocity accounts for frequent, small updates typically encountered in the daily iteration cycles.

In some cases, a correction or addition may be added to the product feature set for later consideration. The iteration cycles depicted in Figure 2-5 continue until all features in the feature set are implemented or until the customer, user, and other stakeholders are satisfied with the outcome; or perhaps until time, money, and resources are exhausted. In the latter case, the most important features have been implemented according to the prioritization of features in the feature set.

It should also be noted that the scope of an adaptive software project includes other elements of project scope, as appropriate to the needs of the project, such as architectural design, independent verification and validation, configuration management, and quality assurance and quality control.

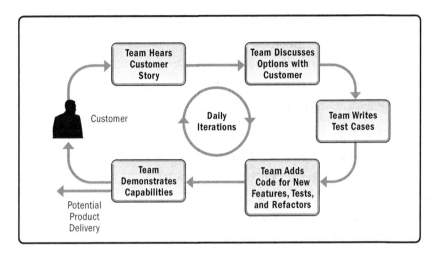

Figure 2-7. External Development Cycles for Adaptive Software Development

2.4.2.5 Highly Adaptive Software Development

Figure 2-7 illustrates a highly adaptive software development method that produces daily demonstrations of working software for a knowledgeable customer who is involved on a continuing, daily basis during development of the software product. The customer relates a user story or scenario for a desired feature of the software. Software team members specify product requirements and write test scenarios for implementation of the desired feature or features. The new feature(s) are added, and the test scenarios are applied.

Some distinctions between the examples illustrated in Figures 2-6 and 2-7 are indicated in Table 2-3 (internal adaptive life cycle versus external highly adaptive life cycle).

Table 2-3. Typical Practices of Internal Adaptive and External Highly Adaptive Software Projects

Internal Adaptive Life Cycle	External Highly Adaptive Life Cycle
Team members "in the loop"	Customer "in the loop"
Daily team stand-up meetings and internal demos	Daily demos for the customer
Team selects feature or features for the next internal iteration	Customer supplies story for the next iteration
Team accepts or revises added features	Customer accepts, request revisions, or rejects added features
Software increments available for delivery into the user environment at predetermined intervals, if desired (1, 2, or 4 weeks)	Software increments available for delivery into the user environment at daily intervals, if desired

Table 2-3 provides two examples of the relationship between the cadence of project iterations and the cadence of product increments. Both examples include daily cadence of iterations but different cadences for producing product increments. Other possibilities exist; for example, the team might produce working increments of software for internal review and demonstration on weekly integration and test cycles. There are many possibilities for the relationship between project iterations and product increments when using adaptive software development methods.

The examples of adaptive software development depicted in Figures 2-5, 2-6, and 2-7 also illustrate a common attribute of adaptive software development: the customer determines the features to be included and therefore determines, from the business viewpoint, value-added expenditure (or not) of additional development time, money, effort, and resources. For the examples in Figures 2-5 and 2-6, the customer can make the determination to continue (or not) when reviewing deliverable product increments at intervals of 1, 2, or 4 weeks. In Figure 2-7, the customer can make the determination to continue (or not) on a daily, or perhaps weekly basis.

3- PROJECT MANAGEMENT PROCESSES FOR A PROJECT

3

PROJECT MANAGEMENT PROCESSES FOR A PROJECT

This section of the *Software Extension to the PMBOK® Guide* describes the ways in which the five Project Management Process Groups of the *PMBOK® Guide* (Initiating, Planning, Executing, Monitoring and Controlling, and Closing) apply to the management of software projects, and includes adaptations and extensions that are commonly used when managing software projects.

The introduction to Section 3 of the *PMBOK® Guide* makes the distinction between project management processes and product-oriented processes as follows:

- **Project management processes.** These processes ensure the effective flow of the project throughout its existence. These processes encompass the tools and techniques involved in applying the skills and capabilities described in the Knowledge Areas (Sections 4 through 13).
- **Product-oriented processes.** These processes specify and create the project's product. Product-oriented processes are typically defined by the project life cycle (as discussed in Section 2.4) and vary by application area as well as the stage of the product life cycle.

Section 2.4 of this *Software Extension* describes life cycles used to manage software projects. Sections 6 through 13 of this *Software Extension* address process-oriented Knowledge Areas and the relationships between project-oriented and product-oriented processes.

As noted in Section 3 of the *PMBOK® Guide,* the five Project Management Process Groups for a project should be used as guides in managing a project while considering the overall approach to be followed for the project. This effort is known as tailoring. Section 2.4 and Sections 4 through 13 of this *Software Extension* provide tailoring guidelines for the processes in the *PMBOK® Guide* that are used to manage a software project.

3.1 Common Project Management Process Interactions

As stated in Section 3.1 of the *PMBOK® Guide*, application of the five Project Management Process Groups is often iterative, with many processes repeated during a project. Section 2.4 of this *Software Extension* indicates that software project life cycles occupy a continuum ranging from highly predictive models to highly adaptive models. Variations along this continuum are based on the manner in which the five Project Management Process Groups are applied.

©2013 Project Management Institute. *Software Extension to the PMBOK® Guide Fifth Edition*   39

As stated in Section 3.2 and Figure 3-3 of the *PMBOK® Guide*: The process flow diagram provides an overall summary of the basic flow and interactions among Process Groups and specific stakeholders. A Process Group includes the project management processes that are linked by the respective inputs and outputs where the result or outcome of one process becomes the input to another. **The Process Groups are not project phases**.

Figure 3-1 in this *Software Extension* is an adaptation of Figure 3-3 of the *PMBOK® Guide* Figure 3-3; the Planning, Executing, and Monitoring and Controlling Process Groups are highlighted. These three Process Groups are often so closely interrelated that they are not distinguishable as separate Process Groups for software project life cycles. For example, initiation and planning for entry to the construction phase of a predictive life cycle or an iteration cycle may involve selecting the set of requirements or features to be implemented, but demonstration of working software code may alter the planned set of requirements or features to be implemented next. Resources used and software demonstrated will provide tangible evidence for monitoring and controlling.

Figure 3-2 of the *PMBOK® Guide* illustrates the level of process interaction among the five Process Groups for a project or project phase; Figure 2-9 of the *PMBOK® Guide* illustrates the cost and staffing level that results from summing the effort for interactions across the five Process Groups. See Section 2.4.2 of this *Software Extension* for a discussion of how the profiles in Figures 2-9 and 3-2 are altered for adaptive life cycle software projects.

Figure 3-2 in this *Software Extension* illustrates the interactions among Process Groups for successive iterations of software development; each cycle involves the application of the five Process Groups in the *PMBOK® Guide*. Project and product scope are defined during initiation and planning of the project; one or both may be modified as the project and product evolve. The product is accepted when the final product scope is achieved or when one or more project constraints (effort, schedule, budget, resources) are exhausted. In the latter case, it is important that the most important features and quality attributes are developed first.

The profile for each iteration cycle in Figure 3-2 indicates effort build-up during the Initiating and Planning Process Groups, level of effort throughout the Executing and Monitoring and Controlling Process Groups, and effort build-down of the iteration cycle during the Closing Process Group. The sum of the overlapping levels of effort across iterations results in an approximately constant level of effort, assuming a fixed number of team members, which is typical of adaptive software development. The cadence of iteration cycles assumes that the team has the skills needed to initiate, plan, execute, monitor and control, and close each iteration, rather than relying on other elements of the organization to provide needed skills, except perhaps as needed on occasion (e.g., consultation with a subject matter expert).

3.2 Project Management Process Groups

According to Section 3.2 of the *PMBOK® Guide*, the five Process Groups have clear dependencies and are typically performed in the same sequence on each project. In contrast, and as indicated in Section 2.4 of this *Software Extension*, the ways in which the five *PMBOK® Guide* Process Groups are applied to software projects may vary from project to project, depending on the life cycles used.

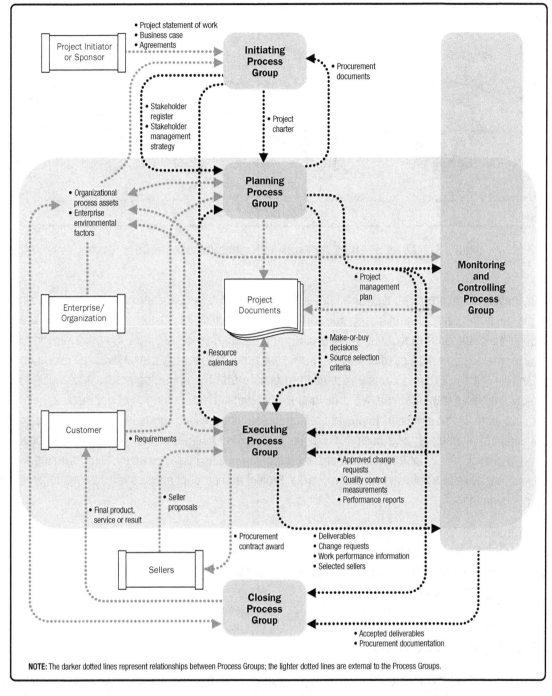

Figure 3-1. Interactions Among Process Groups for Software Development

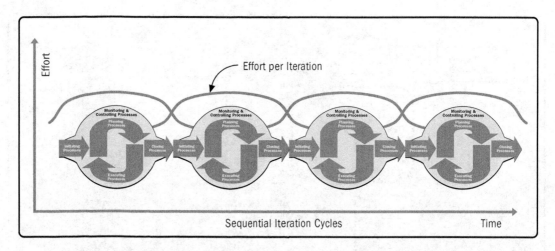

Figure 3-2. Level of Effort for Process Groups Across Iteration Cycles

Software development projects based on adaptive life cycles involve frequent and closely coordinated interactions between the customer and the project—particularly in the translation of customer requirements into planning, which is communicated until execution. Of particular importance, the process flow is not strictly one-directional feed-forward, where information is fed sequentially from one process to the next. In software development, frequent feedback among the five Process Groups is needed to ensure that the emerging software product is consistent with (possibly changing) requirements, features, and expectations. Documentation of decisions is necessary; but documentation alone is not sufficient to provide the understanding needed to implement a software product that meets the needs of a customer or a business. Frequent interpersonal interactions, in addition to documentation, are required to provide clarity for all stakeholders; therefore, emphasis is placed on evolving, working software for each development cycle of a software project life cycle. Project and product scope should be managed to maintain a balance between them.

It is also important to recognize that the life cycle continuum for software projects is not a thin line; it is multidimensional. All of the processes and support functions for software development (e.g., configuration management, quality assurance, documentation, independent testing, etc.) should be adapted to fit the needs of each project life cycle and each software project.

3.3 Initiating Process Group

As stated in Section 3.3 of the *PMBOK® Guide*, internal and external stakeholders who will interact and influence the overall outcome of the project are identified during project initiation. One of the most important stakeholders for a successful software project is a knowledgeable customer, designated customer representative, or user representative who can state needs and desires, and observe demonstrations of the emerging product on a continuing, ongoing basis. Identifying this stakeholder, or stakeholders, during project initiation will permit frequent interactions during the execution and monitoring and controlling of the project. The associated feedback will ensure that the correct features are delivered. During project initiation, it is also important to discuss issues with experienced project managers and technical leaders on similar projects, or perhaps managers and leaders on releases of previous versions of a software product undergoing significant modifications. As indicated previously, an initiating process is typically conducted on each iterative cycle of an adaptive life cycle project.

3.4 Planning Process Group

According to Section 3.4 of the *PMBOK® Guide,* the Planning Process Group consists of those processes performed to establish the total scope of the effort, define and refine the objectives, and develop the course of action required to attain those objectives.

Section 5 of this *Software Extension*, explains that the scope of a software project, the objectives to be obtained, and the courses of action to be followed are often adjusted as a software project evolves. More detailed initial planning is usually accomplished for a predictive life cycle software project than for an adaptive one.

3.5 Executing Process Group

According to Section 3.5 of the *PMBOK® Guide*, results during project execution may require planning updates and rebaselining. Changes may include changes to planned activity durations and changes in resource productivity and availability based on unanticipated risks, problems, and other issues.

Changes during execution are the norm for most software projects. Uncertainty that results from initial lack of information is a major source of risks, problems, and other issues for software projects. Replication of existing software is a simple process compared to replication of physical artifacts; so most software projects are unique undertakings and are, therefore, learning experiences characterized by uncertainty.

3.6 Monitoring and Controlling Process Group

According to Section 3.6 of the *PMBOK® Guide*, the Monitoring and Controlling Process Group consists of those processes required to track, review, and orchestrate the progress and performance of the project; identify any areas in which changes to the plan are required; and initiate the corresponding changes.

Depending on the project life cycle used, monitoring of software projects can vary from traditional techniques (i.e., preplanned milestones, earned value tracking, and technical performance measurement) to reliance on frequent demonstrations of working software. Controlling may include rescoping of project and/or product or changes to tools and techniques.

3.7 Closing Process Group

According to the *PMBOK® Guide*, the techniques presented in the Closing Process Group are equally applicable to software projects. The demonstration of working software is an important element of closing a software project or an iteration cycle. It is important to conduct a retrospective, lessons-learned session; assess team performance; and update the organizational knowledge base during closing of an iteration cycle and during closing of a software project. These activities can provide data for improving future performance.

3.8 Project Information

Section 3.8 of the *PMBOK® Guide* describes three kinds of project information: work performance data, work performance information, and work performance reports. Data is transformed into information that is used to prepare reports. According to the *PMBOK® Guide*, this primary data is compared with other collected data elements, analyzed in context, and aggregated and transformed to become project information. The information can then be communicated verbally or stored and distributed as reports in various document formats. Various kinds of data, information, and reports for software projects are based on the life cycle model being used and are described in Sections 6 through 13 of this *Software Extension*.

Data collected during a software project and the resulting information (including modules, components, functions, and features implemented) can be used to predict attributes such as progress versus plan, and the cost and delivery date of intermediate and final product deliveries.

Data and information can be collected and saved in an organizational database to provide a basis for estimating future software projects that have similar characteristics (i.e., similar domains, customers, software developers, and development tools). Care should be taken to ensure that the attributes of past and future projects are sufficiently similar when using past performance data and information to estimate a future project.

3.9 Role of the Knowledge Areas

As indicated in Section 3.9 of the *PMBOK® Guide*, the 47 project management processes identified in the *PMBOK® Guide* are organized into ten separate Knowledge Areas. These ten Knowledge Areas are presented in Sections 4 through 13 of the *PMBOK® Guide* and describe the inputs, tools and techniques, and outputs for most projects, most of the time. In a similar manner, the ten Knowledge Areas presented in Sections 4 through 13 of this *Software Extension* describe the inputs, tools and techniques, and outputs for most software projects, most of the time as adapted for different project life cycles within the continuum of software project life cycles.

PROJECT INTEGRATION MANAGEMENT

4

Many of the inputs, tools and techniques, and outputs in Section 4 of the *PMBOK® Guide* are applicable to integration management of software projects. This section of the *Software Extension to the PMBOK® Guide* presents additional considerations that are especially important for integration management of software projects.

As stated in the introduction to Section 4 of the *PMBOK® Guide*, Project Integration Management includes the processes and activities needed to identify, define, combine, unify, and coordinate the various processes and project management activities within the Project Management Process Groups.

It is important to note that in this *Software Extension*, Project Integration Management refers to the integration of the processes and activities in this Knowledge Area; it does not refer to the technical process of integrating software components to form a partial or completed software product.

Planning and conducting a software project is mostly a proactive endeavor, rather than integration and coordination of subsidiary plans, as presented in Section 4 of the *PMBOK® Guide*. Sometimes, other departments provide some functional capabilities (e.g., configuration management, independent testing, etc.) however, for the most part, software project managers are responsible for planning and conducting a wide scope of project activities (see Section 5 of this *Software Extension*).

There is no single best way to manage a software project. A wide range of influences impacts the need for emphasis on and the rigor of various project management activities for software projects. Each of the 47 processes in the *PMBOK® Guide* should be addressed to determine the appropriate level of implementation for each project endeavor. Project managers can tailor and adapt the project management processes in the *PMBOK® Guide* and this *Software Extension* to maximize the potential of the project team for achieving the desired level of project performance.

Figure 4-1 provides an overview of Project Integration Management for software projects.

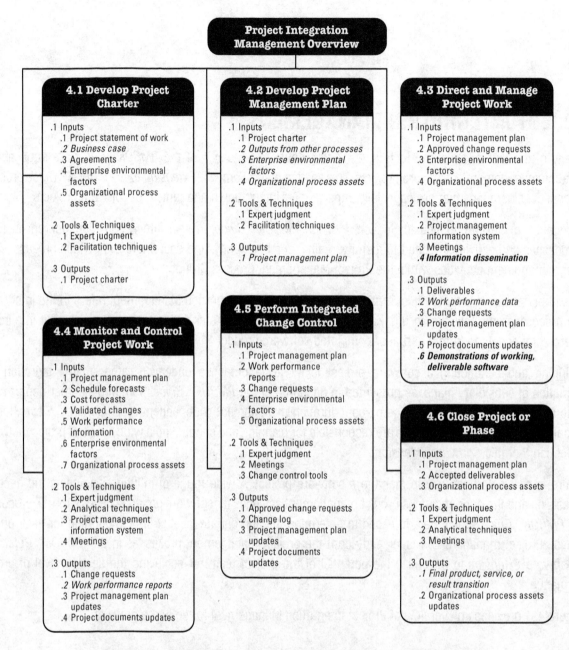

Figure 4-1. Software Project Integration Management Overview

4.1 Develop Project Charter

According to Section 4.1 of the *PMBOK® Guide*, Develop Project Charter is the process of developing a document that formally authorizes the existence of a project and provides the project manager with the authority to apply organizational resources to project activities. The inputs, tools and techniques, and outputs presented in Section 4.1 of the *PMBOK® Guide* are applicable to developing a software project charter.

4.1.1 Develop Project Charter: Inputs

The inputs in Section 4.1.1 of the *PMBOK® Guide* are applicable for developing a software project charter.

4.1.1.1 Project Statement of Work

See Section 4.1.1.1 of the *PMBOK® Guide*.

4.1.1.2 Business Case

See Section 4.1.1.2 of the *PMBOK® Guide*.

In addition, the business case for a software product, and particularly for an enterprise system, should address total cost of ownership, to include anticipated operational and sustainment costs.

4.1.1.3 Agreements

See Section 4.1.1.3 of the *PMBOK® Guide*.

4.1.1.4 Enterprise Environmental Factors

See Section 4.1.1.4 of the *PMBOK® Guide*.

4.1.1.5 Organizational Process Assets

See Section 4.1.1.5 of the *PMBOK® Guide*.

4.1.2 Develop Project Charter: Tools and Techniques

The tools and techniques presented in Section 4.1.2 of the *PMBOK® Guide* are applicable for developing a software project charter with the following additional considerations.

Domain experts should be consulted when developing a software project charter. Expertise in developing similar systems using similar development platforms, systems software, product architecture, and information design (i.e., databases, data interchanges, and data warehouses) may provide valuable insights and expose unrecognized complexities and risk factors. In addition, when software projects involve working with existing software, inputs from experts familiar with the architecture, technical implementation, and/or testing approach can provide assistance in developing the project charter. Those familiar with the project team (when known) can provide inputs concerning team capabilities.

4.1.2.1 Expert Judgment

See Section 4.1.2.1 of the *PMBOK® Guide*.

4.1.2.2 Facilitation Techniques

See Section 4.1.2.2 of the *PMBOK® Guide*.

4.1.3 Develop Project Charter: Outputs

See Section 4.1.3 of the *PMBOK® Guide*.

4.1.3.1 Project Charter

See Section 4.1.3.1 of the *PMBOK® Guide*.

4.2 Develop Project Management Plan

According to Section 4.2 of the *PMBOK® Guide*, Develop Project Management Plan is the process of defining, preparing, and coordinating all subsidiary plans and integrating them into a comprehensive project management plan.

The extent to which this process pertains to software projects depends on the software project life cycle selected, the organizational structure and culture, and the project context. The software project manager may perform all project planning activities, or some planning activities, such as preparing estimates based on historical data, may be performed by a project management office or an internal consulting group. Other planning activities, such as independent testing, may be performed by other functional groups. Project Integration Management ensures that all necessary processes are being performed with sufficient rigor and that sufficient project performance information will be produced so that the software project manager can perform the appropriate Executing and Monitoring and Controlling processes.

Project managers of predictive life cycle software projects tend to put substantial effort into upfront development of the project plan and integration of organizational assets including plans developed by personnel from other organizational units (e.g., configuration management, quality assurance, cost management, and risk management). In adaptive projects, there is typically less upfront effort spent on developing detailed scope, cost, and schedule plans.

Regardless of the life cycle adopted, software projects may also need to integrate a number of additional plans (and perhaps functional groups) such as an information security management plan, information management plan, problem management plan, product launch plan, release plan, and perhaps a team training plan for new technologies or for a new domain. Significant effort is typically spent on defining Monitoring and Controlling processes to ensure coordination among the project members or project teams when the plans are implemented.

Project constraints that influence development of a software project plan include organizational policies, size and criticality of the project, identified risks and risk management strategies complexity of the problem domain and solution domain, and availability of needed resources (including number of team members having appropriate skills). Projects with rigid project and product constraints may require increased emphasis on the Project Risk

Management, Project Integration Management, Project Procurement Management, Project Quality Management, and Project Stakeholder Management processes as described in the corresponding Knowledge Areas of the *PMBOK® Guide* and this *Software Extension*.

Determining the composition of software teams is an important element of project planning for software projects because software is developed by the coordinated intellectual effort of the team members. It is not advisable to plan a large team for a large software project. A preferred approach is to scale up by increasing the number of teams, which limits the number of communication paths within each team. Communication among teams can be controlled by an architectural design that permits the allocation of requirements and interfaces to different teams that can work on components in a concurrent manner with planned integration points.

The project plan includes the integration and verification processes, which typically occur following software construction for predictive life cycles and are integrated into adaptive life cycles. Software projects that have multiple teams typically have team leaders who report to the project manager. In addition to coordinating a team's work, software project team leaders are also developmental or functional contributors; however, they are not considered to be management overhead.

Large complex projects may be organized as multiple subprojects with a project management team, or as multiple distinct projects having a program manager who coordinates the multiple projects, each of which will have a project manager and team leaders for each project. In these cases, it is important to allocate requirements and interfaces to project, subproject, and team (or program, project, and team) so that development of product components can proceed concurrently with a plan for periodic integration of work products. More emphasis is placed on Project Human Resources Management and Project Communications Management processes as the scale of a project grows (see Sections 10 and 13 of the *PMBOK® Guide* and this *Software Extension*).

The form of a software project management plan and the emphasis placed on various aspects of planning and the plan depends on many factors, including but not limited to the project and product scope, product requirements, the choice of software project life cycle model, the organizational assets, the influence of contextual factors, and the nature of the customer relationship.

For example, the choice of a predictive or an adaptive project life cycle model influences the planning for management of scope, time, cost, and product integration, in addition to other factors. A project that uses a geographically distributed project team places emphasis on human resource issues and management of those resources. Perceived complexity of the product and familiarity of the software team with the problem domain and the technology to be used places emphasis on planning for quality control, quality assurance, and risk management. Dealing with vendors and subcontractors places emphasis on planning for procurement activities.

Regardless of the software project life cycle adopted, the development and integration of elements of a software project management plan is rarely a linear process because project elements evolve at different rates and exert different levels of influence on other elements. Conducting a software project is a learning process that results in revision of the project plan and subsidiary plans as understanding grows; replanning of both the project and product is inevitable for software projects, regardless of the life cycle used.

4.2.1 Develop Project Management Plan: Inputs

Section 4.2.1 of the *PMBOK® Guide* indicates that developing a project management plan is the process of defining, preparing, and coordinating all subsidiary plans and integrating them into a comprehensive project management plan (see also Figure 4-5 of the *PMBOK® Guide*). As stated previously, development of a software project plan tends to be a process of planning the primary activities, coordinating development of subordinate plans, and integrating them into a software project management plan. In a mature organization, development of a software project management plan may involve the use of templates and the tailoring of existing organizational assets.

Estimates of cost, schedule, technical infrastructure, and risk provide important inputs for developing a project management plan, as indicated in Section 4.2.1 of the *PMBOK® Guide*. Every software project differs from all past projects because software replication is a simple process that does not require a project, in contrast to replication of physical artifacts so there are typically many unknowns and uncertainties during the initiating and planning stages of a software project. The unknowns and uncertainties often result in imprecise and inaccurate software project estimates.

See Sections 6 and 7 of this *Software Extension* for more information concerning estimation for software projects. ISO/IEC/IEEE Standard 16326 [18] also provides useful information concerning inputs for planning software projects.

4.2.1.1 Project Charter

See Section 4.2.1.1 of the *PMBOK® Guide*.

4.2.1.2 Outputs from Other Processes

Outputs from the processes described in Sections 5 through 13 of the *PMBOK® Guide* and this *Software Extension* are integrated to create a software project management plan.

4.2.1.3 Enterprise Environmental Factors

Enterprise environmental factors, in addition to those in Section 4.2.1.3 of the *PMBOK® Guide*, which may impact planning a software project include availability of skilled human resources; policies for using open-source software; and existing technical assets. Existing technical asset may include software that can be reused; development and testing environments tools; supporting infrastructure and facilities; and the technical infrastructure, which includes networks, data repositories, and simulation and modeling facilities.

4.2.1.4 Organizational Process Assets

Organizational process assets listed in Section 4.2.1.4 of the *PMBOK® Guide* are applicable for software projects. In addition, methods and tools for change control and configuration management are needed to control evolving work products such as software code baselines because software code may be updated and changed frequently during software development. Without effective version control, the incorrect version of a software module may be used as the basis for further work or may be incorrectly integrated into a demonstrable or deliverable product baseline.

Some software projects use formal governance mechanisms to maintain control of software artifacts, such as a software change control board. Other software projects use frequent demonstrations of working software and consultations with the customer or user representative to agree on changes to be made.

4.2.2 Develop Project Management Plan: Tools and Techniques

The tools and techniques in Section 4.2.2 of the *PMBOK® Guide* are applicable for developing a software project management plan. Templates and estimation tools are useful when developing a software project plan.

4.2.2.1 Expert Judgment

See Section 4.2.2.1 of the *PMBOK® Guide*.

4.2.2.2 Facilitation Techniques

See Section 4.2.2.2 of the *PMBOK® Guide*.

4.2.3 Develop Project Management Plan: Outputs

4.2.3.1 Project Management Plan

See Section 4.2.3.1 of the *PMBOK® Guide*. In addition, the following plans may be included as supporting outputs:

- Requirements management plan,
- Configuration management plan,
- Security plans (physical, project, data),
- Quality management plan,
- Enterprise technology insertion plan,
- Information security plan,
- Test and evaluation plan,
- Information management plan,
- Release and deployment plan,
- Technology infrastructure plan, and
- Project-specific training plan for the software team.

Release and deployment plans are important for software projects that involve deployment of a software product to external customer sites. Technology infrastructure plans are important for installation and sustainment of IT infrastructure products.

The level of detail in supporting plans varies with the scope and criticality of the project and product. Supporting plans may be incorporated into the project plan or developed as separate documents referenced within the project plan.

4.3 Direct and Manage Project Work

Software project managers who manage predictive life cycle projects tend to follow more closely the traditional approaches to directing and managing project work included in Section 4.3 of the *PMBOK® Guide* than do managers of adaptive life cycle software projects.

A characteristic attribute of adaptive software teams is that they are self-enabled and self-directed, which places the project manager in a more hands-off position in the day-to-day management of the project team than the manager of a predictive life cycle project team. However, this does not mean the software project manager is left without a role in directing and managing adaptive software projects. Activities engaged in by project managers of adaptive life cycle software projects include, but are not limited to:

- Communicating the project scope, resources, and schedule/budget constraints to the project team and other appropriate stakeholders;
- Providing the resources and facilities needed by the software team;
- Managing project scope, stakeholder expectation, resources, schedule, and budget;
- Creating effective mechanisms to see an ongoing overall picture of progress, status, and issues;
- Controlling changes to project scope, resources, schedule, and budget;
- Consulting with and allocating the work among multiple software development teams;
- Ensuring communication and coordination of work activities among multiple teams and coordinating the integration of resources and components;
- Facilitating ongoing and continuous communications between the customer/user representatives and the software developers;
- Monitoring productivity, product quality, and team performance while making adjustments as needed;
- Ensuring effective interactions with other organizational units, such as independent testing and user training;
- Facilitating demonstrations of evolving product capabilities for appropriate stakeholders;
- Facilitating delivery of early product capabilities into the user environment, as desired;
- Facilitating delivery and acceptance of the final product and closing the project;
- Coordinating dependencies with related projects, which may be elements of a common development program or milestone dependencies with related IT infrastructure projects; and
- Managing risk.

Managers of all software projects engage in these activities, whether using a predictive or adaptive life cycle, although the details vary with the life cycle model used.

4

4.3.1 Direct and Manage Project Work: Inputs

See Section 4.3.1 of the *PMBOK® Guide* for inputs that are generally applicable inputs for directing and managing software project work.

4.3.1.1 Project Management Plan

See Section 4.3.1.1 of the *PMBOK® Guide*.

4.3.1.2 Approved Change Requests

See Section 4.3.1.2 of the *PMBOK® Guide*.

4.3.1.3 Enterprise Environmental Factors

See Section 4.3.1.3 of the *PMBOK® Guide*.

4.3.1.4 Organizational Process Assets

See Section 4.3.1.4 of the *PMBOK® Guide*.

4.3.2 Direct and Manage Project Work: Tools and Techniques

The tools and techniques presented in Section 4.3.2 of the *PMBOK® Guide* are generally applicable tools and techniques for directing and managing software project execution. In addition to these, information dissemination is an important tool/technique for directing and managing software project execution (see Section 4.3.2.4 of this extension).

4.3.2.1 Expert Judgment

See Section 4.3.2.1 of the *PMBOK® Guide*.

4.3.2.2 Project Management Information System

See Section 4.3.2.2 of the *PMBOK® Guide*.

4.3.2.3 Meetings

See Section 4.3.2.3 of the *PMBOK® Guide*.

4.3.2.4 Information Dissemination

Because software is an intangible product, tools and techniques for disseminating project information are particularly important for software projects. Providing appropriate and timely information to team members, managers, customer, users, other stakeholders, and everyone who affects or is affected by a software project, at the level appropriate for each constituency, is an important activity for a software project manager. The kind of information to be disseminated includes, but is not limited to:

- Current overall status of the project;

- Risks and risk status (watch list, monitored, confronted);

- Current work assignments;

- Daily progress and remaining work;

- Forecasts of future project status;

- Number of requirements, features, stories, or use cases written/demonstrated/delivered;

- Number of test cases and test scenarios written/passed;

- Product components/features implemented versus cost or staff-hours;

- Resolutions and action items from the last retrospective meeting; and

- Status of servers and other infrastructure equipment (up, down, in maintenance).

See Section 10 (Project Communications Management) for additional information concerning information dissemination.

Some software projects use large displays (i.e., information radiators) posted in locations where software developers and other team members can easily see them; the displays are typically posted in locations where it is difficult to avoid seeing them. The purpose of visual displays is to communicate essential project information that personnel need to know without anyone having to ask questions. This approach facilitates increased communication with less confusion and misinterpretation for the project team and other stakeholders. Well-designed visual displays are:

- Large and readily visible,

- Understood at a glance, and

- Changed periodically and kept current.

Visual displays are more effective when the purpose is clear and the information is succinctly presented. Although visual displays are usually paper-based and posted in the team room or in a hallway, they can be presented on large screen monitors or on readily accessible web pages. Visual displays can be used to inform stakeholders beyond the project team concerning project status and other issues that may be of concern to them.

4.3.3 Direct and Manage Project Work: Outputs

The outputs presented in Section 4.3.3 of the *PMBOK® Guide* are applicable for directing and managing software project execution. Additional outputs are provided in Sections 4.3.3.2 and 4.3.3.6 of this *Software Extension*.

4

4.3.3.1 Deliverables

See Section 4.3.3.1 of the *PMBOK® Guide*.

4.3.3.2 Work Performance Data

See Section 4.3.3.2 of the *PMBOK® Guide*.

Productivity and progress indicators such as velocity and burndown and burnup charts provide work performance data for adaptive life cycle software projects (see the Glossary for definitions of these terms).

4.3.3.3 Change Requests

See Section 4.3.3.3 of the *PMBOK® Guide*.

4.3.3.4 Project Management Plan Updates

See Section 4.3.3.4 of the *PMBOK® Guide*.

4.3.3.5 Project Documents Updates

See Section 4.3.3.5 of the *PMBOK® Guide*.

4.3.3.6 Demonstrations of Working, Deliverable Software

In addition to the outputs contained in Section 4.3.3 of the *PMBOK® Guide*, frequent and ongoing demonstrations of working, deliverable software are the most important indicators of tangible progress for software projects.

4.4 Monitor and Control Project Work

The inputs, tools and techniques, and outputs for monitoring and controlling project work in Section 4.4 of the *PMBOK® Guide* are applicable for monitoring and controlling software project work. In addition, increments of working software code can be evaluated against the project and product constraints, the team performance, and the overall goals of the project to trigger change control events, as necessary, when those events exceed control limits. A scope management plan, perhaps including a prioritization scheme and business rules, can be helpful in managing scope changes that fall outside of the control limits of the project or product.

4.4.1 Monitor and Control Project Work: Inputs

4.4.1.1 Project Management Plan

See Section 4.4.1.1 of the *PMBOK® Guide.*

4.4.1.2 Schedule Forecasts

See Section 4.4.1.2 of the *PMBOK® Guide.*

4.4.1.3 Cost Forecasts

See Section 4.4.1.3 of the *PMBOK® Guide.*

4.4.1.4 Validated Changes

See Section 4.4.1.4 of the *PMBOK® Guide.*

4.4.1.5 Work Performance Information

See Section 4.4.1.5 of the *PMBOK® Guide.*

4.4.1.6 Enterprise Environmental Factors

See Section 4.4.1.6 of the *PMBOK® Guide.*

4.4.1.7 Organizational Process Assets

See Section 4.4.1.7 of the *PMBOK® Guide.*

4.4.2 Monitor and Control Project Work: Tools and Techniques

The tools and techniques for monitoring and controlling project work in Section 4.4.2 of the *PMBOK® Guide* are applicable tools and techniques for monitoring and controlling software projects.

4.4.2.1 Expert Judgment

See Section 4.4.2.1 of the *PMBOK® Guide.*

4.4.2.2 Analytical Techniques

See Section 4.4.2.2 of the *PMBOK® Guide*.

4.4.2.3 Project Management Information System

See Section 4.4.2.3 of the *PMBOK® Guide*.

4.4.2.4 Meetings

See Section 4.4.2.4 of the *PMBOK® Guide*.

4.4.3 Monitor and Control Software Project Work: Outputs

The outputs for monitoring and controlling project work in Section 4.4.3 of the *PMBOK® Guide* are applicable outputs for monitoring and controlling software projects, with the following extension to 4.4.3.2.

4.4.3.1 Change Requests

See Section 4.4.3.1 of the *PMBOK® Guide*.

4.4.3.2 Work Performance Reports

Work performance reports for software project, in addition to those in Section 4.4.3.2 of the *PMBOK® Guide* include:

- Updates to estimates (product size, delivered quality, delivery date, final cost);
- Team productivity measures such as velocity metrics and burndown and burnup charts;
- Feature backlogs; and
- Configuration management reports.

4.4.3.3 Project Management Plan Updates

See Section 4.4.3.3 of the *PMBOK® Guide*.

4.4.3.4 Project Documents Updates

See Section 4.4.3.4 of the *PMBOK® Guide*.

4.5 Perform Integrated Change Control

See Section 4.5 of the *PMBOK® Guide,* which is applicable for performing integrated change control when managing software projects, with the following extensions.

4.5.1 Perform Integrated Change Control: Inputs

The inputs for performing integrated change control, as presented in the *PMBOK® Guide,* are applicable for performing integrated change control for software projects.

Variations that trigger change control processes differ for different software project life cycles. Control limits for schedule, cost, defects, and product scope are usually established during initiation and planning for predictive software project life cycle projects; exceeding a control limit triggers a change control process. For adaptive project life cycles, formal change control is not usually required for occasional anomalies, as long as the vision and goals of the project can be achieved within the constraints on project and product scope.

4.5.1.1 Project Management Plan

See Section 4.5.1.1 of the *PMBOK® Guide.*

4.5.1.2 Work Performance Reports

See Section 4.5.1.2 of the *PMBOK® Guide.*

4.5.1.3 Change Requests

See Section 4.5.1.3 of the *PMBOK® Guide.*

4.5.1.4 Enterprise Environmental Factors

See Section 4.5.1.4 of the *PMBOK® Guide.*

4.5.1.5 Organizational Process Assets

See Section 4.5.1.5 of the *PMBOK® Guide.*

4.5.2 Perform Integrated Change Control: Tools and Techniques

The tools and techniques for performing integrated change control, as presented in Section 4.5.2 of the *PMBOK® Guide,* are applicable for performing integrated change control for software projects.

All proposed changes should be evaluated for impacts on project and product scope, the software team, customers, users, and other operational stakeholders. Changing the color of an icon on a user display may not be important, or it may render the application unusable when some users are unable to detect certain colors or when compliance with disability regulations concerning color blindness may be required. Adding an additional choice on a web page may have no impact on present capabilities or it may render a data interchange capability inoperable. Therefore, some changes are minor and others may have significant impacts; all proposed changes need to be evaluated for impact.

For predictive software life cycle projects, a change control process typically includes change requests and change control boards; the change control board may schedule the request at an indicated level of priority, defer it, or deny it. For adaptive life cycle projects, a change request is another element of the product feature set. An iteration feature set includes both requests for new features and requests for modifications to existing features; the content of new and modified features may determine the priority of the features in an iteration feature set.

4.5.2.1 Expert Judgment

See Section 4.5.2.1 of the *PMBOK® Guide*.

4.5.2.2 Meetings

See Section 4.5.2.2 of the *PMBOK® Guide*.

4.5.2.3 Change Control Tools

See Section 4.5.2.3 of the *PMBOK® Guide*.

4.5.3 Perform Integrated Software Change Control: Outputs

See Section 4.5.3 of the *PMBOK® Guide* for outputs applicable to performing integrated change control for software projects.

4.5.3.1 Approved Change Requests

See Section 4.5.3.1 of the *PMBOK® Guide.*

4.5.3.2 Change Log

See Section 4.5.3.2 of the *PMBOK® Guide*.

4.5.3.3 Project Management Plan Updates

See Section 4.5.3.3 of the *PMBOK® Guide*.

4.5.3.4 Project Documents Updates

See Section 4.5.3.4 of the *PMBOK® Guide*.

4.6 Close Project or Phase

According to Section 4.6 of the *PMBOK® Guide*, Close Project or Phase is the process of finalizing all activities across all five Project Management Process Groups to formally complete the project or phase. The inputs, tools and techniques, and outputs for closing a project in Section 4.6 of the *PMBOK® Guide* are applicable to closing a software project, project phase, or iteration cycle.

Two items are particularly important when closing a software project: historical productivity data and lessons learned. This information should be captured in organizational data repositories. Historical data provides a basis for estimating future, similar projects. Historical data and lessons learned can be used to identify trends, both positive and negative, during the life cycle of a project. Positive trends can indicate areas for organizational process improvement by indicating good practices used on the project that should be adopted throughout the organization. Negative trends and lessons learned indicate areas for needed process improvements throughout the software organization. Adherence to requirements for legal review and approval may be an important additional element of the closing process for software projects.

For purposes of future sustainment and possible reuse of the software, the software project manager, and others, as appropriate, should arrange for continuing configuration control of the software assets, such as requirements, source code, and associated architecture and design documentation for the life of the software product.

4.6.1 Close Project or Phase: Inputs

The inputs for closing a project or phase in Section 4.6.1 of the *PMBOK® Guide* are applicable inputs for closing a software project, phase, or iteration cycle.

4.6.1.1 Project Management Plan

See Section 4.6.1.1 of the *PMBOK® Guide*.

4.6.1.2 Accepted Deliverables

See Section 4.6.1.2 of the *PMBOK® Guide*.

4.6.1.3 Organizational Process Assets

See Section 4.6.1.3 of the *PMBOK® Guide*.

4.6.2 Close Project or Phase: Tools and Techniques

The tools and techniques for closing a project or phase in Section 4.6.2 of the *PMBOK® Guide* are applicable for closing a software project, phase, or iteration cycle.

4.6.2.1 Expert Judgment

See Section 4.6.2.1 of the *PMBOK® Guide*.

4.6.2.2 Analytical Techniques

See Section 4.6.1.2 of the *PMBOK® Guide*.

4.6.2.3 Meetings

See Section 4.6.2.3 of the *PMBOK® Guide*.

4.6.3 Close Project or Phase: Outputs

The outputs in Section 4.6.3 of the *PMBOK® Guide* are applicable outputs for closing a software project, phase, or iteration cycle.

4.6.3.1 Final Product, Service, or Result Transition

See Section 4.6.3.1 of the *PMBOK® Guide*.

Archiving of software work products, including delivered source code and related documentation plus project performance data, is an important activity during the transition process from software development to software delivery.

4.6.3.2 Organizational Process Assets Updates

See Section 4.6.3.2 of the *PMBOK® Guide*.

5

PROJECT SCOPE MANAGEMENT

Most of the material in Section 5 of the *PMBOK® Guide* is applicable to scope management for software projects. This section of the *Software Extension* presents additional considerations for managing software project scope.

As stated in the introduction to Section 5 of the *PMBOK® Guide:* Project Scope Management includes the processes required to ensure that the project includes all the work required, and only the work required, to complete the project successfully. This section of the *Software Extension to the PMBOK® Guide* presents additional considerations for managing the scope of a software project.

Also from the introduction to Section 5 of the *PMBOK® Guide*:

"In the project context, the term scope can refer to:

- **Product scope.** The features and functions that characterize a product, service, or result; and/or
- **Project scope.** The work performed to deliver a product, service, or result with the specified features and functions. The term project scope is frequently viewed as including product scope."

For software, product scope includes features and quality attributes that are needed and desired by users, customers, and other stakeholders. Product scope can be used to estimate project scope (i.e., schedule, budget, resources, and technology). Alternatively, constraints on project scope may determine product scope (features and quality attributes). Constraints on both project scope and product scope may require trade-offs among features, quality attributes, schedule, budget, resources, and technology.

Project and product scope determine the effort needed to develop or modify a software product. Effort is the primary cost factor for most software projects, because software is the direct product of effort. Additional costs may include the cost of elements such as user training, product documentation, hardware and software platforms, and perhaps a dedicated testing facility. Team effort is also used as the basis for determining the schedule for a software project; a project estimated to require 60 person-months of effort might be scheduled as 10 months for 6 people. Teams for adaptive life cycle projects often have a fixed number of team members and a fixed duration for each iteration cycle; the scope of work to be completed during an iteration is thus adjusted for the duration, the number of team members, and availability of other resources. See Sections 6 and 7 of this *Software Extension* for cost and time management considerations for software projects. Although presented in separate sections of this *Software Extension*, schedule and cost (effort) are closely intertwined for software projects.

Section 2 of this *Software Extension* presents the continuum of life cycles for software projects that lie within a spectrum from highly predictive life cycles to highly adaptive life cycles. This section describes the common elements of and the distinctions between project scope management for predictive and adaptive life cycles for software projects.

Figure 5-1 provides an overview of Project Scope Management in this *Software Extension*.

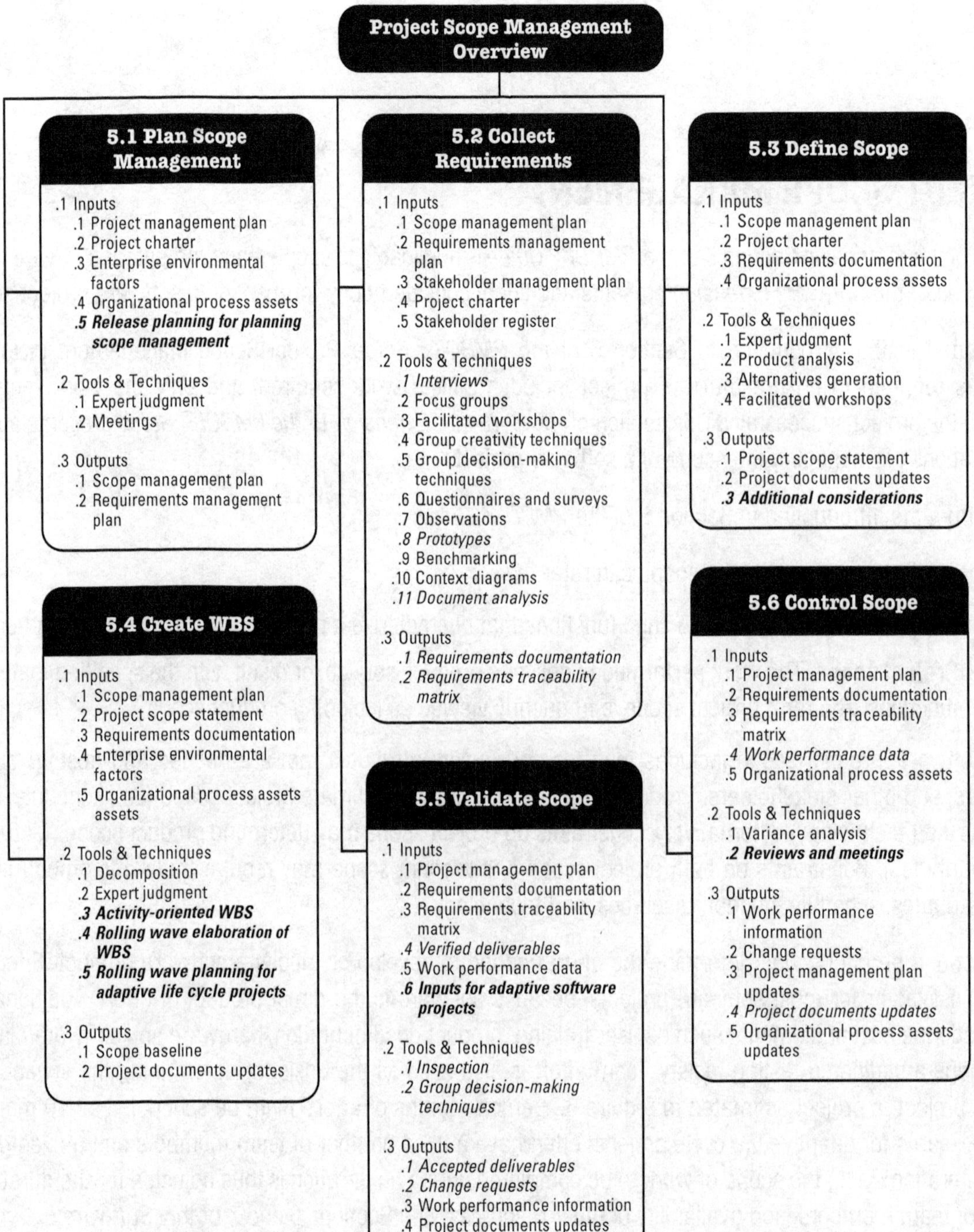

Project Scope Management Overview

5.1 Plan Scope Management

.1 Inputs
.1 Project management plan
.2 Project charter
.3 Enterprise environmental factors
.4 Organizational process assets
.5 Release planning for planning scope management

.2 Tools & Techniques
.1 Expert judgment
.2 Meetings

.3 Outputs
.1 Scope management plan
.2 Requirements management plan

5.4 Create WBS

.1 Inputs
.1 Scope management plan
.2 Project scope statement
.3 Requirements documentation
.4 Enterprise environmental factors
.5 Organizational process assets assets

.2 Tools & Techniques
.1 Decomposition
.2 Expert judgment
.3 Activity-oriented WBS
.4 Rolling wave elaboration of WBS
.5 Rolling wave planning for adaptive life cycle projects

.3 Outputs
.1 Scope baseline
.2 Project documents updates

5.2 Collect Requirements

.1 Inputs
.1 Scope management plan
.2 Requirements management plan
.3 Stakeholder management plan
.4 Project charter
.5 Stakeholder register

.2 Tools & Techniques
.1 Interviews
.2 Focus groups
.3 Facilitated workshops
.4 Group creativity techniques
.5 Group decision-making techniques
.6 Questionnaires and surveys
.7 Observations
.8 Prototypes
.9 Benchmarking
.10 Context diagrams
.11 Document analysis

.3 Outputs
.1 Requirements documentation
.2 Requirements traceability matrix

5.5 Validate Scope

.1 Inputs
.1 Project management plan
.2 Requirements documentation
.3 Requirements traceability matrix
.4 Verified deliverables
.5 Work performance data
.6 Inputs for adaptive software projects

.2 Tools & Techniques
.1 Inspection
.2 Group decision-making techniques

.3 Outputs
.1 Accepted deliverables
.2 Change requests
.3 Work performance information
.4 Project documents updates

5.3 Define Scope

.1 Inputs
.1 Scope management plan
.2 Project charter
.3 Requirements documentation
.4 Organizational process assets

.2 Tools & Techniques
.1 Expert judgment
.2 Product analysis
.3 Alternatives generation
.4 Facilitated workshops

.3 Outputs
.1 Project scope statement
.2 Project documents updates
.3 Additional considerations

5.6 Control Scope

.1 Inputs
.1 Project management plan
.2 Requirements documentation
.3 Requirements traceability matrix
.4 Work performance data
.5 Organizational process assets

.2 Tools & Techniques
.1 Variance analysis
.2 Reviews and meetings

.3 Outputs
.1 Work performance information
.2 Change requests
.3 Project management plan updates
.4 Project documents updates
.5 Organizational process assets updates

Figure 5-1. Software Project Scope Management Overview

5.1 Plan Scope Management

Section 5.1 of the *PMBOK® Guide* indicates that planning scope management is the process of planning for, defining, and documenting stakeholder needs to meet the project objectives. The details of planning scope management for a software project depend on the life cycle model used to manage the project. Predictive software project life cycles rely on initially collecting and documenting the software product requirements (to the extent possible) and developing the software architecture; these are used to determine the scope of the project, which provides the basis for developing a work breakdown structure (WBS). A predictive life cycle for a software project is most likely to result in a successful project when stable software requirements can be developed in sufficient detail during project initiation and planning; there is a fixed definition of scope that results in a detailed initial WBS; and the product is in a familiar product domain. Many software projects require innovations that cannot be initially foreseen and planned, perhaps because the user community is not sure what is needed or how it can be provided, or perhaps new technology is involved (new hardware, new infrastructure software), or environmental factors, such as new policies and regulations, should be considered. Planning an adaptive life cycle project, in which the project scope and product scope evolve together as features are iteratively elaborated, is appropriate for these kinds of software projects.

5.1.1 Plan Scope Management: Inputs

The inputs for planning the scope of a software project in Section 5.1.1 of the *PMBOK® Guide* are suitable inputs for planning scope management for software projects. Two additional inputs that are applicable for planning scope management of adaptive life cycle software projects are presented in Section 5.1.1.5 of this *Software Extension*.

5.1.1.1 Project Management Plan

See Section 5.1.1.1 of the *PMBOK® Guide*.

5.1.1.2 Project Charter

See Section 5.1.1.2 of the *PMBOK® Guide*.

5.1.1.3 Enterprise Environmental Factors

See Section 5.1.1.3 of the *PMBOK® Guide*.

5.1.1.4 Organizational Process Assets

See Section 5.1.1.4 of the *PMBOK® Guide*.

5.1.1.5 Release Planning for Planning Scope Management

Release planning for a software project can also provide an input for Plan Scope Management of a software project. As shown in Figure 5-2, the product scope for a software project can be specified as a sequence of feature sets (i.e., requirements) specified during project initiation and planning. Each feature set is developed as deliverable software that can be released for demonstration to external stakeholders, and released into the user environment, when desired. The product increments in each feature set can be developed and demonstrated to internal stakeholders and to external stakeholders, when planned or desired. Planning the features sets provides an input for planning scope management. For predictive life cycle projects, the increments for each feature set may also be planned initially.

For adaptive life cycle software projects, the number and content of the feature sets are typically specified during project initiation and planning. The number and content of increments for each feature set are typically planned as the project evolves, but the number and content of both feature sets and increments may be adjusted as the project evolves. The release plan may evolve in a rolling wave manner, as described in Section 5.4.2.5 of this *Software Extension*, which includes another example of planning feature sets for adaptive life cycle software projects.

Also note, in Figure 5-2, that the number of increments may differ for different feature sets for both predictive and adaptive software project life cycles. Development of each increment many involve multiple iteration cycles, in

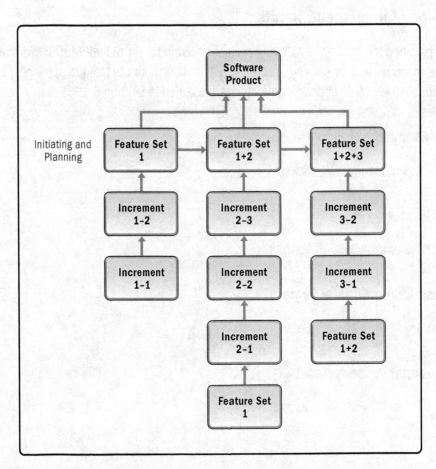

Figure 5-2. Release Planning for an Adaptive Software Project Life Cycle

both cases. As described in Section 2.4 of this *Software Extension*, development iterations and product increments are independent factors.

5.1.2 Plan Scope Management: Tools and Techniques

The tools and techniques in Section 5.1.2 of the *PMBOK® Guide* can be used to plan scope management for both predictive and adaptive life cycle software projects.

5.1.2.1 Expert Judgment

See Section 5.1.2.1 of the *PMBOK® Guide.*

5.1.2.2 Meetings

See Section 5.1.2.2 of the *PMBOK® Guide.*

5.1.3 Plan Scope Management: Outputs

The outputs for planning scope management of a software project include the scope management plan and the requirements management plan, as indicated in Section 5.1.3 of the *PMBOK® Guide*. In addition, the project plan may include a release plan (see 5.1.1.5 of this *Software Extension*).

5.1.3.1 Scope Management Plan

See 5.1.3.1 of the *PMBOK® Guide.*

5.1.3.2 Requirements Management Plan

See 5.1.3.2 of the *PMBOK® Guide.*

5.2 Collect Requirements

The inputs, tools and techniques, and outputs for Collect Requirements in Section 5.2 of the *PMBOK® Guide* are applicable for collecting requirements for software projects.

The Collect Requirements process is often referred to as "Elicit Requirements" in software engineering. Software requirements provide the basis for establishing project and product scope and for determining needed resources. Requirements are collected (elicited), to the extent possible, during the initiation and planning phases of all software projects. Additional requirements may emerge, especially during the iterative cycles of adaptive software project life cycles [19].

Initially, in predictive life cycle software projects, there is an attempt to develop a set of software requirements that is complete, correct, consistent, and detailed. The requirements provide the basis for determining the scope of the project and for developing the WBS and the work packages. Project scope is then managed by controlling changes to the software requirements and the work activities needed to implement those requirements. The impact of changes to product requirements on the project schedule, budget, resources, and technology may require revision of the project scope and is reflected in changes to the WBS. Change control boards and a version control system are typically utilized in predictive life cycle software projects to manage the changing scope of a software project.

5.2.1 Collect Requirements: Inputs

The inputs for collecting requirements in Section 5.2.1 of the *PMBOK® Guide* are applicable to collecting requirements for software projects.

5.2.1.1 Scope Management Plan

See Section 5.2.1.1 of the *PMBOK® Guide*.

5.2.1.2 Requirements Management Plan

See Section 5.2.1.2 of the *PMBOK® Guide*.

5.2.1.3 Stakeholder Management Plan

See Section 5.2.1.3 of the *PMBOK® Guide*.

5.2.1.4 Project Charter

See Section 5.2.1.4 of the *PMBOK® Guide*.

5.2.1.5 Stakeholder Register

See Section 5.2.1.5 of the *PMBOK® Guide*.

5.2.2 Collect Requirements: Tools and Techniques

The tools and techniques in Section 5.2.2 of the *PMBOK® Guide* are applicable tools and techniques for collecting requirements for both predictive and adaptive software projects with the indicated adaptations and extensions. Persona modeling is also used as a tool for collecting software requirements. See Section 13 of this *Software Extension*.

5.2.2.1 Interviews

See Section 5.2.2.1 of the *PMBOK® Guide*.

For IT projects, applicable business rules and business processes can be identified through interviews. The Business Analysis Body of Knowledge (BABOK) can also provide guidance for collecting business requirements.[3]

5.2.2.2 Focus Groups

See Section 5.2.2.2 of the *PMBOK® Guide*.

5.2.2.3 Facilitated Workshops

See Section 5.2.2.3 of the *PMBOK® Guide*.

5.2.2.4 Group Creativity Techniques

See Section 5.2.2.4 of the *PMBOK® Guide*.

5.2.2.5 Group Decision-Making Techniques

See Section 5.2.2.5 of the *PMBOK® Guide*.

5.2.2.6 Questionnaires and Surveys

See Section 5.2.2.6 of the *PMBOK® Guide*.

5.2.2.7 Observations

See Section 5.2.2.7 of the *PMBOK® Guide*.

5.2.2.8 Prototypes

See Section 5.2.2.8 of the *PMBOK® Guide*.

Prototyping is a particularly effective technique for collecting software requirements either predictively or adaptively. In addition, demonstration of working software is a primary technique for eliciting the next set of requirements to be implemented when product increments are developed, either predictively or adaptively.

5.2.2.9 Benchmarking

See Section 5.2.2.9 of the *PMBOK® Guide*.

---

[3] For additional information, refer to www.IIBA.org

5.2.2.10 Context Diagrams

See Section 5.2.2.10 of the *PMBOK® Guide*.

5.2.2.11 Document Analysis

See Section 5.2.2.11 of the *PMBOK® Guide*.

Use cases and user stories are commonly used to collect and analyze features and functional requirements for software.

5.2.3 Collect Requirements: Outputs

The outputs in Section 5.2.3 of the *PMBOK® Guide* are applicable as outputs for collecting software requirements. Documentation guidelines for software requirements are presented in IEEE Standard 830 [20] and IEEE Standard 1362 [21].

For adaptive life cycles, the customer, a customer representative, or a knowledgeable user provides the software requirements in an emergent manner. Adaptive projects typically have a backlog of requirements for potential assignment to future iteration feature sets (the product feature set in Figure 2-5 of this extension). Product feature sets are easier to modify (add, delete, modify, reprioritize features) than are the baselined requirements, architecture, and WBS for a highly predictive software project.

5.2.3.1 Requirements Documentation

See Section 5.2.3.1 of the *PMBOK® Guide*.

Software requirements for predictive life cycle software projects are typically documented in a repository of baselined requirements. Software requirements for future iterations of an adaptive life cycle can be maintained in product feature backlogs, candidate feature lists, story lists, or in a more automated requirements management system.

5.2.3.2 Requirements Traceability Matrix

See Section 5.2.3.2 of the *PMBOK® Guide*.

Requirements documentation, including traceability, is particularly important for software projects because of the intangible nature of software. A requirements traceability matrix provides visibility from software requirements to intermediate work products (e.g., design documentation, test plans, test results), and to the components of the deliverable product.

5.3 Define Scope

According to Section 5.3 of the *PMBOK® Guide*, Define Scope is the process of developing a detailed description of project and product. The nature of software and the fact that software development is the result of coordinated human effort results in a close relationship between process and product scope for both predictive and adaptive life cycle software projects. Some of the inputs, tools and techniques, and outputs for defining the scope of a software project are the same for predictive and adaptive life cycles and some are different. The similarities and differences are presented in this section of this *Software Extension*.

The *PMBOK® Guide* states that since all of the requirements identified in Collect Requirements will not be included in the product, Define Scope involves choosing the requirements that will be part of the product scope. For software projects, this issue is commonly dealt with by prioritizing the requirements using criteria that include the wants and needs of the customer and user communities, and the value added by each requirement. Risks, assumptions, and constraints are also taken into consideration when defining software project and product scope.

5.3.1 Define Scope: Inputs

For predictive software projects, the inputs described Section 5.3.1 of the *PMBOK® Guide* and those listed below are used as inputs to define project and product scope; an attempt is made to initially define the project and product scope completely, correctly, and consistently, and in detail. For adaptive life cycle software projects, the project and product scopes are initially defined to the extent possible, at a high level, but the product scope typically evolves during iterative development. The initial project scope may be adjusted as the product scope emerges.

5.3.1.1 Scope Management Plan

See Section 5.3.1.1 of the *PMBOK® Guide*.

5.3.1.2 Project Charter

See Section 5.3.1.2 of the *PMBOK® Guide*.

5.3.1.3 Requirements Documentation

See Section 5.3.1.3 of the *PMBOK® Guide*.

5.3.1.4 Organizational Process Assets

See Section 5.3.1.4 of the *PMBOK® Guide*.

5.3.2 Define Scope: Tools and Techniques

The tools and techniques listed in Section 5.3.2.1 through 5.3.2.4 are applicable for defining the scope of software project and product.

5.3.2.1 Expert Judgment

See Section 5.3.2.1 of the *PMBOK® Guide.*

5.3.2.2 Product Analysis

See Section 5.3.2.2 of the *PMBOK® Guide.*

5.3.2.3 Alternatives Generation

See Section 5.3.2.3 of the *PMBOK® Guide.*

5.3.2.4 Facilitated Workshops

See Section 5.3.2.4 of the *PMBOK® Guide.*

5.3.3 Define Scope: Outputs

The outputs for defining scope in Section 5.3.3 of the *PMBOK® Guide* are applicable outputs from defining software project and product scope. Section 5.3.3.3 of this *Software Extension* presents additional considerations for defining scope output for adaptive life cycle software projects.

5.3.3.1 Project Scope Statement

See Section 5.3.3.1 of the *PMBOK® Guide.*

5.3.3.2 Project Documents Updates

See Section 5.3.3.2 of the *PMBOK® Guide.*

5.3.3.3 Additional Considerations

For an ideal predictive life cycle software project, the initial project and product scope statement is a static document, although this is rarely the case in practice. In an adaptive life cycle software project, the scope statement is planned to be an evolving document that is bounded by overall project scope constraints. Planning for systematic evolution of project and product scope is a primary factor that distinguishes adaptive software project life cycles from predictive life cycles.

Iterative development cycles and development of product increments can be used during the software construction stage of both predictive and adaptive software projects. The scope of requirements or features that can be implemented during an iteration cycle is determined by the specified time period (the time box) and the production rate of the development team. The production rate can be based on accumulated experience using measures such as velocity and burndown rate when the time box and the number of team members are fixed from iteration to iteration. Short-duration development cycles provide rapid feedback and the ability to revise and reprioritize the product scope based on demonstrations of tested working software; this may be easier to accomplish for adaptive life cycle projects than for predictive life cycle projects.

Another aspect of iterative development that develops product increments on some of the iterative cycles (perhaps all) is the learning environment in which customers and users clarify and prioritize requirements and product features based on value-adding priorities and periodic demonstrations of working software.

5.4 Create WBS

The inputs, tools and techniques, and outputs for Create WBS in Section 5.4 of the *PMBOK® Guide* are equally applicable for creating work breakdown structures for predictive life cycle software projects. Comparable techniques for adaptive software projects are described in Section 5.4.2.5 of this *Software Extension*.

Section 5.4 of the *PMBOK® Guide* includes the following statement: "In the context of the WBS, work refers to work products or deliverables that are the result of activity and not to the activity itself." The *PMBOK® Guide* distinguishes between organizing a WBS by phase or by major deliverables at the second level.

For software projects, the top level of the WBS subdivides the project by life-cycle process or activity. The work products and deliverables are shown as outputs of activities and tasks at lower levels in the WBS. This form of WBS is referred to as an activity-oriented WBS (Section 5.4.2.3 of this *Software Extension* provides an example).

Activity-oriented work breakdown structures are desirable for most software development projects because software is the product of the cognitive processes of software developers and does not involve fabrication of physical work products or deliverables in media such as wood, metal, plastic, or silicon. Work packages for the tasks in a software WBS include specification of the work activities and the work products or deliverables to be created or modified by those work activities, as well as the acceptance criteria for the work products or deliverables. Activity-oriented work breakdown structures are also applicable for other kinds of knowledge-based work.

Considerations for developing an activity-oriented WBS for a predictive life cycle software project can proceed top-down as follows: (a) by first specifying the project activities at the top level and decomposing each top-level element into subordinate activities and tasks; (b) by first identifying the lowest-level tasks to be performed and grouping them into successively larger groupings (activities); or (c) by working "middle out" by identifying intermediate-level activities and decomposing them downward and grouping them upward. In practice, all three approaches are typically used to produce an activity-oriented WBS. Predefined templates for work breakdown structures and work packages, plus examples designed to fit the local situation, make the task of constructing a software WBS much easier than starting without guidance.

The *PMBOK® Guide* distinguishes between organizing a WBS by phase or by major deliverables. Using the technique of embedding the work to produce deliverables in an activity-oriented WBS and specifying the deliverables and acceptance criteria in the work packages, as described in Section 5.4.2.3 of this *Software Extension*, merges this distinction for software projects and other kinds of activity-oriented projects.

5.4.1 Create WBS: Inputs

The inputs in Section 5.4.1 of the *PMBOK® Guide* are equally applicable for creating an activity-oriented software WBS.

5.4.1.1 Scope Management Plan

See Section 5.4.1.1 of the *PMBOK® Guide*.

5.4.1.2 Project Scope Statement

See Section 5.4.1.2 of the *PMBOK® Guide*.

5.4.1.3 Requirements Documentation

See Section 5.4.1.3 of the *PMBOK® Guide*.

5.4.1.4 Enterprise Environmental Factors

See Section 5.4.1.4 of the *PMBOK® Guide*.

5.4.1.5 Organizational Process Assets

See Section 5.4.1.5 of the *PMBOK® Guide*.

5.4.2 Create WBS: Tools and Techniques

The decomposition technique for creating a WBS described in Section 5.4.2 of the *PMBOK® Guide* is equally applicable for creating an activity-oriented WBS for a software project. Additional considerations are presented in Sections 5.4.2.2, 5.4.2.3, and 5.4.2.4 of this extension.

5.4.2.1 Decomposition

See Section 5.4.2.1 of the *PMBOK® Guide*.

5.4.2.2 Expert Judgment

See Section 5.4.2.2 of the *PMBOK® Guide*.

5.4.2.3 Activity-Oriented WBS

An example of an activity-oriented WBS is illustrated in this section of the *Software Extension*; it is descriptive of an approach to creating a WBS for a software project; it is not intended to be prescriptive. The top level of an activity-oriented WBS for a software project includes the full scope, at a high level, of all the work required to complete the project successfully, as illustrated in Figure 5-3. The top level of an activity-oriented WBS is reflected in, and can provide an input for refining the project scope statement. The subordinate levels can provide an input for refining the product scope statement because the elements of work to produce the product components are embedded in an activity-oriented WBS. The lowest level elements of work for the software construction activity of the WBS produce specific deliverables. The tasks for Activity 3.2 in Figure 5-3 include work to reuse, construct, and buy some software components. For brevity of presentation, the example includes only the subordinate elements of Construct Software.

Embedding product scope in an activity-oriented software WBS is depicted in Figure 5-3, which illustrates a partial WBS for developing the software for an automated teller machine; the product components are indicated in bold font. The figure in Section 5.4.2.4 of this *Software Extension* illustrates further decomposition of the "Construct FINAT" element of the WBS in Figure 5-3.

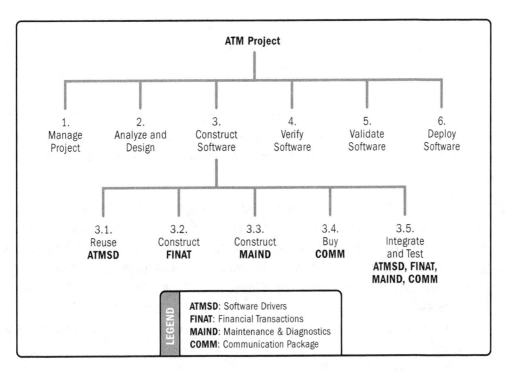

Figure 5-3. Partially Decomposed Activity-Oriented WBS

The *PMBOK® Guide* distinguishes between project scope and product scope. The two scopes can be integrated in an activity-oriented WBS for software projects because of the nature of software and the way in which software is developed or modified. As illustrated in Figure 5-3 product structure is embedded in the activity-oriented software WBS.

Work packages can be used to document the tasks in a software project WBS. Factors documented in a work package for constructing software components include:

- Estimated duration,
- Number of personnel by skill level,
- Additional resources needed,
- Software component or components to be developed or modified,
- Acceptance criteria for the software component or components developed or modified, and
- Risk factors.

Risk factors are potential problems that may inhibit successful completion of the software component or components using the allocated effort and additional resources. Other factors that can be included in an activity-oriented work package include predecessor and successor task for the task being documented and work products to be placed under version control.

5.4.2.4 Rolling Wave Elaboration of WBS

According to Section 6.2.2.2 of the *PMBOK® Guide*: rolling wave planning is an iterative planning technique in which the work to be accomplished in the near term is planned in detail, while the work in the future is planned at a more general level. It is a form of progressive elaboration. Therefore, work can exist at various levels of detail depending on where it is in the project life cycle.

Rolling wave planning is a valuable technique for progressively elaborating the work to be accomplished when using an activity-oriented WBS for a predictive life cycle software project, based on the following considerations (the equivalent of rolling wave planning for adaptive life cycle software projects is presented in Section 5.4.2.5 of this *Software Extension*).

Every software project results in a unique product, either new or modified, because replication of existing software is a simple process as compared to the replication of physical artifacts. Most software projects thus require innovation and creative problem solving to satisfy new and evolving needs. For predictive life cycle software projects, an activity-oriented WBS is elaborated in a rolling wave manner as the details of constructing the software product are elaborated with increased understanding of the problem to be solved. Some rolling wave modifications of work to be accomplished using an activity-oriented WBS may be accomplished within the overall scope constraints of schedule, budget, resources, and technology, while other elaborations may require renegotiation of the project scope constraints.

An example of rolling wave elaboration of the WBS for the ATM project (see Figure 5-3) is illustrated in Figure 5-4, where the details of constructing the financial transaction component have been added, perhaps after some prototyping and feasibility analysis once the project was underway. The work package for the financial transaction component in Figure 5-3 (FINAT) is decomposed into work packages shown in Figure 5-4 for the four subordinate software components plus the FINAT integration and test task. Note that the product components are denoted in boldface font. Also, note the decision to reuse existing recorder software from another software product. A work package for a software construction task includes the work needed to accomplish detailed design, coding, unit testing, and integration and testing of the composite software module (e.g., the validator module in Figure 5-4).

Rolling wave elaboration of an activity-oriented software WBS is typically accomplished periodically, perhaps monthly, to accommodate increased understanding of the problem to be solved. Rolling-wave elaboration also may be accomplished as circumstances dictate, such as changes to requirements, schedule, budget, resources, or technology.

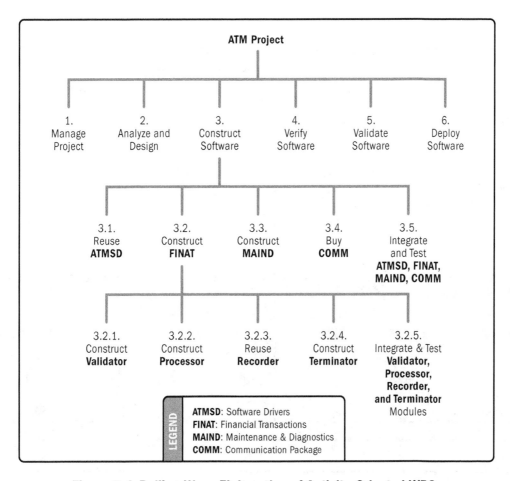

Figure 5-4. Rolling Wave Elaboration of Activity-Oriented WBS

5.4.2.5 Rolling Wave Planning for Adaptive Life Cycle Projects

The scope of an adaptive life cycle software project can be progressively elaborated in a rolling wave manner, as illustrated in Figure 5-5, which is the equivalent of a rolling wave WBS. The small "boxes" in each quarter (Q1 – Q4) are feature sets at the top level with increments of functionality for the features sets in the subordinate levels. As indicated, the feature sets and increments of functionality are progressively elaborated during planning for subsequent quarters of calendar time.

As stated in conjunction with Figure 5-2 of this *Software Extension*, it may be possible to specify an initial release plan during the planning process for an adaptive software project. In other cases, the release plan may evolve in a rolling wave manner. The elaboration in Figure 5-4 may have been developed initially or as a rolling wave elaboration across the quarters. This form of elaboration and presentation could also be used for a predictive life cycle software project that develops the product in deliverable increments of functionality (called feature sets in Figure 5.5).

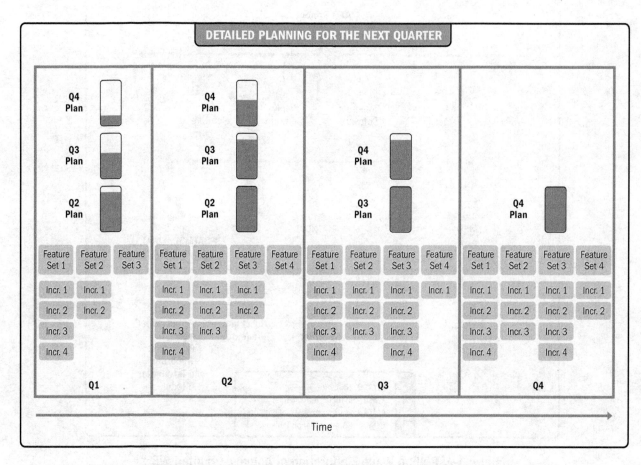

Figure 5-5. Rolling Wave Elaboration of an Adaptive Life Cycle Software Project

©2013 Project Management Institute. *Software Extension to the PMBOK® Guide Fifth Edition*

5.4.3 Create WBS: Outputs

The outputs for creating a WBS in Section 5.4.3 of the *PMBOK® Guide* are equally applicable outputs from creating an activity-oriented software WBS.

5.4.3.1 Scope Baseline

See Section 5.4.3.1 of the *PMBOK® Guide.*

5.4.3.2 Project Documents Updates

See Section 5.4.3.2 of the *PMBOK® Guide.*

5

5.5 Validate Scope

According to Section 5.5 of the *PMBOK® Guide*, Validate Scope covers formalizing acceptance of the completed project deliverables. In software engineering, a distinction is made between verification and validation. Verification is concerned with determining, in an objective manner, that the deliverable software is correct, complete, and consistent with respect to the product requirements, design constraints, and other product parameters. Validation is concerned with determining, in an objective manner, that the deliverable software will satisfy the needs and expectations of customers, users, and other stakeholders when installed in the operational environment. Colloquially, verification answers the question "did we build the software correctly?" and validation answers the question, "did we build the correct software?"

5.5.1 Validate Scope: Inputs

The inputs for validating scope in Sections 5.5.1.1 to 5.5.1.5 of the *PMBOK® Guide* are applicable for validating the scope of predictive life cycle software projects. An additional input, described in Section 5.5.1.6 of this *Software Extension*, is concerned with inputs for validating the scope of adaptive software project life cycle projects.

The primary input for validating scope of a software project is working deliverable software: other deliverables may include an acceptance test plan, user training materials, installation and operating instructions, and guidance for maintainers. The intended users, operators, and maintainers use these inputs to validate the acceptability of the software. These work products may be in printed form or accessible online.

5.5.1.1 Project Management Plan

See Section 5.5.1.1 of the *PMBOK® Guide.*

5.5.1.2 Requirements Documentation

See Section 5.5.1.2 of the *PMBOK® Guide*.

5.5.1.3 Requirements Traceability Matrix

See Section 5.5.1.3 of the *PMBOK® Guide*.

5.5.1.4 Verified Deliverables

See Section 5.5.1.4 of the *PMBOK® Guide*.

Inputs for verification may include formally documented requirements, one or more requirements traceability matrices, design documentation, and the software code, all of which may be updated incrementally as they evolve during iterative cycles. In some cases, a suite of development work products including the technical specifications, design documentation, traceability matrices, test plans, and test results, as maintained in automated application life-cycle management systems, may also be inputs for verification of scope.

5.5.1.5 Work Performance Data

See in Section 5.5.1.5 of the *PMBOK® Guide*.

5.5.1.6 Inputs for Adaptive Software Projects

For adaptive life cycle software projects, validation occurs incrementally during and at the end of iterative cycles that produce working deliverable increments of the software product; the inputs are the test cases, test scenarios, and demonstration scenarios developed before and during each iteration cycle. Additional inputs for validating the scope of an adaptive life cycle software project may include formally documented requirements, one or more requirements traceability matrices, design documentation, and the software code, all of which may be updated incrementally as they evolve during iteration cycles. A formal validation plan may be developed initially and applied throughout the project life cycle, or validation may be an element that is built into each iterative cycle without a formal validation plan.

5.5.2 Validate Scope: Tools and Techniques

The tools and techniques for validating scope in Section 5.5.2 of the *PMBOK® Guide* are applicable for validating the scope of both predictive and adaptive software projects. Product scope can be validated using analysis, reviews, acceptance testing, and demonstrations. Reviews include formal inspections, peer reviews of working software, management reviews of validation status, and reviews with external stakeholders. Test-driven development (TDD) is a method of validating the scope of small increments of software. TDD is described in conjunction with Figure 2-6 and in Section 9.2.3.8 of this *Software Extension*.

Ideally, a software test involves preparation of test inputs, test conditions, and an objective statement of the desired test results; execution of the test in a specified environment under specified conditions; and observation and recording of the test results. A validation demonstration differs from a validation test in that a test has objectively stated success criteria, whereas a demonstration relies on the subjective observations of witnesses to determine the success or failure of the demonstrated software features.

For predictive life cycle software projects, validation of product scope is a major phase that occurs at the end of developing a product increment and during software delivery. For adaptive life cycles, continuous validation occurs during and at the end of each iteration cycle. A major validation effort may accompany delivery of the final product at the end of the final iteration cycle. A formal validation plan may be developed initially and applied throughout an adaptive project life cycle, or validation may be an element that is built into each iterative cycle without a formal validation plan.

5.5.2.1 Inspection

See Section 5.5.2.1 of the *PMBOK® Guide*.

A software inspection is a formalized review process that involves preparation for the inspection; roles to be played by the inspectors; checklists and forms; a moderated meeting; and documented follow-up activities. A software inspection differs from a software walkthrough in the formality of the inspection process, including record keeping, and the systematic follow-up to ensure that defects discovered during an inspection are fixed [16 (p. 289–298 and Appendix 7B)].

5.5.2.2 Group Decision-Making Techniques

See Section 5.5.2.2 of the *PMBOK® Guide*.

For adaptive life cycle software projects, validation of scope for tested, deliverable product increments occurs by group decision-making of the customer, user representatives, and other stakeholders, as appropriate.

5.5.3 Validate Scope: Outputs

The outputs for Validate Scope in Section 5.5.3 of the *PMBOK® Guide* are applicable outputs for validating the scope of a software project with the following clarifications.

5.5.3.1 Accepted Deliverables

See Section 5.5.3.1 of the *PMBOK® Guide*.

Adaptive life cycle software projects produce validated, deliverable software at the end of each iteration cycle that produces a working demonstrable product increment. A customer may choose to accept delivery of some, all, or none of the intermediate deliverables of an adaptive life cycle project.

5.5.3.2 Change Requests

See Section 5.5.3.2 of the *PMBOK® Guide*.

Change requests for software projects may be handled informally or, depending on the formality of the validation process, may be documented and handled using a Perform Integrated Change Control process (see Section 4.5 of the *PMBOK® Guide*).

5.5.3.3 Work Performance Information

See Section 5.5.3.3 of the *PMBOK® Guide*.

5.5.3.4 Project Documents Updates

See Section 5.5.3.4 of the *PMBOK® Guide*.

5.6 Control Scope

According to Section 5.6 of the *PMBOK® Guide*, Control Scope is the process of monitoring the status of the project and product scope and managing changes to the scope baseline.

5.6.1 Control Scope: Inputs

The inputs for controlling scope in Section 5.6.1 of the *PMBOK® Guide* are applicable to controlling the scope of a software project, with the extensions indicated below.

5.6.1.1 Project Management Plan

See Section 5.6.1.1 of the *PMBOK® Guide*.

5.6.1.2 Requirements Documentation

See Section 5.6.1.2 of the *PMBOK® Guide*.

5.6.1.3 Requirements Traceability Matrix

See Section 5.6.1.3 of the *PMBOK® Guide*.

5.6.1.4 Work Performance Data

See Section 5.6.1.4 of the *PMBOK® Guide*.

For adaptive life cycle software projects, work performance data includes velocity, which is used to help establish a realistic scope of work for subsequent iterations.

5.6.1.5 Organizational Process Assets

See Section 5.6.1.5 of the *PMBOK® Guide.*

5.6.2 Control Scope: Tools and Techniques

5

The tools and techniques for controlling scope in Section 5.6.2 of the *PMBOK® Guide* are applicable for controlling the scope of predictive life cycle software projects because those projects typically use traditional project management techniques, such as change requests and change control boards, in addition to variance analysis (described in Section 5.6.2.1 of the *PMBOK® Guide.*)

As previously stated, a predictive, plan-driven life cycle for a software project is most likely to result in a successful project when the customer is familiar enough with the problem domain to ensure stable and detailed software requirements can be developed in sufficient detail during project initiation and planning, when the team is well acquainted with the product, and when the problem and solution domain are familiar to all involved. These conditions facilitate control of project and product scope.

An important aspect of adaptive life cycles for software projects is that the customer, in consultation with the project manager and software team, determines the scope of product features to be included in each development cycle. The features are scoped to accommodate the time and resources available. The scope of the product continues to expand during successive development cycles until the customer requests are fully satisfied, or until time and resources are exhausted. In the latter case, the working, deliverable software will incorporate the most value-adding features, which were specified by the customer as input to the iterative development cycles.

The project scope for an adaptive life cycle software project, including schedule, budget, and resources, may be fixed or may grow adaptively based on value-added considerations of continuing or terminating product development.

It should also be noted that the scope of an adaptive life cycle software project includes other elements of project scope as appropriate to the needs of the project, such as a scope management plan, initial analysis and design, independent verification and validation, configuration management, and quality assurance, and quality control. The continuum of software project life cycles is not a thin line, but is multidimensional to accommodate additional aspects of scope control.

5.6.2.1 Variance Analysis

See Section 5.6.2.1 of the *PMBOK® Guide.*

5.6.2.2 Reviews and Meetings

Predictive life cycle software projects rely on milestone reviews to control of scope. Formal reviews may include demonstrations of working software increments, to provide an input for revising project and product scope, when necessary. Revisions result in a new scope baseline.

Adaptive life cycle projects typically use short iteration cycles and frequent demonstrations of working software to provide the input for ongoing control of project and product scope. The customer, in consultation with the project manager and the software development team, determines the features to be developed in each iteration cycle; those features expand the defined product scope and may even change the high-level scope. The project scope may be sufficient to accommodate expanding product scope, or may be adjusted as necessary. Alternatively, some desired features might be omitted because of constraints on the project scope.

5.6.3 Control Scope: Outputs

The outputs in Section 5.6.3 of the *PMBOK® Guide* are applicable to controlling the scope of a software project, with the following additional considerations.

- The outputs of scope control for a software project vary with governance model and the life cycle used within the continuum of software project life cycles. For predictive life cycles, the primary outputs of scope control are the decisions of the change control board to deny or accept change requests; acceptance may be scheduled for immediate or delayed response. For adaptive life cycles, the primary output of scope control is the decision of the customer concerning the next set of features to be implemented and the changes to be made to the current working software. The development team, after consulting with the project manager and the customer, may decide to spend the next iteration cycle modifying the software architecture and doing significant refactoring of the existing software base before continuing the iterative development cycles.

- The output of scope control may require the project manager, higher management, and the customer (or customers) to make significant changes to project scope (schedule, budget, resources) and product scope (features, functional requirements, quality attributes, technology, mission). These changes may be required by factors that are beyond the control of the project manager, such as a changing operational environment, changes in the software development organization's or customer's strategic vision, changes in technology or infrastructure, or changes to competitors' products.

- The outputs for controlling scope in Section 5.6.3 of the *PMBOK® Guide* are applicable for controlling the scope of software projects, both predictive and adaptive.

5.6.3.1 Work Performance Information

See Section 5.6.3.1 of the *PMBOK® Guide*.

5.6.3.2 Change Requests

See Section 5.6.3.2 of the *PMBOK® Guide*.

5.6.3.3 Project Management Plan Updates

See Section 5.6.3.3 of the *PMBOK® Guide*.

5.6.3.4 Project Documents Updates

See Section 5.6.3.4 of the *PMBOK® Guide*.

For an adaptive life cycle software project, document updates may include updates to the product feature set, iteration plan, and release plan.

5.6.3.5 Organizational Process Assets Updates

See Section 5.6.3.5 of the *PMBOK® Guide*.

PROJECT TIME MANAGEMENT

Most of the material in Section 6 of the *PMBOK® Guide* is applicable to time management for software projects. This section of the *Software Extension to the PMBOK® Guide* presents additional considerations for managing software project time.

Section 6 of the *PMBOK® Guide* includes seven processes that constitute Project Time Management, which include the processes required to manage the timely completion of a project. This section of the *Software Extension* to the *PMBOK® Guide* indicates the activities in Section 6 of the *PMBOK® Guide* that are applicable to time management for software projects and describes extensions that are important for software projects.

Project Time Management for software projects is driven by risk, resource availability, business value, and the scheduling method(s) used. When possible, a software project schedule should remain flexible throughout the project to adjust for knowledge gained, increased understanding of risk, and value-added. Understanding the different scheduling methods and selecting one or more appropriate methods for dealing with scheduling risks are critical for project success. Most of the development cost for a software project is human effort, and effort is the product of people and time, therefore this section and Section 7 of this *Software Extension* (Project Cost Management) are closely associated. Scheduling methods and time management procedures that are appropriate for software projects are discussed in this section.

A schedule management plan specifies a scheduling method and a scheduling tool. It also establishes the criteria for developing and controlling the project schedule, plus the format that will be used to display schedule information. A schedule management plan is based on life cycle decisions (see Section 2.4 of this *Software Extension*) and scope considerations (see Section 5 of this *Software Extension*).

Establishing a schedule, like most software decisions, should involve consideration of the risks associated with the project, the development environment, the organization culture, organizational process assets, and accommodation of the customer, users, and other stakeholders. For example, a customer may want delivery of some usable software in a very short timeframe, but some initial time to develop the software architecture or information model to reduce the risk of delivering unacceptable software may be needed. When human life or the company's reputation are stake, more upfront design and increased emphasis on quality-related processes are warranted (see Section 8 of this *Software Extension*). Using risk to determine a software project schedule involves the risk-related processes addressed in Section 11 of this *Software Extension*.

The project environment is a significant influence on the appropriateness of a scheduling method. When the method is not supported by the culture of the organization or is not aligned with the management infrastructure and incentives, the project may fail to meet schedule commitments regardless of any risk-mitigating effects it might provide.

Value delivered to the customer is an important factor for all projects. In most cases, the nature of software allows value to be provided in increments rather than in a single delivery at the end of the project; this enables the scheduling method to take advantage of changes that occur during a software development project. It may be that highly valued capabilities can be provided early in a project rather than only at completion. It may also be possible to provide less-valued capabilities while waiting for more-valued, but difficult, capabilities to evolve. However, even when the customer is able to use partial functionality, this option is eliminated when the scheduling method and the architecture are not structured to produce progressive increments of value.

In addition to the methods described in Section 6 of the *PMBOK® Guide*, examples of other scheduling methods used for software projects include:

- **Structured scheduling.** This method involves development of project milestones during the initiation and planning phases of a software project. Structured scheduling can be used when some of the following conditions apply: well-understood product requirements; related precedent work within the organization; strict architectural requirements; specified limits on the number, size, or timing of deployments; critical backward compatibility issues; or heavy dependencies on new infrastructure. Structured scheduling is often used for products with high safety, security, or regulatory constraints; for major version releases of high-profile products; or for very large projects with significant amounts of multi-group coordination.

- **Schedule as independent variable (SAIV).** This is a date-certain scheduling method. It is used when there is a specific date after which the value of the product declines precipitously. Examples are time to market considerations (e.g., announced version release), an immovable event for which the product is required (e.g., trade show, holiday sales), or a date by which the enterprise is required to institute some element of a regulatory change (e.g., preparing tax returns). Prioritizing requirements or features and a scheduling strategy that will ensure availability of the most-valued functionality by a required deadline is an example of SAIV scheduling. This is similar to "time boxing" in adaptive life cycles when time constrains the work that can be done within an iterative cycle or an incremental product cycle. More discussion is provided in Section 6.3.2.5 of this *Software Extension*.

- **Iterative scheduling with a backlog.** This is a form of rolling wave planning for software projects based on adaptive life cycles, where the requirements are prioritized, allocated to iterations, and refined just prior to construction of product features. Adjustments to an iterative schedule occur throughout the project life cycle; adjustments are based on the ongoing learning and adaptation that results from emergent requirements. This approach is often used to deliver incremental value to the customer or when multiple teams can concurrently develop a large number of features that that have few interconnected dependencies among features. This scheduling method is appropriate for many software projects, as indicated by the widespread and growing use of adaptive life cycles for software projects.

- **On-demand scheduling.** This approach is based on the theory-of-constraints and pull-based scheduling concepts from lean manufacturing. On-demand scheduling does not preschedule the development of product or product increments, but rather pulls work from a backlog or intermediate queue of work to be done immediately as resources become available. It provides the customer with a statistically based estimate of time-to-complete for any given task (often referred to as lead time), and can be used to continually assess backlogged task-value to maximize value for customers. On-demand scheduling is often used for projects that evolve the product incrementally in operational or sustainment environments, and where tasks may be made relatively similar in size and scope or can be bundled by size and scope. This approach may use classes of service to allow flexibility in resource utilization, ensuring that critical or time-sensitive tasks are fast-tracked, while less schedule-critical tasks are perhaps delayed but not put off indefinitely. The goals of on-demand scheduling are to minimize the time taken to accomplish work, to minimize estimation activities, and to maximize the value of work accomplished.

- **Portfolio management scheduling.** This method involves scheduling of projects based on prioritizing investments in software as established by criteria determined at the organizational level. Scheduling of projects and the activities within projects are not based on the size or scope of the work but rather on importance to the organization. Scheduling based on portfolio management is determined by value created for the organization vs. the time and/or cost of a development project. This method is often used for strategic management of large enterprise systems or commercial services.

Figure 6-1 provides an overview of Project Time Management for software projects.

6.1 Plan Schedule Management

The inputs, tools and techniques, and outputs presented in Section 6.1 of the *PMBOK® Guide* are generally applicable for planning a software project schedule, when the issues outlined above are taken into account.

6.1.1 Plan Schedule Management: Inputs

The inputs in Section 6.1.1 of the *PMBOK® Guide* are applicable for planning software project schedule management.

6.1.1.1 Project Management Plan

See Section 6.1.1.1 of the *PMBOK® Guide*.

6.1.1.2 Project Charter

See Section 6.1.1.2 of the *PMBOK® Guide*.

6.1.1.3 Enterprise Environmental Factors

See Section 6.1.1.3 of the *PMBOK® Guide*.

Enterprise environmental factors that may impact planning software project schedule management include software project portfolios and enterprise architectures.

Project Time Management Overview

6.1 Plan Schedule Management

.1 Inputs
.1 Project management plan
.2 Project charter
.3 Enterprise environmental factors
.4 Organizational process assets
.5 Safety and security issues

.2 Tools & Techniques
.1 Expert judgment
.2 Analytical techniques
.3 Meetings

.3 Outputs
.1 Schedule management plan

6.5 Estimate Activity Durations

.1 Inputs
.1 Schedule management plan
.2 Activity list
.3 Activity attributes
.4 Activity resource requirements
.5 Resource calendars
.6 Project scope statement
.7 Risk register
.8 Resource breakdown structure
.9 Enterprise environmental factors
.10 Organizational process assets
.11 Additional inputs

.2 Tools & Techniques
.1 Expert judgment
.2 Analogous estimating
.3 Parametric estimating
.4 Three-point estimating
.5 Group decision-making techniques
.6 Reserve analysis

.3 Outputs
.1 Activity duration estimates
.2 Project documents updates

6.2 Define Activities

.1 Inputs
.1 Schedule management plan
.2 Scope baseline
.3 Enterprise environmental factors
.4 Organizational process assets
.5 Additional factors

.2 Tools & Techniques
.1 Decomposition
.2 Rolling wave planning
.3 Expert judgment
.4 Story breakdown structures
.5 Storyboards
.6 Use cases

.3 Outputs
.1 Activity list
.2 Activity attributes
.3 Milestone list

6.6 Develop Schedule

.1 Inputs
.1 Schedule management plan
.2 Activity list
.3 Activity attributes
.4 Project schedule network diagrams
.5 Activity resource requirements
.6 Resource calendars
.7 Activity duration estimates
.8 Project scope statement
.9 Risk register
.10 Project staff assignments
.11 Resource breakdown structure
.12 Enterprise environmental factors
.13 Organizational process assets
.14 Additional inputs

.2 Tools & Techniques
.1 Schedule network analysis
.2 Critical path method
.3 Critical chain method
.4 Resource optimization techniques
.5 Modeling techniques
.6 Leads and lags
.7 Schedule compression
.8 Scheduling tool
.9 Incremental product planning

.3 Outputs
.1 Schedule baseline
.2 Project schedule
.3 Schedule data
.4 Project calendars
.5 Project management plan updates
.6 Project documents updates
.7 Release and iteration plan updates

6.3 Sequence Activities

.1 Inputs
.1 Schedule management plan
.2 Activity list
.3 Activity attributes
.4 Milestone list
.5 Project scope statement
.6 Enterprise environmental factors
.7 Organizational process assets
.8 Architectural and IV & V constraints
.9 Safety and security analyses

.2 Tools & Techniques
.1 Precedence diagramming method (PDM)
.2 Dependency determination
.3 Leads and lags
.4 SAIV and time boxing
.5 Work in progress limits and classes of service
.6 Feature set evaluation
.7 Service-level agreements

.3 Outputs
.1 Project schedule network diagrams
.2 Project documents updates
.3 Feature sets
.4 Release plans
.5 Architectural and nonfunctional dependencies

6.4 Estimate Activity Resources

.1 Inputs
.1 Schedule management plan
.2 Activity list
.3 Activity attributes
.4 Resource calendars
.5 Risk register
.6 Activity cost estimates
.7 Enterprise environmental factors
.8 Organizational process assets

.2 Tools & Techniques
.1 Expert judgment
.2 Alternative analysis
.3 Published estimating data
.4 Bottom-up estimating
.5 Project management software
.6 Service-level agreements
.7 Other tools and techniques

.3 Outputs
.1 Activity resource requirements
.2 Resource breakdown structure
.3 Project documents updates

6.7 Control Schedule

.1 Inputs
.1 Project management plan
.2 Project schedule
.3 Work performance data
.4 Project calendars
.5 Schedule data
.6 Organizational process assets

.2 Tools & Techniques
.1 Performance reviews
.2 Project management software
.3 Resource optimization techniques
.4 Modeling techniques
.5 Leads and lags
.6 Schedule compression
.7 Scheduling tool
.8 Evidence-based reviews
.9 Retrospectives
.10 Cumulative flow diagrams
.11 Workflow board with daily walkthrough
.12 Reprioritization reviews
.13 Burnup and burndown charts
.14 Variance analysis

.3 Outputs
.1 Work performance information
.2 Schedule forecasts
.3 Change requests
.4 Project management plan updates
.5 Project documents updates
.6 Organizational process assets updates
.7 Additional outputs

Figure 6-1. Project Time Management Overview

6.1.1.4 Organizational Process Assets

See Section 6.1.1.4 of the *PMBOK® Guide*

Organizational process assets for software projects may include governance policies and project life cycles predefined for use within the software development organization.

6.1.1.5 Safety and Security Issues

Public safety and cyber security issues may provide inputs for planning schedule management because they may impact the sequencing of some project activities in order to satisfy safety and security regulations, standards, policies, and requirements during a software project.

6.1.2 Plan Schedule Management: Tools and Techniques

The tools and techniques in Section 6.1.2 of the *PMBOK® Guide* are applicable for planning software project schedule management.

6.1.2.1 Expert Judgment

See Section 6.1.2.1 of the *PMBOK® Guide*.

6.1.2.2 Analytical Techniques

See Section 6.1.2.2 of the *PMBOK® Guide*.

6.1.2.3 Meetings

See Section 6.1.2.3 of the *PMBOK® Guide*.

6.1.3 Plan Schedule Management: Outputs

The output in Section 6.1.3 of the *PMBOK® Guide* is applicable for planning software project schedule management.

6.1.3.1 Schedule Management Plan

See Section 6.1.3.1 of the *PMBOK® Guide*.

6.2 Define Activities

According to Section 6.2 of the *PMBOK® Guide*, Define Activities is the process of identifying the specific actions to be performed to produce the project deliverables. Defining activities for software projects is based on the requirements or features, the project scope, the project environment, and project life cycle selected.

As described in Section 2 of this *Software Extension*, software project activities, processes, and stages are detailed in ISO/IEC/IEEE Standard 12207.

6.2.1 Define Activities: Inputs

The inputs for defining activities in Section 6.2.1 of the *PMBOK® Guide* are applicable for defining inputs for software project activities. The extension and adaption of these inputs are provided below.

6.2.1.1 Schedule Management Plan

See Section 6.2.1.1 of the *PMBOK® Guide*.

6.2.1.2 Scope Baseline

See 6.2.1.2 of the *PMBOK® Guide*. In addition, an organization's enterprise architecture, when applicable, is a scope factor that may influence the definition of software project activities.

6.2.1.3 Enterprise Environmental Factors

See Section 6.2.1.3 of the *PMBOK® Guide*.

6.2.1.4 Organizational Process Assets

In addition to those listed in Section 6.2.1.4 of the *PMBOK® Guide,* organizational process assets that may provide inputs for defining activities for a software project include governance documents, the project life cycle model, team velocity measures, scheduling techniques such as SAIV (described in the introduction to this section of this *Software Extension*), the cadence of iterations, and workflow measures such as time-in-process statistics for on-demand scheduling.

Organization factors such as mission and vision statements provide input metadata for scheduling software projects so that project, program, and portfolio information can be rolled up into strategic plans.

6.2.1.5 Additional Factors

Other factors that may provide inputs for defining software project activities include existing work orders and enhancement requests; technical debt remaining from previous work, incomplete functionality, and needed rework; business process changes; and activities external to a software project such as database or operating system upgrades.

6.2.2 Define Activities: Tools and Techniques

The tools and techniques for defining activities in Section 6.2.2 of the *PMBOK® Guide* are generally applicable for defining software project activities. In addition to these, Sections 6.2.2.5, 6.2.2.6, and 6.2.2.7 of this *Software Extension* are tools and techniques for defining software project activities.

6.2.2.1 Decomposition

See Section 6.2.2.1 of the *PMBOK® Guide*.

6.2.2.2 Rolling Wave Planning

See Section 6.2.2.2 of the *PMBOK® Guide*.

6.2.4.3 Expert Judgment

See Section 6.2.2.3 of the *PMBOK® Guide*.

6.2.2.4 Story Breakdown Structures

Adaptive development methods for software projects are sometimes based on "user stories" that describe desired software capabilities from the users' point of view. Features needed to support the stories are specified and work activities to construct the features are identified, based on development methods described in Section 2.4 of this *Software Extension*.

Complex stories may be defined as *epics* (stories described at a high level) that are refined into detailed stories at a later date. Stories that are associated by a common factor, such as software functionality, data source, or security level may be grouped within a *theme*. Other project work activities (procurement, documentation, risk management, training, etc.) may also be identified using epics, themes, and stories.

6.2.2.5 Storyboards

Storyboards can be used to define software project activities in a similar manner to those used in movie and television production. They provide a pictorial overview of the project that illustrates the order in which work activities are to be completed.

6.2.2.6 Use Cases

Use cases provide scenarios of operation (step-by-step interactions) between a user (called an actor) and the software. A use-case scenario can be specified as an itemized list of steps or using a UML/SysML diagram: a sequence diagram, an activity diagram, or state diagram. Software tools are available for these notations; some tools support various forms of analysis and can generate code templates for software construction. Use cases can include business rules, alternate paths, and exception scenarios, in addition to the primary scenario. They can be used to identify features to be implemented, as shown in Figure 6-2; features are used to identify the work activities needed to construct the features.

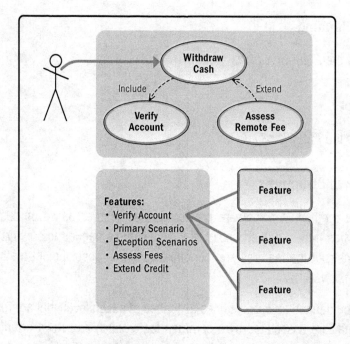

Figure 6-2. Identifying Features for a Use Case

6.2.3 Define Activities: Outputs

The outputs in Section 6.2.3 of the *PMBOK® Guide* are applicable outputs from defining software project activity. Extension and adaptations are described below.

6.2.3.1 Activity List

Activity lists for software projects may include coordination with entities external. The software development team may need access to testing facilities and infrastructure equipment, and/or access to multiple user environments. These project elements may be outside the scope of control of the software project manager and may require external scheduling to avoid negative impact to the software project schedule. See Section 6.2.3.1 of the *PMBOK® Guide* for additional information.

6.2.3.2 Activity Attributes

See Section 6.2.3.2 of the *PMBOK® Guide*. In addition, attributes that may be included as outputs from defining activities in a software project activity list include but are not limited to the following:

- Dependencies and enabling precedent activities,
- Stakeholder value or priority,
- Estimated effort, size, complexity, and/or risk,
- Security and/or safety standards and constraints, and
- Special competencies required of project team members and others.

6.2.3.3 Milestone List

Milestone lists, as described in Section 6.2.3.3 of the *PMBOK® Guide* are applicable outputs from defining software project activities.

Milestones for software projects are defined in various ways for various development environments and project life cycles. For example, some software project life cycles define *anchor points*, which are points in time when major phase transitions occur in the project life cycle.

In predictive software development, milestones may be set to denote requirements and architectural design reviews, customer reviews, and product delivery. Often each milestone includes validation or acceptance criteria, but not always.

On-demand scheduling methods do not usually have specified milestones; progress is measured by customer satisfaction within the time-to-complete cadence. Calendar-based coordination conferences may be held to discuss project performance, but these are rarely associated with a specific goal or technical criterion.

A useful technique for reducing project risk is to define joint milestones with interdependent projects such as hardware procurement, installation and configuration of the development and installation platforms, and related software projects. This type of program/portfolio management is often critical to the successful delivery of software products, especially on a constrained schedule.

6.3 Sequence Activities

According to Section 6.3 of the *PMBOK® Guide,* Sequence Activities is the process of identifying and documenting relationships among the project activities. Sequencing activities for software projects differs somewhat from those in Section 6.3 of the *PMBOK® Guide* because the sequencing methods used may be based on value-added, technical risk, software architecture, and specific expertise availability, as well as other technical and staffing dependencies.

Dependencies on database structure, infrastructure needs, and other architecture and design concerns exist in many software projects. However, for a new application domain, or for a large, complex software project in a new or existing domain, there is often a need to establish and refine the operational concepts, to build prototypes, and/or to define an architecture or infrastructure before specifying the functional requirements for the product. How much time is needed for these activities and how concurrently they can be accomplished depends on the familiarity, size, and complexity of the software product. Sequencing of project activities also depends on the risk profiles, and, in particular, on the likelihood of changes to the product requirements during the project.

Software architecture has a significant impact on sequencing of project activities in several areas. First, the time needed to development a software architecture is not easily estimated, and therefore, scheduling of any software development activities directly related to (some part of) the architectural design may need to be delayed until (that part of) the architecture is completed. In some instances, only some of the architectural decisions remain to be made, so early investment in activities that prove the effectiveness of an architectural solution or that build an initial architectural structure may be effective. These activities are sometimes called building an architectural backbone or skeleton.

The intent of these activities is to verify that the key architectural decisions are feasible and that solutions can be developed for the software requirements or user features. For example, exception handling, data assurance, and security patterns need to be established early for consistency across the software components. Second, software architecture provides the ability to define pieces of the product that can be independently developed and tested, perhaps with addition of mockups, stubs, and dummy software that will allow testing and demonstration of incomplete software. Architectural design needs to precede software construction so that methods such as test-driven development have a framework to build on. This is of particular significance in larger software systems that are required to interact with other software systems that are external to, and beyond the control of the software project manager.

In a similar way, nonfunctional requirements may impact the sequencing of activities by requiring time to implement crosscutting strategies (such as error-handling and failure modes). The need for certification of software components due to regulatory, safety, or security requirements may also affect sequencing of work activities because of the time required for certification activities. It is usually more cost-effective to bundle scheduled changes to certified code so that recertification activities are not repeated unnecessarily.

Software schedules are frequently revised. Unscheduled prototyping and code experimentation may be needed to support decision making. These activities may not be identified during initial scheduling, so the ripple effects they cause can impact sequencing of other activities. Rework to fix discovered defects is another activity that may not be anticipated but is necessary for successful project completion. This unanticipated work (sometimes referred to as *dark matter*) can often take precedence over other work and is sometimes tracked independently. Section 6.7 of this *Software Extension* describes the role of burnup and burndown charts in relation to scheduling issues.

Adjustment to schedule sequencing for adaptive life cycle software projects is more dynamic and typically occurs more frequently than for predictive life cycle projects; adaptive scheduling generally provides more opportunities to absorb unplanned work. A schedule plan is created to provide structure for the adaptive iterations, their content, and any points in time for release of intermediate versions of the final software product. However, the plan is revisited often to incorporate changes related to feedback based on factors such as demonstrations of the evolving product, productivity (velocity) data, unscheduled work, and retrospective findings.

Managers of adaptive software projects usually schedule the sequence of work activities prior to the start iterative development but, as stated, the scope of this initial sequencing is typically refined as the project evolves. In some cases, higher levels of features and story breakdowns are used to coordinate lower levels—with the unscheduled work absorbed into the estimates for the higher-level activities.

On-demand scheduling techniques allow the work to flow to whatever suitable staff resources become available. This is sometimes referred to as late binding of the work to the available resources. The available staff resources dynamically select (or are assigned to) the next work to be done based on value added of the queued work activities. Value is defined by project specific risks and constraints (e.g., cost of delay, value to customer, class of service, or criticality of service).

Rather than date-certain scheduling of events or a specified time box when a certain number of tasks are to be completed, on-demand scheduling establishes a regular cadence of events, such as completion of demonstrable increments of software. The pace of the cadence is determined through measures such as velocity or statistical based lead-time or transit time for an activity. The cadence then provides an indication of how long a customer or software project manager can expect to wait for a particular activity to be completed. Work-in-progress limits are used to maintain resource viability and to smooth out workflow; these are adjusted according to statistical measures maintained throughout the development process. Visual indicators (i.e., workflow charts) can be used to provide visibility and help identify and resolve bottlenecks to make better use of available resources.

6.3.1 Sequence Activities: Inputs

The inputs in Section 6.3.1 of the *PMBOK® Guide* are applicable inputs for sequencing software project activities, with the modification of 6.3.1.7 and extensions of 6.3.1.8 and 6.3.1.9 (see below).

6.3.1.1 Schedule Management Plan

See Section 6.3.1.1 of the *PMBOK® Guide*.

6.3.1.2 Activity List

See Section 6.3.1.2 of the *PMBOK® Guide*.

6.3.1.3 Activity Attributes

See Section 6.3.1.3 of the *PMBOK® Guide*.

6.3.1.4 Milestone List

See Section 6.3.1.4 of the *PMBOK® Guide*.

6.3.1.5 Project Scope Statement

See Section 6.3.1.5 of the *PMBOK® Guide*.

6.3.1.6 Enterprise Environmental Factors

See Section 6.3.1.6 of the *PMBOK® Guide*.

6.3.1.7 Organizational Process Assets

See also Section 6.3.1.7 of the *PMBOK® Guide*. Governance models often have milestones, templates, and environmental factors that can provide inputs to sequencing activities for software projects. The enterprise architecture, when applicable, may also impact sequencing. Organizational parameters for valuing software investments may be of use in identifying the value of functionality to be provided and thus impact sequencing.

6.3.1.8 Architectural and IV&V Constraints

Architectural constraints (e.g., what needs to be built first) and independent verification and validation (IV&V) planning may provide inputs that will impact sequencing. In the latter case (IV&V) there may be scheduling constraints for product features needed to verify and validate cross functional, multi-system, multi-platform, or multi-environment requirements.

6.3.1.9 Safety and Security Analyses

Safety and cyber security issues may impact the sequencing of some software activities to meet requirements, policies, and standards. Certification activities are expensive, so certification requirements as inputs to schedule sequencing should try to minimize the number of certification cycles in the schedule.

6.3.2 Sequence Activities: Tools and Techniques

The tools and techniques for sequencing project activities in Section 6.3.2 of the *PMBOK® Guide* are applicable for sequencing software project activities. In addition to these, the tools and techniques in 6.3.2.5 through 6.3.2.8 of this *Software Extension* are applicable for sequencing software project activities.

6.3.2.1 Precedence Diagramming Method (PDM)

See Section 6.3.2.1 of the *PMBOK® Guide*.

6.3.2.2 Dependency Determination

See Section 6.3.2.2 of the *PMBOK® Guide*.

6.3.2.3 Leads and Lags

See Section 6.3.2.3 of the *PMBOK® Guide*.

6.3.2.4 SAIV and Time Boxing

Using SAIV (schedule as independent variable) for sequencing software project activities can help to ensure that the most valuable features or functionality are available when time is exhausted, provided the most important features have been implemented first. The SAIV concept is applied in a variety of situations, including time boxing and date-certain scheduling. As shown in Figure 6-3, product scope can be determined when cost and time have been set. SAIV can be applied to software increments, intermediate releases, or completed products.

This method depends on the ability to prioritize items of work for valued-added requirements, stories, or features. The value-added may change over time, but adaptive life cycles allow for that change by frequently reassessing value. This assumes that the customer or other stakeholders are either available or are represented by surrogates whenever values are reassessed.

6.3.2.5 Work in Progress Limits and Classes of Service

See on-demand scheduling in Section 6.1 of this *Software Extension*.

6.3.2.6 Feature Set Evaluation

A feature set includes a collection of features that deliver business value; feature sets are often derived from user stories. Figure 6-4 illustrates construction and evaluation of software for the features in an iteration feature set. Activities needed to implement features are usually sequenced one feature at a time. Evaluation of an implemented feature may affect sequencing of other features or feature sets.

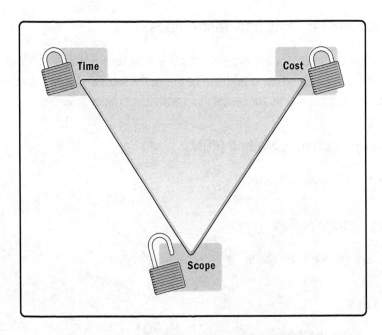

Figure 6-3. Schedule as Independent Variable

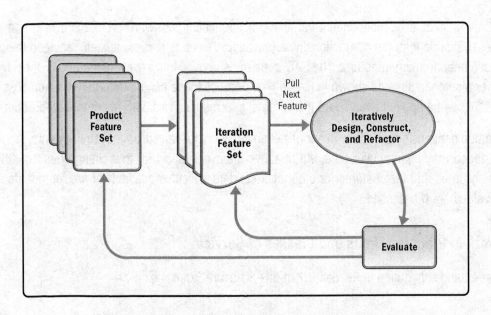

Figure 6-4. Sequencing of Feature Set Construction

6.3.2.7 Service-Level Agreements

There may be a service-level agreement between a project manager and a customer (or other stakeholder) that specifies the amount of work to be accomplished over a specified period of time. This establishes the project capacity and may impact sequencing of activities.

6.3.3 Sequence Activities: Outputs

The outputs from sequencing activities in the *PMBOK® Guide* are applicable as outputs from sequencing software project activities. In addition, the outputs specific to software project sequencing activities are described in Sections 6.3.3.3, 6.3.3.4, and 6.3.3.5 of this *Software Extension*.

6

6.3.3.1 Project Schedule Network Diagrams

See Section 6.3.3.1 of the *PMBOK® Guide*.

6.3.3.2 Project Documents Updates

See Section 6.3.3.2 of the *PMBOK® Guide*.

6.3.3.3 Features Sets

A feature set includes a collection of features that deliver business value; feature sets are often derived from user stories.

6.3.3.4 Release Plans

A release plan specifies the overall project schedule of releases for delivery of software capabilities; it may be one of the outputs of sequencing activities for software projects. Release delivery may be for customer/user evaluation or for delivery into the users' environment. The release plan is highly dependent upon the production rate of the software team. Comparing estimated time to the actual time taken to accomplish work over a period of several iterative development cycles provides a baseline for estimating the time for future releases.

6.3.3.5 Architectural and Nonfunctional Dependencies

The outputs of sequencing software project activities may be influenced by architectural and nonfunctional dependencies intended to avoid duplication of work or rework by other project teams or initiatives. In turn, these dependencies may need to be updated based on the scheduled project activities.

6.4 Estimate Activity Resources

According to Section 6.4 of the *PMBOK® Guide* estimating resources for project activities involves estimating the type and quantities of material, people, equipment, or supplies required to perform each activity.

Because software is developed by the coordinated intellectual work activities of software developers, software projects are dependent on human resources more than any other software project resource. The skills and abilities of software developers are significant factors in estimating the number of software developers needed. Studies have shown 10:1 and greater variations in productivity among software developers having similar educational backgrounds and work experiences [9].

Determining the roles required for a software project can be determined by reviewing the product requirements, the project objectives, stakeholder's goals, and budget and schedule constraints. As a software project evolves, requirements will be refined, user stories, and features will be identified, and the human resources needed to satisfy the project goals will be compared to the current team's collective skills. Gaps may indicate that different roles or more team members for present roles are required. Likewise, the teams' production rate (velocity) and quality metrics may provide insights into team role requirements as the project progresses. In some cases, the software project manager may be given a collection of team members without the opportunity to identify needed project roles or to adjust the roles as the project evolves. In other cases, the project manager may be asked to specify the roles that need to be filled, the number of members needed for each role, and the timing for filling the roles.

Other resource requirements for software projects may include resources for additional architectural studies and several kinds of support activities (e.g., configuration management, quality assurance, documentation, user training). Test facilities, software for testing, multi-configuration test suites, and multiple target environments or platforms for deployment are examples of other resources that may be required.

6.4.1 Estimate Activity Resources: Inputs

The inputs described in Section 6.4.1 of the *PMBOK® Guide* are applicable inputs for estimating software project activity resources. As stated in Section 6.4 of this *Software Extension*, software developers are the most important resources for a software project. Historical data concerning a team's production rate is a valuable input for estimating software project activity resources, because software productivity varies widely among software teams and software developers (even among those having similar educations and work experiences). Software project managers who use adaptive life cycles have the opportunity to collect production rate data on a frequent, ongoing basis and may be able to adjust human resources as the project progresses.

Other inputs for estimating software project activity resources involve using a results chain or other form of analysis to identify key assumptions and resources outside of the software development activities that may impact estimation of activity resources for a software project (such as coordination among multiple customers or development of multiple variants of the software) .

6.4.1.1 Schedule Management Plan

See Section 6.4.1.1 of the *PMBOK® Guide*.

6.4.1.2 Activity List

See Section 6.4.1.2 of the *PMBOK® Guide*.

6.4.1.3 Activity Attributes

See Section 6.4.1.3 of the *PMBOK® Guide*.

6.4.1.4 Resource Calendars

See Section 6.4.1.4 of the *PMBOK® Guide*.

6.4.1.5 Risk Register

See Section 6.4.1.5 of the *PMBOK® Guide*.

6.4.1.6 Activity Cost Estimates

See Section 6.4.1.6 of the *PMBOK® Guide*.

6.4.1.7 Enterprise Environmental Factors

See Section 6.4.1.7 of the *PMBOK® Guide*.

6.4.1.8 Organizational Process Assets

See Section 6.4.1.8 of the *PMBOK® Guide*.

6.4.2 Estimate Activity Resources: Tools and Techniques

The tools and techniques for estimating activity resources in the *PMBOK® Guide* are applicable for estimating activity resources for software projects. In addition to these, the tools and techniques in 6.4.2.6 and 6.4.2.7 of this *Software Extension* apply to estimating software project activity resources.

6.4.2.1 Expert Judgment

See Section 6.4.2.1 of the *PMBOK® Guide*.

6.4.2.2 Alternative Analysis

See Section 6.4.2.2 of the *PMBOK® Guide*.

6.4.2.3 Published Estimating Data

See Section 6.4.2.3 of the *PMBOK® Guide*.

6.4.2.4 Bottom-Up Estimating

See Section 6.4.2.4 of the *PMBOK® Guide*.

6.4.2.5 Project Management Software

See Section 6.4.2.5 of the *PMBOK® Guide*.

6.4.2.6 Service-Level Agreements

There may be an agreement between the project manager and the customer or other stakeholder that specifies the amount of work to be accomplished over a specified period of time. This establishes the development capacity and may impact resource estimation.

6.4.2.7 Other Tools and Techniques

Other tools and techniques for estimating software project activity resources include use of algorithmic estimation models and function point/story point/use-case estimation tools. See Section 7 of this *Software Extension*.

6.4.3 Estimate Activity Resources: Outputs

The outputs listed in Section 6.4.3 of the *PMBOK® Guide* are applicable outputs from estimating software project resources.

6.4.3.1 Activity Resource Requirements

See Section 6.4.3.1 of the *PMBOK® Guide*.

6.4.3.2 Resource Breakdown Structure

See Section 6.4.3.2 of the *PMBOK® Guide*.

6.4.3.3 Project Documents Updates

See Section 6.4.3.3 of the *PMBOK® Guide*.

6.5 Estimate Activity Durations

The difficulty in estimating software project activity durations is the result of many factors: intangibility of software, broad variance in productivity of software developers, need for changes to meet emergent requirements, the often unprecedented nature of the software product, unknown competencies of the software team, unknown hardware or software defects, and the need to incorporate legacy software, commercial software, customer-supplied software, or open-source software into the software product. Even when these factors are taken into consideration, the result may be accurate for the known work, but cannot account for the unidentified, unknown work that will need to be performed.

A major challenge for estimating software activity durations is the nonlinear nature of scaling software work; a product twice as big or twice as complex, however measured, typically requires more than twice as much work, and more than twice as much time because of the increased interdependencies of the work activities and the increased communication among individual software developers and software teams. Adding additional work activities may result in significant delays in the delivery of each increment of value and may result in schedule perturbations, which future complicates the ability to accurately update estimated activity durations. The software project life cycle and method, or methods, used to estimate activity durations should account for the significant risk of likely estimation errors.

Because effort is the product of people and time, the schedule durations of software project activities depend on estimated effort and available of skilled personnel resources. Section 7.2.2 of this *Software Extension* provides information on additional ways to estimate effort for software projects.

6.5.1 Estimate Activity Durations: Inputs

The inputs in Section 6.5.1 of the *PMBOK® Guide* are applicable inputs for estimating software project activity durations. Section 6.5.1.11 below describes additional inputs.

6.5.1.1 Schedule Management Plan

See Section 6.5.1.1 of the *PMBOK® Guide*.

6.5.1.2 Activity List

See Section 6.5.1.2 of the *PMBOK® Guide*.

6.5.1.3 Activity Attributes

See Section 6.5.1.3 of the *PMBOK® Guide.*

6.5.1.4 Activity Resource Requirements

See Section 6.5.1.4 of the *PMBOK® Guide.*

6.5.1.5 Resource Calendars

See Section 6.5.1.5 of the *PMBOK® Guide.*

6.5.1.6 Project Scope Statement

See Section 6.5.1.6 of the *PMBOK® Guide.*

6.5.1.7 Risk Register

See Section 6.5.1.7 of the *PMBOK® Guide.*

6.5.1.8 Resource Breakdown Structure

See Section 6.5.1.8 of the *PMBOK® Guide.*

6.5.1.9 Enterprise Environmental Factors

See Section 6.5.1.9 of the *PMBOK® Guide.*

6.5.1.10 Organizational Process Assets

See Section 6.5.1.10 of the *PMBOK® Guide.*

6.5.1.11 Additional Inputs

In addition to the inputs presented in Section 6.5.1 of the *PMBOK® Guide,* customer stories and features organized into lists, groups, or sets are useful inputs for estimating software project activity durations. Velocity and rework metrics are also useful inputs.

6.5.2 Estimate Activity Durations: Tools and Techniques

The tools and techniques presented in Section 6.5.2 of the *PMBOK® Guide* are applicable for estimating software project activity durations. Service level agreements are also useful (see Section 6.4.2.6 of this *Software Extension*).

6.5.2.1 Expert Judgment

See Section 6.5.2.1 of the *PMBOK® Guide*.

6.5.2.2 Analogous Estimating

See Section 6.5.2.2 of the *PMBOK® Guide*.

6.5.2.3 Parametric Estimating

See Section 6.5.2.3 of the *PMBOK® Guide*.

6.5.2.4 Three-Point Estimating

See Section 6.5.2.4 of the *PMBOK® Guide*.

6.5.2.5 Group Decision-Making Techniques

See Section 6.5.2.5 of the *PMBOK® Guide*.

6.5.2.6 Reserve Analysis

See Section 6.5.2.6 of the *PMBOK® Guide*.

6.5.3 Estimate Activity Durations: Outputs

The outputs for estimating project activity durations in Section 6.5.3 of the *PMBOK® Guide* are applicable for software projects.

6.5.3.1 Activity Duration Estimates

See Section 6.5.3.1 of the *PMBOK® Guide*.

6.5.3.2 Project Documents Updates

See Section 6.5.3.2 of the *PMBOK® Guide*.

6.6 Develop Schedule

The form of a software project schedule may be the same as described in Section 6.5 of the *PMBOK® Guide* or it may take a different form altogether. In addition to the approach described in the *PMBOK® Guide*, a more flexible approach facilitates the expected changes that inevitably occur in a software project schedule. Software project schedules and plans change, driven by customer requests, project feedback, and by the emergence of previously unidentified work activities. The form of software project schedule used may be unfamiliar to some stakeholders. For example, a prioritized backlog of work may be the preferred method for illustrating and managing the sequence of project activities instead of a network diagram. The approach of maintaining a prioritized backlog of work activities is similar to rolling wave planning, where a top-level schedule is maintained for the entire project and only the proximate elements of the schedule are completed in detail as the project evolves.

6.6.1 Develop Schedule: Inputs

The inputs for developing a project schedule in the *PMBOK® Guide* are applicable inputs for developing a software project schedule. Additional inputs are described in Section 6.6.1.14.

6.6.1.1 Schedule Management Plan

See Section 6.6.1.1 of the *PMBOK® Guide*.

6.6.1.2 Activity List

See Section 6.6.1.2 of the *PMBOK® Guide*.

6.6.1.3 Activity Attributes

See Section 6.6.1.3 of the *PMBOK® Guide*.

6.6.1.4 Project Schedule Network Diagrams

See Section 6.6.1.4 of the *PMBOK® Guide*.

6.6.1.5 Activity Resource Requirements

See Section 6.6.1.5 of the *PMBOK® Guide.*

6.6.1.6 Resource Calendars

See Section 6.6.1.6 of the *PMBOK® Guide.*

6.6.1.7 Activity Duration Estimates

See Section 6.6.1.7 of the *PMBOK® Guide.*

6.6.1.8 Project Scope Statement

See Section 6.6.1.8 of the *PMBOK® Guide.*

6.6.1.9 Risk Register

See Section 6.6.1.9 of the *PMBOK® Guide.*

6.6.1.10 Project Staff Assignments

See Section 6.6.1.10 of the *PMBOK® Guide.*

6.6.1.11 Resource Breakdown Structure

See Section 6.6.1.11 of the *PMBOK® Guide.*

6.6.1.12 Enterprise Environmental Factors

See Section 6.6.1.12 of the *PMBOK® Guide.*

6.6.1.13 Organizational Process Assets

See Section 6.6.1.13 of the *PMBOK® Guide.*

6.6.1.14 Additional Inputs

Additional inputs for developing a software project schedule include activity lists, features and feature sets, and stories. Other inputs include historical data on project team cadence and velocity, and service level agreements for on-demand scheduling.

6.6.2 Develop Schedule: Tools and Techniques

The tools and techniques for developing a project schedule in Section 6.6.2 of the *PMBOK® Guide* are applicable for developing a software project schedule, with the modification of Section 6.6.2.8. In addition, the extensions described in Sections 6.6.2.7 and 6.6.2.9 (below) are applicable when developing a software project schedule.

6.6.2.1 Schedule Network Analysis

See Section 6.6.2.1 of the *PMBOK® Guide*.

6.6.2.2 Critical Path Method

See Section 6.6.2.2 of the *PMBOK® Guide*.

6.6.2.3 Critical Chain Method

See Section 6.6.2.3 of the *PMBOK® Guide*.

6.6.2.4 Resource Optimization Techniques

See Section 6.6.2.4 of the *PMBOK® Guide*.

6.6.2.5 Modeling Techniques

See Section 6.6.2.5 of the *PMBOK® Guide*.

6.6.2.6 Leads and Lags

See Section 6.6.2.6 of the *PMBOK® Guide*.

6.6.2.7 Schedule Compression

Compressing the schedule of a software project without doing other tradeoffs results in a nonlinear increase in the number of people needed to meet the schedule because the number of communication paths among more project members increases exponentially; more effort will be spent on communication and coordination of work activities. A well-known rule of thumb states that software projects rarely succeed when the project schedule is compressed more than 25%, regardless of the number of people added to the project because increased communication and coordination becomes counter-productive. And, the well-known Brooks Law states "adding manpower to a late project makes it later." [22]

For adaptive software projects, the schedule can be compressed by reducing the number of features planned during an iterative cycle to those that can be delivered with the given number of team members in the planned time frame. Another method for compressing the schedule is to limit the level of functionality within features to a minimally viable subset.

6.6.2.8 Scheduling Tool

See Section 6.6.2.8 of the *PMBOK® Guide*.

6.6.2.9 Incremental Product Planning

Managers of software projects often schedule development of features and quality attributes (the product scope) as deliverable increments of software. This approach can be used for the construction phase of a predictive life cycle and for the iterative development cycles of an adaptive life cycle. The project schedule is ordered by the priority of incremental product development cycles that are typically weekly, monthly, or quarterly. The scheduling sequence for increments of working, deliverable software can be reviewed and revised during periodic incremental product planning meetings.

For adaptive life cycles, the project manager and the project team plan the work activities for the next incremental delivery cycle in enough detail to accomplish the work, typically making adjustments based on daily reviews as the work is accomplished. Using this method of incremental product planning, the anticipated unknowns may indicate that the selected increments are too large for delivery within scheduled development cycles. When this occurs, the team partitions the increments to be delivered into what can be delivered, which requires an adjustment in the prioritization of work activities and the product backlog.

6.6.3 Develop Schedule: Outputs

The outputs from developing a project schedule in Section 6.6.3 of the *PMBOK® Guide* are applicable outputs from developing a software project schedule. In addition, the output in 6.6.3.7 applies to software project schedules.

6.6.3.1 Schedule Baseline

See Section 6.6.3.1 of the *PMBOK® Guide*.

6.6.3.2 Project Schedule

See Section 6.6.3.2 of the *PMBOK® Guide*.

6.6.3.3 Schedule Data

See Section 6.6.3.3 of the *PMBOK® Guide*.

6.6.3.4 Project Calendars

See Section 6.6.3.4 of the *PMBOK® Guide.*

6.6.3.5 Project Management Plan Updates

See Section 6.6.3.5 of the *PMBOK® Guide.*

6.6.3.6 Project Documents Updates

See Section 6.6.3.6 of the *PMBOK® Guide.*

6.6.3.7 Release and Iteration Plan Updates

Updates to the release and iteration plans are additional outputs from developing a schedule for the construction phase of a predictive life cycle or for the iteration cycles of an adaptive life cycle software project.

6.7 Control Schedule

Controlling a software project schedule is a challenging proposition because of the dynamics of software projects. To control schedule variance, a software project manager needs to understand the following: the rate that teams are delivering completed software increments; the current rate of completion for work in process, the risks and dependencies that can impact the schedule; the impact of technical variance on the schedule; and options for reprioritizing product scope, by reducing, deferring, or removing lower priority features from the product scope.

Technical variance in software can have a substantial impact on the project schedule—particularly when the root causes of technical variance are addressed late in a software project. See Section 8.1.3.3 of this *Software Extension* for more information on measuring software to discern technical variance and Section 8.3.2 of this *Software Extension* for options to control technical variance.

Schedule variance can be corrected by improving the velocity of a software development team; velocity is the rate of delivering increments of working software within fixed timeframes (i.e., the time box) and with a fixed number of team members. A retrospective meeting at the end of each iteration cycle allows a team to reflect on, and identify opportunities to improve their velocity. Section 9.2.4.5 of this *Software Extension* provides information on how teams use retrospectives to improve their velocity. Section 8.3.2 of this *Software Extension* provides techniques such as continuous integration to improve velocity.

Other changes to control schedule variance may include reprioritization of the backlog of remaining work or adjusting the engagement model with the customer. See Section 5.3.3.3 of this *Software Extension* for more information on aligning scope with schedule on projects that use an adaptive life cycle. Schedule control may also involve making changes to team structures and managing the workflow within the teams.

6.7.1 Control Schedule: Inputs

The inputs for controlling a project schedule in Section 6.7.1 of the *PMBOK® Guide* are applicable inputs for controlling software project schedules, with the modification of 6.7.1.3 below.

6.7.1.1 Project Management Plan

See Section 6.7.1.1 of the *PMBOK® Guide*.

6.7.1.2 Project Schedule

See Section 6.7.1.2 of the *PMBOK® Guide*.

6.7.1.3 Work Performance Data

The cadence of recent work completed, current velocity metrics, and service-level agreements for on-demand scheduling can provide inputs for controlling the schedule of an adaptive life cycle software project.

6.7.1.4 Project Calendars

See Section 6.7.1.4 of the *PMBOK® Guide*.

6.7.1.5 Schedule Data

See Section 6.7.1.5 of the *PMBOK® Guide*.

6.7.1.6 Organizational Process Assets

See Section 6.7.1.6 of the *PMBOK® Guide*.

6.7.2 Control Schedule: Tools and Techniques

The tools and techniques presented in Section 6.7.2 of the *PMBOK® Guide* for controlling a project schedule are applicable to controlling the schedule of a software project with the indicated modifications and the addition of 6.7.2.9 through 6.7.2.14 (below).

6.7.2.1 Performance Reviews

In many software projects, performance reviews, as described Section 6.7.2.1 of the *PMBOK® Guide*, are part of the technical review cycle. In most cases, the best measurement of performance is the value created/delivered over time. However, care should be taken when reviewing software performance to ensure that all the ancillary activities that are not specifically related to the software development are progressing as well. Ancillary activities include infrastructure support, testing environments, test case development, interface control, configuration management, equipment or supply acquisition, deployment planning, and logistics activities.

6.7.2.2 Project Management Software

See Section 6.7.2.2 of the *PMBOK® Guide*.

6.7.2.3 Resource Optimization Techniques

See Section 6.7.2.3 of the *PMBOK® Guide*.

6.7.2.4 Modeling techniques

See Section 6.7.2.4 of the *PMBOK® Guide*.

6.7.2.5 Leads and Lags

See Section 6.7.2.5 of the *PMBOK® Guide*.

6.7.2.6 Schedule Compression

As described in Section 6.6.2.6 of this *Software Extension*, schedule compression for software projects results in a nonlinear increase in the required number of team members. Increased communication and coordination among more team members and less time to do adequate development and testing may result in decreased software quality. An alternative to reducing quality is to reduce the number of lower-valued features to be included in the software product, and/or to reduce the functionality within features to a minimally viable level.

6.7.2.7 Scheduling Tool

See Section 6.7.2.7 of the *PMBOK® Guide*.

6.7.2.8 Evidence-Based Reviews

Evidence-based reviews for software projects have been recommended in various standards (including ISO/IEC/IEEE Standards 1028 and 12207). They include the following guidelines:

- Base reviews on *evidence* (e.g., demonstration of working software) provided by the developer and validated by independent experts. A laundry list of work activities completed is not evidence.

- Provide evidence to indicate that when the system is built to the specified architecture, it will:
  - Support the operational concept;
  - Satisfy the requirements—that is, capability, interfaces, level of service, quality attributes, and evolution;
  - Be buildable within the budget and schedule in the project plan;
  - Generate a viable return on investment; and
  - Generate satisfactory outcomes for all of the success-critical stakeholders.
  - Resolve all major risks or include them in a risk management plan.

6.7.2.9 Retrospectives

Retrospectives are a variant of the performance reviews listed in Section 6.7.2.1 of the *PMBOK® Guide* but they are typically held more frequently than traditional performance reviews—usually after each iteration cycle.

6.7.2.10 Cumulative Flow Diagrams

Cumulative flow diagrams (CFDs) are effective inputs for controlling a software project schedule. They provide a simple method of tracking work-in-progress and visually tracking the trend line for the projected delivery of implemented features. CFDs allow teams and managers to react early to developing problems and, in addition, they provide visibility into the overall project life cycle. Because CFDs plot both the total product scope and the progress of individual items, they visually communicate progress as well as the proportion of total completeness. Figure 6-5 provides an example of using a CFD to track cumulative flow for development of software features.

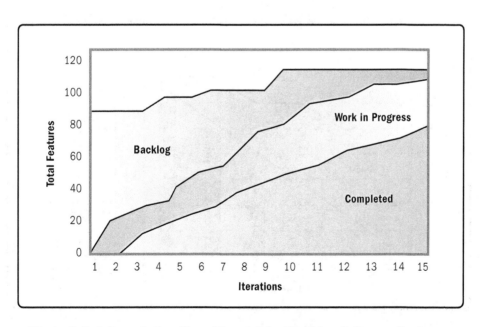

Figure 6-5. A Cumulative-Flow Diagram for Tracking Software Features

6.7.2.11 Workflow Board with Daily Walkthrough

A workflow board is a visual depiction of work flowing through a software project when using an on-demand scheduling approach. Daily walkthroughs provide immediate feedback on blockages and resource issues for the entire team, effectively supporting decisions.

6.7.2.12 Reprioritization Reviews

Reprioritization reviews are elements of an iterative scheduling process. Lack of satisfactory progress may require adjustment of priorities among planned work activities.

6.7.2.13 Burnup and Burndown Charts

A burnup or burndown chart visually illustrates the progress of a software team as measured by completed features, stories, or other work units. A burnup chart is illustrated in Figure 6-6; a burndown chart is illustrated in Section 10.2.3.7 of this *Software Extension*.

As indicated in Figure 6-6, the number of features is plotted on the vertical axis and tracked across iterations on the horizontal axis. The bars indicate the number of features developed during iterations. The dark line indicates the number of features planned for completion in the iterations. *Dark matter* indicates unanticipated and unplanned features that were added. The top "stair step" line indicates the growth of product features from 10 to 14. This growth is acceptable, provided it was initiated by the customer and provided the customer authorized additional time and increased resources (when needed) for development of the added features.

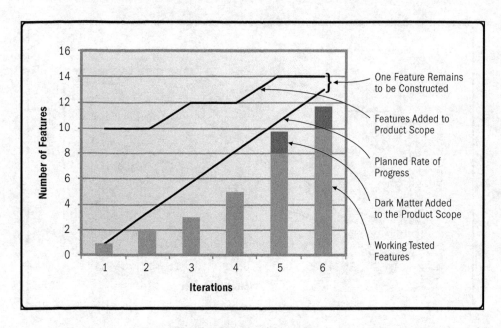

Figure 6-6. Burnup Chart

6.7.2.14 Variance Analysis

As stated in Section 6.7.1.3 of this *Software Extension*, the cadence of recent work completion, current velocity metrics, and service-level agreements for on-demand scheduling can be analyzed to control schedule variance in work performance data when using an adaptive software project life cycle. As a project evolves, the trend in velocity during iterations can be used as an indicator of the final completion date.

6.7.3 Control Schedule: Outputs

6

The outputs for controlling a project schedule in Section 6.7.3 of *PMBOK® Guide* are applicable for controlling a software project schedule, with the addition of the output in Section 6.7.3.7.

6.7.3.1 Work Performance Information

See Section 6.7.3.1 of the *PMBOK® Guide*.

6.7.3.2 Schedule Forecasts

See Section 6.7.3.2 of the *PMBOK® Guide*.

6.7.3.3 Change Requests

See Section 6.7.3.3 of the *PMBOK® Guide*.

6.7.3.4 Project Management Plan Updates

See Section 6.7.3.4 of the *PMBOK® Guide*.

6.7.3.5 Project Documents Updates

See Section 6.7.3.5 of the *PMBOK® Guide*.

6.7.3.6 Organizational Process Assets Updates

See Section 6.7.3.6 of the *PMBOK® Guide*.

6.7.3.7 Additional Outputs

Velocity measures and iteration and release plan updates are useful outputs for controlling the schedule of an adaptive life cycle software project, as are service level agreement adjustments for on-demand scheduling.

7

PROJECT COST MANAGEMENT

Most of the material in Section 7 of the *PMBOK® Guide* is applicable to cost management for software projects. This section of the *Software Extension to the PMBOK® Guide* presents additional considerations for managing software project cost.

As stated in the introduction to Section 7 of the *PMBOK® Guide*, Project Cost Management includes the processes involved in estimating, budgeting, funding, managing, and controlling costs so that a project can be completed within the approved budget. This section of the *Software Extension to the PMBOK® Guide* discusses cost management for software projects.

Large corporations and government agencies develop many new software products and modify hundreds of existing products each year. Small companies may develop or modify fewer software products, but those products may be the essence of the company's business. As a result, project cost management is a mainstream activity for every organization that builds software; it has become a critical process for the success and survival of many organizations.

As indicated in Section 6 of this *Software Extension*, effort and schedule are closely related for software projects because effort is the product of people and time. Because staff-hours is the primary cost factor for software development, effort estimation is used as the basis for estimating the cost of a software project. Additional costs may be included as an overhead percentage on the cost of effort. Many companies do not disclose the resource rates (dollar-value) to the project manager. A software project manager can manage project costs in units of staff-hours instead of monetary units when the resource rate for the staff-hours is not provided.

The effort required to develop or modify software is almost entirely dependent on the skills, abilities, and motivations of individual team members, the interactions among team members, technical leadership, project management, and the culture and organizational processes in the software development environment. Cost management for software projects includes making initial estimates and updating them periodically, and may include identifying and forecasting the cost of maintaining and evolving a software product plus licensing or updating commercially acquired components over many years. Managing software project costs with this amount of variability is difficult even when a software project manager has a significant amount of experience.

This section of the *Software Extension* addresses effort estimation, in addition to other aspects of managing software project cost, to help software project managers understand the impact of the variability of software cost drivers on software project costs. When using adaptive life cycle models, which maintain flexibility as late into the development process as possible, software project managers still need to estimate the effort (cost) and schedule of their projects. However, the volatility of project attributes, such as rapidly evolving technology, changing and emerging architecture and requirements, and the varying productivity of software developers, has a significant impact on cost estimation and cost management.

The *PMBOK® Guide* states that the ability to influence costs is greatest at the early stages of the project, making early scope definition of a project critical to estimating and managing costs. A stable software architecture and enabling technologies (such as configuration management, quality assurance, and testing tools) have a strong influence on software cost—especially on the cost of late changes. Flexible or scalable architecture, continuous testing, and enabling technologies can also reduce the long-term cost of using, maintaining, and supporting a software product.

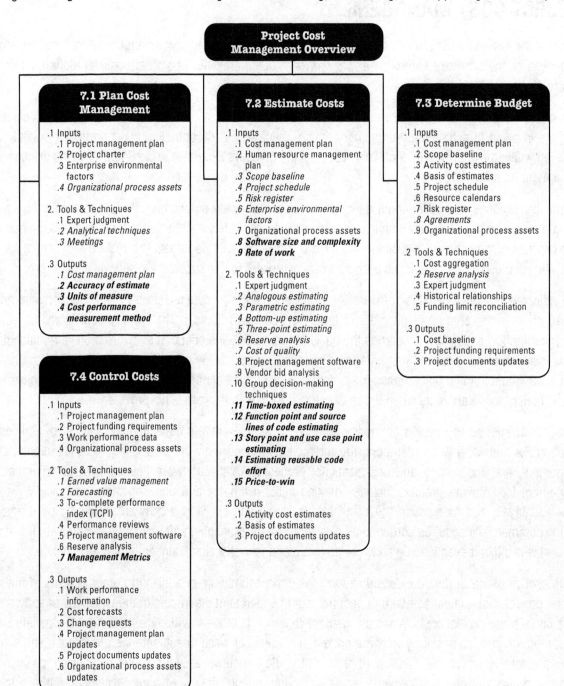

Figure 7-1. Project Cost Management Overview

The financial benefit of conducting a software project can be continuously evaluated during evolution of the product. Each adjustment to product scope and implementation details can be based on predicting the prospective value of the product. Delivery into the operational environment of a planned product increment can provide financial return and other benefits during software development. Scope management for software projects is addressed in Section 5 of this *Software Extension.*

Figure 7-1 provides an overview of Project Cost Management for software projects; it is an adaptation of Figure 7-1 in the *PMBOK® Guide.*

7.1 Plan Cost Management

As stated in the *PMBOK® Guide,* Plan Cost Management is a process that establishes the policies, procedures, and documentation for planning, managing, executing, and controlling project costs. This includes identifying incremental funding models and establishing change control to manage variations from the cost control plan. The inputs, tools and techniques, and outputs for planning cost management in Section 7.1 of the *PMBOK® Guide* are applicable to planning cost management for software projects, with the indicated additions and extensions.

7.1.1 Plan Cost Management: Inputs

The inputs in Section 7.1.1 of the *PMBOK® Guide* are applicable for planning cost management for software projects, with the modification of 7.1.1.4.

7.1.1.1 Project Management Plan

See Section 7.1.1.1 of the *PMBOK® Guide.*

7.1.1.2 Project Charter

See Section 7.1.1.2 of the *PMBOK® Guide.*

7.1.1.3 Enterprise Environmental Factors

See Section 7.1.1.3 of the *PMBOK® Guide.*

7.1.1.4 Organizational Process Assets

In addition to those assets described in 7.1.1.4 of the *PMBOK® Guide,* organizational process assets for software project cost management include direct-cost drivers, governance policies, and the product portfolio, when they exist.

- **Cost Drivers.** Size and complexity of software are highly correlated with the effort for software projects and drive software cost; large and/or complex products require more effort. Other cost drivers include skills and abilities of software developers; maintaining relationships with customers and other stakeholders; infrastructure technology; development tools and environments; and costs of other organizational entities such as configuration management and independent testing. Historical values of these cost drivers and their impact on effort (i.e., cost) are often maintained as an organizational asset for various domains for which the organization develops software.

Measures of software size are presented subsequently in this section of the *Software Extension*; complexity is discussed here. There are two forms of complexity for software projects: complexity of the problem domain and complexity of the solution domain; both affect the effort, and therefore the cost of a software project. Problem complexity is determined in part by the problem domain and in part by the familiarity of the software developers with that domain. Data processing software for a small organization is thought to be a less complex domain than interplanetary navigation or instrumentation software for experiments in nuclear physics. However, software developers who are experienced in software for interplanetary navigation may find that domain simpler for them than business data processing for which they have no experience. Solution complexity depends on whether known algorithms, data representations, and computational methods can be used or whether new algorithms, data representations, and/or computational methods will have to be developed to solve the problem. A complex problem domain and/or a complex solution domain can greatly increase the amount of effort needed to provide a satisfactory solution to a problem.

- **Governance Policies.** In some organizations, organizational governance policies may specify objectives, processes, and procedures that can have a significant impact on cost management for IT and software projects. Governance policies may impose a standard process for software development or the software testing and review processes that need to be accounted for in a software project cost estimate. For software that has safety, security, health, or financial impact for the users, governance policies or regulations that have to be built into the software may impact cost. These may result in complex software that checks to ensure computations are being performed properly (checks and balances in intermediate results, user intervention in completing or safely terminating a software process), or imposes limits on access to authorized groups of people who perform some functions, or preserves audit records of those who perform certain functions (such as adjusting a paycheck).

  Operating policies and procedures, and the resulting software functions and controls, may be based on IT governance standards and guidance from sources such as COBIT (Control Objectives in Information and Related Technology), COSO (Committee of Sponsoring Organizations of the Treadway Commission), ITIL® (Information Technology Infrastructure Library), ISO/IEC 20000 (IT Service Management) or ISO/IEC 27000 (Systems and Software Security Engineering). Other inputs to planning software project cost include fiduciary requirements or government regulations that mandate the financial and security controls to be built into the software system. For example, ensuring compliance to policies such as the Sarbanes Oxley Act (SOX Compliance), Basel-III, or the Health Insurance Portability and Accountability Act (HIPAA) may need to be included in the software project cost management plan.

- **Portfolio.** Priorities and constraints in an organization's portfolio of projects and programs that includes software projects and software programs may provide inputs to planning cost management for a software project. The availability of reuse, COTS, or open source software will influence how much of the desired software will be original development and how much will be modification and integration of existing software. Even when other sources of software components are available, an organization may decide to build new software, thereby developing wholly owned Intellectual Property (IP) for future reuse or resale.

7.1.2 Plan Cost Management: Tools and Techniques

The tools and techniques in Section 7.1.2 of the *PMBOK® Guide* are also applicable for planning cost management for software projects, with the modifications to Sections 7.1.2.2 and 7.1.2.

7.1.2.1 Expert Judgment

See Section 7.1.2.1 in the *PMBOK® Guide*.

7.1.2.2. Analytical Techniques

Some organizations use analytical techniques to establish decision thresholds and financial control limits to be used as inputs for planning cost management for software projects. Historical data from predictive life cycle software projects are typically analyzed using statistical techniques. Performance data from adaptive life cycle software projects are collected and analyzed for each cycle of software development.

7.1.2.3. Meetings

After the preliminary cost management plan is drafted and proposed control limits are established, a meeting is typically held with the project sponsors to reach agreement on the cost management plan.

7.1.3 Plan Cost Management: Outputs

The outputs in Section 7.1.3 of the *PMBOK® Guide* are also applicable as outputs from planning cost management for software projects, with the following modification to 7.1.3.1. In addition, the outputs in Sections 7.1.3.2 through 7.1.3.4 also apply to planning software project cost management.

7.1.3.1 Cost Management Plan

The cost management plan for a software project typically includes the accuracy of the cost estimate, units of measure, and the cost performance measurement methods to be used.

7.1.3.2 Accuracy of Estimate

Software estimation is error-prone; predicting the accuracy of an estimate is difficult because of the many factors that can affect an estimate. The values of many of these factors are unknown during initial planning. A rough order-of-magnitude preliminary estimate is typically generated during the initiation phase of a software project, when requirements are immature, the actual parameters of software development are being formulated, and the development team may or may not have been identified. Estimation accuracy can deviate by as much as ±150% or more at this point. Productivity, skills, and motivation are widely variable among software developers, so effort data from previous projects may not be directly applicable as a basis of estimation. A budgetary estimate may be created when the requirements or feature set and high-level design are stable and the project team and schedule have been set. At this point, the estimate may deviate by ±50%, depending on the complexity of the design, the stability of the requirements, and the known characteristics of the team that will develop the software. A definitive estimate for a development cycle of 2 to 4 weeks may be accurate to within ±10% of actual cost; however, that depends on factors such as the stability of the design and accurate translation of features into product requirements. Increasing accuracy of a software estimate is sometimes referred to as the "cone of uncertainty." Providing a confidence level for an estimate can be used to qualify estimation risk.

Early, inaccurate estimates made to a high level of detail may not be worth the time and effort it takes to develop them. Early, order-of-magnitude estimates are more likely to be more useful, provided they are refined as the project evolves and uncertainties are resolved.

7.1.3.3 Units of Measure

The cost management plan for a software project typically includes definitive units of measure for the project metrics, such as person-hours or person-days for effort measurement, and function points or objects as surrogates for effort measurement. User stories, use cases, features, and test cases are also used to calculate effort based on historical data of effort per function point, object, user story, use case, and so forth. Note that number of lines of software code written does not necessarily correspond to the business value of software or as a measure of the completion of required software features. Units of measure such as function points, objects, user stories, use cases, and so forth each require a measurement scale (e.g., counting rules for function points or objects).

7.1.3.4 Cost Performance Measurement Method

Methods of performance measurement are specified as outputs in a software cost management plan. The construction phase of a predictive life cycle and the iterations of adaptive life cycles use performance trends based on estimated amount of work needed versus the actual effort performed to develop an increment of working, deliverable software. This can be reflected in measures such as productivity in function points per staff-day or velocity in features delivered per staff-week, and shown in visual presentations such as burndown charts and continuous flow diagrams.

7.2 Estimate Costs

The inputs, tools and techniques, and outputs for estimating project costs in Section 7.2 of the *PMBOK® Guide* are applicable for estimating costs of software projects, with the following clarifications and extensions.

Software project managers tend to use multiple estimation approaches and then reconcile the differences among the estimates because estimating costs for software projects is an error-prone process. Estimates of software project cost may need to include a number of additional factors beyond development and deployment costs, such as licensing fees for vendor software included in the software product and infrastructure upgrades for internal systems. Some of these costs may be captured in corporate overhead, such as the infrastructure resources and tools for software development. For other projects, infrastructure resources and tools may be seen as direct charges to the software project, or assessed on a per seat basis for the project team.

- **Project direct-cost factors.** The dynamics of individual performance, team skills, size and complexity of the software product, and integration with other systems are primary direct-cost factors for software projects. Other direct costs may include specific software tools required by the customer, travel for a geographically distributed software team or remote customer, and hardware and/or operating systems specified by the customer. Hardware simulators may be needed to support development and testing of the software.

- **Fiduciary requirements and government regulations.** Meeting statutory or regulatory constraints may need to be included in a software project cost estimate.

- **Standards compliance.** Some software projects may include costs for conforming to standards that are part of the organizational governance framework. However, conformance to process standards is usually considered to reduce project risk and cost of rework, resulting in lower overall project life cycle costs.

- **Organizational changes.** The cost of organizational changes that may impact the actual cost of a software project is typically included in the cost estimate.

- **Cost and value risk.** For some software projects, the probability that the product may not return the value anticipated can impact the cost planning of the project or lead to incremental estimates at milestones when the investment in the project is reevaluated.

- **Funding costs.** Additional cost estimation factors may include total cost of ownership (TOC), payback period, break-even point, and return on investment. For software projects, it may be possible to deliver one or more subset version of the final product during the development life cycle. This can provide early payback to the sponsoring organization. The impact of the time-value of money can be reflected in the business case.

7.2.1 Estimate Costs: Inputs

The inputs for estimating project costs in Section 7.2.1 of the *PMBOK® Guide* are applicable inputs for software projects, with the modification of Sections 7.2.1.3 through 7.2.1.6 and addition of Sections 7.2.1.8 and 7.2.1.9 (see below).

7.2.1.1 Cost Management Plan

See Section 7.2.1.1 in the *PMBOK® Guide*.

7.2.1.2 Human Resource Plan

See Section 7.2.1.2 in the *PMBOK® Guide*.

7.2.1.3 Scope Baseline

Theoretically, a fixed scope and stable requirements can result in an accurate initial cost estimate for a software project. In reality, many successful software projects use feature driven delivery (FDD) where high-level scope and a set of candidate features, use cases, or epics (overarching user stories) are defined early in the project and evolved, as uncertainties are resolved. Using an adaptive approach for a software project intentionally limits upfront planning to high-level scope, which in itself may not be a sufficient basis for an accurate initial cost estimate. For adaptive software projects, constraints on total time and overall cost may be specified initially, with the possibility of later revision.

7.2.1.4 Project Schedule

As described in Section 6 of this *Software Extension*, predictive software projects tend to develop detailed schedules that include major milestones and other review and evaluation times. Adaptive software projects are based on minimal initial plans, including the details of the project schedule; details of the schedule versus priorities of features to be implemented are elaborated as the project evolves. Statistical methods may be used to account for schedule uncertainty for both predictive and adaptive software projects.

7.2.1.5 Risk Register

As described in Section 11 of this *Software Extension*, all software projects (predictive or adaptive) can benefit from initial and ongoing risk management. A risk register can be used as an input to cost estimation by documenting identified risk factors and the mitigation strategies to be pursued. Confidence in a cost estimate is dependent on the probability of and the potential impact of identified risk factors, such as the availability of functional specialists and subject matter experts when they will be needed. Opportunity management is also pursued to identify opportunities for cost savings and additional cost-benefit returns. Risk analysis is particularly important in estimating the cost and price to bid for a competitively sourced software project.

There is a large number of variables that can impact an estimate; assumptions about the variables need to be documented and tracked in the risk register.

7.2.1.6 Enterprise Environmental Factors

The level and maturity of architecture for an enterprise-wide software product have a significant impact on the effort and schedule for software development. Conformance to existing enterprise architecture often lowers the amount of effort and time required for software development, while it imposes constraints on the solution, particularly in the use of COTS or other non-developmental software items. Once architectural decisions are made, some development tasks can be performed concurrently, thus allowing shorter schedules at higher completion rates.

7.2.1.7 Organizational Process Assets

See Section 7.2.1.7 in the *PMBOK® Guide*.

7.2.1.8 Software Size and Complexity

Software size and complexity are two of the most important factors that affect software cost, so they are primary inputs to most software cost and schedule estimation models. Deriving appropriate estimates of size and complexity is neither straightforward nor trivial, because of the inherent difficulty of quantifying software attributes. Even during late stages of software development, estimation of software size, complexity and the resulting effort, schedule, and cost are often inaccurate. Estimation techniques that depend on size and complexity estimates include:

- Analogy,
- Expert judgment (including Delphi),
- Use of historical data,
- Rules of thumb, and
- Estimation algorithms (calibrated using local historical data).

Because of the uncertainties associated with estimation of size and complexity, estimators typically use more than one approach to estimating effort, schedule, and cost.

Often, software estimates are made for small units and rolled up (bottom-up estimation). The cost of integration and testing of the software components need to be added when bottom-up estimates are made only for the work to be performed to develop each software component.

7.2.1.9 Rate of Work

Stable software development teams that have all of the needed skills (i.e., cross-functional teams) and who have worked together over time can establish a predictable rate for producing working, deliverable software. The rate of production is called velocity; it can be used to provide accurate estimates for developing software increments.

7.2.2 Estimate Costs: Tools and Techniques

Software project managers use most of the estimation tools and techniques listed in Section 7.2.2 of the *PMBOK® Guide*, but different approaches are used in different situations.

After determining the project scope and product scope, and planning for software project cost management, the software project manager and project team estimate the cost to develop and deliver the software product. The first level of estimation is typically a preliminary high-level estimate based on requirements, stories, use cases, or features to be implemented. The goal of initial estimation is to quickly converge on an order-of-magnitude estimate. This first estimate is used to drive initial planning. Analogies, historical data, and expert judgment are typically used at this point.

Experts may be asked, either individually or as a group (perhaps using a Delphi process), to develop initial estimates. Since each expert may use personal experiences and a different estimation method, some perspective on the accuracy of individual estimates is provided. This approach may be time consuming, and is only as good as the experts' judgment. It can be especially useful when a software project involves new technologies.

- **Estimation units.** The units of measure adopted by a project team or a software organization used to estimate project work may be expressed in units of effort (e.g., staff-days) or ideal time for a fixed number of software developers (e.g., development-days).

- **Work units.** A work unit is a relative measure that is compared to the work needed for similar work products. Implementation of function points, for example, can be used to determine the relative amount of work required to implement a software feature, compared to implementing function points for other similar features. After a team has worked through several iterative cycles together and achieved a consistent velocity, their work units can be more accurately aligned to units of actual time and effort.

- **Story points.** Some adaptive methods utilize *story points* or *use case points* as a basis of estimation. A story point is an approximation of the complexity of software functions to be implemented, expressed in a narrative of user interactions with the system (the user story). Story points are comparisons of the complexity of a new story to a well-defined base story commonly understood by the team. Story points are then awarded from a range of values in comparison to the base story. Some teams use a story point range defined as a modified Fibonacci sequence (i.e., 1, 2, 3, 5, 8, 13, 20, 40, 100) to scale the complexity of stories. If the base story represents 5 story points, then a 3-point story would take 60% of the base story's work to complete. Note that these are relative rather than absolute values, and may differ from team to team and project to project, limiting their applicability across an organization or across the software industry.

- **Ideal time.** This is the time expected for an "ideal" software developer or development team to deliver a feature or complete a task, without regard to actual time used for distractions, overhead functions, and lost time for holidays or to recover from disasters such as missing code planned for reuse. Ideal time is sometimes expressed as full-time equivalent (FTE) days or weeks. Many organizations estimate project schedules based on 60% to 80% FTE availability of the software developers.

The tools and techniques for estimating project costs in Section 7.2.2 of the *PMBOK® Guide* are applicable to estimating costs of software projects. The following adaptations and extensions (Sections 7.2.2.11 through 7.2.2.15) also apply.

7.2.2.1 Expert Judgment

See Section 7.2.2.1 of the *PMBOK® Guide*.

7.2.2.2 Analogous Estimating

A software project team that has worked together to develop software in the past can use their experience to estimate the number of work units they can deliver in a given amount of time. Some algorithmic approaches use historical values of productivity to estimate future projects (e.g., function points developed per staff-day). Early estimates are often based on nominal measures such as simple, average, and difficult complexity.

Software development teams, when using an adaptive approach, develop the ability to estimate their velocity based on their experience. A team's velocity (amount of software developed over a given period of time) can be used to estimate future effort. Velocity becomes a more accurate predictor after a team has completed several iterations together; it may not be applicable for a team that has not worked together until some performance data on the current project is collected.

7.2.2.3 Parametric Estimating

Parametric estimation tools for software projects typically include an estimation algorithm with adjustment factors for specific cost drivers. Most estimation tools for software projects use some measure of product size as the primary input variable, such as estimated number of function points or number of use cases. Parametric estimation tools can be calibrated for the specific software development organization, infrastructure tools, complexity of the software to be developed, and experience or ability of the team, or a provided calibration that most closely matches the characteristics of the project being estimated can be used.

Calibration of a parametric estimation tool using local, historical data is preferred to the use of provided calibrations because local data will include factors unique to the local organization and the software produced by the organization; also, since the methods and tools used on projects are frequently changed for newer technology.

7.2.2.4 Bottom-Up Estimating

Bottom-up estimation is often used to estimate effort and cost of software projects. Estimates are made for individual software components and rolled up. The cost of integration and testing of the software components need to be added when bottom-up estimates are made only for the effort needed to develop the software components. Additional costs for project management, quality assurance, configuration management, and other project cost factors should also be included.

7.2.2.5 Three-Point Estimating

Estimating software size or effort can be based on expert judgment and the three-point PERT algorithm. Using this approach, experts estimate the size or effort for individual software components as small, (e.g., 20% probable), medium (50% probable), or large (e.g., 80% probable)—the percentages for small and large depend on parameters in the PERT algorithm. The PERT algorithm is used to estimate the mean and standard deviation of size or effort for each software component and the mean and standard deviation for the collection of components; probability distributions for effort or size can be calculated from the mean and standard deviation. Also, the mean and standard deviation of a size estimate can be used as inputs to a parametric estimation algorithm to compute a probability distribution for effort. Other forms of statistical estimation, including Monte Carlo simulation, can be used to overcome some of the undesired effects of three-point estimation, such as nodal bias or merge bias that occurs when applying three-point estimation to an activity network.

7.2.2.6 Reserve Analysis

Estimates can be made to establish cost and schedule reserves to be included in the project estimate and the project budget. Past projects can be analyzed to support the amount of reserve that should be included for a new project by determining the difference between the known effort (cost) at the start of the previous projects and the amount of effort (cost) that was eventually required to complete the project.

7.2.2.7 Cost of Quality (COQ)

Estimating the cost of quality can be used as a technique to improve software cost estimation because cost of quality can exert a significant impact on the cost of a software project. For example, requirements for high quality (e.g., safety-critical or mission-critical software) can multiply the effort and, therefore, the cost of software development. Initially identifying quality-critical features and functions can reduce overall cost, as opposed to attempting to test quality into the software at the end of the project. Failure Modes and Effects and Criticality Analysis (FMECA) and the processes in RTCA DO-178B/C for safety-critical avionics software are systems engineering tools that support identification of quality-critical cost factors. Also, results chains and business process analyses can identify high-cost, but possibly low-value, quality requirements. These quality requirements can be expensive to implement and, in some cases, are undetectable by the user in the operating environment.

At the same time, failing to estimate and include the cost of resources needed to meet legitimate requirements for performance, safety, security, and other nonfunctional requirements can inhibit market or customer acceptance and cause huge additional costs in rework at the end of a project when the rework is most expensive.

Cost of quality also includes the cost to fix functional or technical defects found during a project. These costs include effort associated with reestablishing the development or testing environment to verify fixes after the fact, updating project artifacts related to the defective code, and the cost of interrupting the flow of value-added work. These costs of rework can be considerable and are very difficult to anticipate at the beginning of a project.

For adaptive life cycle software projects with stable teams and a history of delivery, historical velocity (analogy estimating) will include much of the cost of quality for software developed in similar projects because the dynamics of individual performance, team skills, motivation, and other factors are included in historical velocity. For other projects, expert judgment, estimating models, and reserve analysis from prior projects can be used to establish a management reserve to handle the uncertainty associated with the cost of quality.

A key to reducing these costs in adaptive life cycle projects is gathering feedback early in the process. See Section 8 of *the PMBOK® Guide* and this *Software Extension* for more information on the cost of quality for software projects.

7.2.2.8 Project Management Software

See Section 7.2.2.8 of the *PMBOK® Guide*.

7.2.2.9 Vendor Bid Analysis

See Section 7.2.2.9 of the *PMBOK® Guide*.

7.2.2.10 Group Decision-Making Techniques

See Section 7.2.2.10 of the *PMBOK® Guide*.

7.2.2.11 Time-Boxed Estimating

Adaptive projects that are time-boxed with an evolving product scope should ensure that their cost estimates are not just Level of Effort (LOE) aggregates. The current production rate and the resources that will be used determine cost. For example, if a backlog of software features is required to be delivered in 12 months and 5 people are available, then the available effort is 60 person-months. Although this approach sometimes produces an accurate estimate, care should be taken because it may provide unrealistic estimates unless the requirements and features to be included are scaled to what can be done by those 5 people in 12 months.

7.2.2.12 Function Point and Source Lines of Code Estimating

Historically, the estimated number of source lines of code or function points was used as the primary input variable for effort estimation. Function point estimates are considered more accurate and more easily applied from one project to another, since source lines of code vary significantly by programming language and by programmer for the same function. More recent input measures include stories, story points, use cases, features, and architectural objects. ISO/IEC 20926, *Software and systems engineering—Software measurement—IFPUG functional size measurement method 2009*, provides guidance for software size estimation.

7.2.2.13 Story Point and Use Case Point Estimating

As mentioned in Section 7.2.2 of this *Software Extension*, story points and use case points are sometimes used as inputs to cost estimation algorithms. Historical productivity data can be used to prepare an estimate; for example, staff-days per historical story point can be multiplied by estimated story points to produce an estimated number of staff-days.

7.2.2.14 Estimating Reusable Code Effort

Software project estimators consider whether software code will be developed or whether existing code will be reused as is, adapted from a previous project, acquired from open sources, or some combination thereof. The amount of effort required to reuse code without modification may be small. Integration testing to check that the reused code was integrated correctly may be all that is required. Additional effort may be required to modify the existing code base to accommodate the reused code. Adapted code requires some amount of redesign, recoding, and testing as newly developed code. The amount of effort required depends on the amount of modification required. It is possible that the adapted code may have the correct design but requires conversion because the new software is in a different programming language, or the adapted code may require some amount of redesign to change or add capabilities. Some estimation models include parameters to account for the estimated effort of reuse.

7.2.2.15 Price-to-Win

Estimating the cost of performing a software project is the basis for estimating the price, that is, what the customer will pay. Especially in competitive acquisitions, price is computed as cost plus profit or fee. The ideal price-to-win is a price the customer is willing to pay, is lower than competitors are expected to bid, but not so low that it will be rejected by the customer's evaluators as unreasonable or as showing that the supplier does not understand the project. Price-to-win should be balanced with cost-to-build to produce a realistic bid. Risk analysis is performed on the price-to-win bid (as described further in Section 11 of this *Software Extension*) so that the risk of having to perform the project at the bid price is acceptable to the supplier's organization. (This discussion ignores the competitive strategy of bidding a small project at a price with a low probability of being profitable, or even below the most likely cost, with the intention of gaining experience, customer confidence, or intellectual property for future, more profitably priced projects.)

7.2.3 Estimate Costs: Outputs

The outputs in Section 7.2.3 of the *PMBOK® Guide* are applicable outputs from estimating software project costs.

7.2.3.1 Activity Cost Estimates

See Section 7.2.3.1 of the *PMBOK® Guide*.

7.2.3.2 Basis of Estimates

See Section 7.2.3.2 of the *PMBOK® Guide*.

7.2.3.3 Project Documents Updates

See Section 7.2.3.3 of the *PMBOK® Guide*.

7.3 Determine Budget

The inputs, tools and techniques, and outputs for determining budget in Section 7.3 of the *PMBOK® Guide* are applicable for software projects.

7.3.1 Determine Budget: Inputs

The inputs for determining budget in Section 7.3.1 of the *PMBOK® Guide* are applicable inputs for determining the budget for a software project.

7.3.1.1 Cost Management Plan

See Section 7.3.1.1 of the *PMBOK® Guide*.

7.3.1.2 Scope Baseline

See Section 7.3.1.2 of the *PMBOK® Guide*.

7.3.1.3 Activity Cost Estimates

See Section 7.3.1.3 of the *PMBOK® Guide*.

7.3.1.4 Basis of Estimates

See Section 7.3.1.4 of the *PMBOK® Guide*.

7.3.1.5 Project Schedule

See Section 7.3.1.5 of the *PMBOK® Guide*.

7.3.1.6 Resource Calendars

See Section 7.3.1.6 of the *PMBOK® Guide*.

7.3.1.7 Risk Register

See Section 7.3.1.7 of the *PMBOK® Guide*.

7.3.1.8 Agreements

See Section 7.3.1.8 of the *PMBOK® Guide*.

Service level agreements, when applicable, should be included as an input to determining a software project budget.

7.3.1.9 Organizational Process Assets

See Section 7.3.1.9 of the *PMBOK® Guide*.

7.3.2 Determine Budget: Tools and Techniques

The tools and techniques for determining budget in Section 7.3.2 of the *PMBOK® Guide* are applicable tools and techniques for determining the budget for a software project, with modification of 7.3.2.2.

7.3.2.1 Cost Aggregation

See Section 7.3.2.1 of the *PMBOK® Guide*.

7.3.2.2 Reserve Analysis

A software project budget is based on the sum of estimates for all identified work activities plus an additional reserve for work that will potentially emerge. During the project, reserved budget is either applied to meet contingencies or preserved as surplus or profit. Ideally, as a project progresses and the risks and uncertainties are resolved, the amount of reserve needed is reduced to zero by the end of a project. When charted over time, the amount of reserve needed should resemble a cone (the "cone of uncertainty," large at the beginning of the project and narrowing to zero by the end of the project). The reserve may be divided between the amount that the project manager can use directly (contingency reserve) and the management reserve, which will require authorization to be applied to the project.

7.3.2.3 Expert Judgment

See Section 7.3.2.3 of the *PMBOK® Guide*.

7.3.2.4 Historical Relationships

See Section 7.3.2.4 of the *PMBOK® Guide*.

7.3.2.5 Funding Limit Reconciliation

See Section 7.3.2.5 of the *PMBOK® Guide*.

7.3.3 Determine Budget: Outputs

The outputs for determining budget in Section 7.3.1 of the *PMBOK® Guide* (7.3.3.1 through 7.3.3.3) are applicable to determining the budget for software projects.

7.3.3.1 Cost Baseline

See Section 7.3.3.1 of the *PMBOK® Guide*.

7.3.3.2 Project Funding Requirements

See Section 7.3.3.2 of the *PMBOK® Guide*.

7.3.3.3 Project Documents Updates

See Section 7.3.3.3 of the *PMBOK® Guide*.

7.4 Control Costs

The inputs, tools and techniques, and outputs for controlling costs in Section 7.4 of the *PMBOK® Guide* are applicable to controlling costs of software projects, with the following clarifications.

Effective software project managers constantly monitor changes to evolving stakeholder requirements and other conditions to analyze potential impact on project cost. Some changes will be *in scope* and require no changes to effort allocations (and therefore cost) while other changes may be *out of scope* and will require changes to effort (cost) and schedule. This is especially important for adaptive life cycle software projects because stakeholder requirements typically evolve in a dynamic manner, and changes can occur rapidly as a project evolves. Also, different organizations and their customers use different cost accrual methods for measuring software project success. For example, a project deliverable may be considered as value-adding after successful integration and verification testing, while others may consider it value-adding only after successful user acceptance testing and product delivery into the operational environment.

7.4.1 Control Costs: Inputs

The inputs for controlling costs of software projects in Section 7.4.1 of the *PMBOK® Guide* are applicable for controlling costs of software projects.

7.4.1.1 Project Management Plan

See Section 7.4.1.1 of the *PMBOK® Guide*.

7.4.1.2 Project Funding Requirements

See Section 7.4.1.2 of the *PMBOK® Guide*.

7.4.1.3 Work Performance Data

See Section 7.4.1.3 of the *PMBOK® Guide*.

7.4.1.4 Organizational Process Assets

See Section 7.4.1.4 of the *PMBOK® Guide*.

7.4.2 Control Costs: Tools and Techniques

The tools and techniques for controlling costs in Section 7.4.2 of the *PMBOK® Guide* are applicable for controlling costs of software projects, with the following modification of Sections 7.4.2.1 and 7.4.2.2, and the addition of Section 7.4.2.7.

7.4.2.1 Earned Value Management

Earned value management, when applied to projects that produce physical artifacts, is concerned with measuring cost and schedule progress against an overall plan for cost, schedule, and rate of generating work products. Frequent testing and demonstration of working software increments supports use of earned-value techniques during the construction phase of a predictive life cycle software project and during production of software increments in an adaptive life cycle software project because working, demonstrable software can be used in both cases as a measure of progress. However, the intangible nature of other software work products such as requirements, design documentation, and test plans makes it difficult to measure and report work progress at the level of granularity required to generate accurate earned value reports on a periodic basis.

7.4.2.2 Forecasting

Desirable attributes of a software development forecasting method include providing credible estimates in a short amount of time, quickly communicating the need for decisions or actions, and empowering the project sponsors to choose how the software development funds are to be spent. Earned value tracking, burndown charts, and cumulative flow diagrams (CFDs) provide indicators of the costs expended to-date on a project and provide forecasts of project cost at completion. These mechanisms typically report cost in units of labor (i.e., staff-hours) or in monetary units that account for labor costs plus additional costs.

The information is presented as calculated amounts, but it is the visibility of the charts that is most valuable to project managers, software teams, and other stakeholders. The charts indicate cumulative progress, how much effort or money is being expended on the project, and how much remains to be done. This is important because it represents the amount of effort or money needed to keep the project operational on track regardless of the amount of work assigned.

A simple calculation of the resources that are needed, the percentage of allocation, and all costs associated can be placed on the earned value, burndown, or cumulative flow chart. Often there is a major effort to re-estimate and rebaseline a large project and significant customer discussions may occur concerning scope adjustment and prioritization or deferral of product features. On smaller projects, it may be simpler to use extrapolation to determine adjustments to the cost and schedule needed to deliver the desired software functionality. The project manager and key stakeholder then adjust the functionality to be developed so that it can be completed within the specified budget and time, or adjust the budget and time, or some combination thereof.

7.4.2.3 To-Complete Performance Index (TCPI)

See Section 7.4.2.3 of the *PMBOK® Guide*.

7.4.2.4 Performance Reviews

See Section 7.4.2.4 of the *PMBOK® Guide*.

7.4.2.5 Project Management Software

See Section 7.4.2.5 of the *PMBOK® Guide*.

7.4.2.6 Reserve Analysis

See Section 7.4.2.6 of the *PMBOK® Guide*.

7.4.2.7 Management Metrics

Earned value graphs, burndown charts, and cumulative flow diagrams provide visual indicators of software cost measurement for project control. They are based on planned versus actual cost, time, and product features.

- **Earned value graphs.** An earned value graph for a project displays budgeted and actual costs plus estimated and actual schedule progress on the vertical axis versus time on the horizontal axis. Cumulative trend lines based on periodic earned value reports display the deviations of planned versus actual cost and planned versus schedule progress as well as the projections of estimated actual cost and estimated completion date versus the estimated actual cost and estimated completion date.

- **Burnup and Burndown charts.** A burndown chart is a graphical representation of remaining work versus time. The remaining work (i.e., the backlog) is typically displayed on the vertical axis, with time along the horizontal. A burndown chart can be used to visualize project completion. A set of previous burndown charts can provide trends for the project. A burnup chart is illustrated in Figure 6-6 of this *Software Extension* and a burndown chart is shown in Section 10.2.3.7 of this *Software Extension*.

- **Cumulative flow diagrams.** As illustrated in Figure 6-5 of this *Software Extension*, cumulative flow diagrams (CFDs) provide a method for tracking the progress of an adaptive life cycle software project. CFDs communicate progress while indicating the degree of completion because they show the total scope, work in progress, and work completed. CFD diagrams can be correlated with resource expenditures to support cost control.

7.4.3 Control Costs: Outputs

The outputs in Section 7.4.3 of the *PMBOK® Guide* are applicable to controlling the costs for software projects.

7.4.3.1 Work Performance Information

See Section 7.4.3.1 of the *PMBOK® Guide*.

7.4.3.2 Cost Forecasts

See Section 7.4.3.2 of the *PMBOK® Guide*.

7.4.3.3 Change Requests

See Section 7.4.3.3 of the *PMBOK® Guide*.

7.4.3.4 Project Management Plan Updates

See Section 7.4.3.4 of the *PMBOK® Guide*.

7.4.3.5 Project Documents Updates

See Section 7.4.3.5 of the *PMBOK® Guide*.

7.4.3.6 Organizational Process Assets Updates

See Section 7.4.3.6 of the *PMBOK® Guide*.

PROJECT QUALITY MANAGEMENT

Most of the material in Section 8 of the *PMBOK® Guide* is applicable to quality management for software projects. This section of the *Software Extension to the PMBOK® Guide* presents additional considerations for managing software project quality.

According to the *PMBOK® Guide*: Project Quality Management includes the processes and activities of the performing organization that determine quality policies, objectives, and responsibilities so that the project will satisfy the needs for which it was undertaken. This section of the *Software Extension to the PMBOK® Guide* provides additional considerations for managing software project quality.

Project Quality Management processes in the *PMBOK® Guide* include:

- **Plan Quality Management**—The process of identifying quality requirements and/or standards for the project and its deliverables and documenting how the project will demonstrate compliance with quality requirements.

- **Perform Quality Assurance**—The process of auditing the quality requirements and the results from quality control measurements to ensure that appropriate quality standards and operational definitions are used.

- **Control Quality**—The process of monitoring and recording results of executing the quality activities to assess performance and recommend necessary changes.

Software Quality Assurance (SQA) is an ongoing process that audits other software processes to ensure that those processes are being followed (including but not limited to planning for and following software quality management plans). SQA also determines the degree to which the desired results from software quality control are being obtained. The charter of SQA typically includes examination of the degree to which all processes used to develop and modify software are being followed; approaches for improving those processes may be recommended. Guidance for conducting software quality audits are included in IEEE Std 1028 – Software Reviews and Audits [23].

Software Quality Control (SQC) is concerned with applying methods, tools, and techniques to ensure that the software work products (including but not limited to software code) satisfy the quality requirements for a software product under development or modification.

There are two levels of SQA and SQC in most organizations that develop software: internal SQA and SQC that occur within the software development team, or teams; and external SQA and SQC that occur at the level of the organizational unit in which a software project resides. A separate functional unit within an organization, which may have two distinct units for SQA and SQC, typically conducts external SQA and SQC activities. Sometimes a third level of independent quality control is applied to safety-critical software (i.e., independent verification and validation).

Within software teams, internal SQA takes the form of introspection, retrospective meetings, and lessons-learned reviews to determine whether or not the specified processes are being followed and to find ways to improve those processes. Performance measures are also reviewed and compared to norms and expectations.

SQA at the organizational level examines internal and external SQC methods, tools, techniques, and results for software projects within the organization. The other activities of external SQA may differ for predictive and adaptive software project life cycles. For a predictive life cycle, external SQA determines the degree to which processes such as initiating and planning a software project, eliciting and documenting requirements, preparing design documentation, conducting milestone reviews, and adhering to processes and procedures for change control, test planning, software construction, and testing are being followed and the results that are being obtained.

External SQA for adaptive life cycle software projects typically involves determining the degree to which processes and procedures are being followed for the particular adaptive life cycle used and the results being obtained. Processes examined include development of initial project and product scope, identification and involvement of key stakeholders, inclusion of a knowledgeable customer or key stakeholder who is available on a continuing basis, appropriate numbers and skills of teams and team members, and the other elements of agility described in Section 2.4.2.4 of this *Software Extension*. SQA also examines measurement results related to team velocity, cadence of iteration cycles, and burnup/burndown rates. Measurement results are compared to historical values for the team or teams, and to historical and current values for other software projects within the organization.

Commonly used methods of SQC include reviews, inspections, and testing both within teams and externally by independent agents. For a predictive life cycle software project, external SQC typically has a prominent role to play at the end of each incremental development stage (when software increments are developed) and in particular, prior to software delivery/deployment for software projects in the organization. When SQC is applied near the end of a predictive software project, significant rework, increased cost, and schedule delays are often encountered. This can result in pressure on the project manager and the software development team members by key stakeholders. The result can be inadequate software testing and suppression of software quality findings. Developing the software in tested, demonstrable increments can reduce these problems. External SQC for adaptive life cycle software projects may be applied to some or all of the working, demonstrable increments of software produced and for the final, deliverable software product.

Most of the tools and techniques in Section 8 of the *PMBOK® Guide* for project quality management are applicable to managing project quality for software projects, with the following adaptations and extensions that are unique to, or especially important for planning software project quality management, performing software quality assurance, and controlling software quality. This section of the *Software Extension* also discusses how software quality is defined and how software project managers, their teams, and others plan for and perform software quality management. Both project quality and product quality should be considered to ensure the quality of the delivered software product, and to improve software project quality management for software projects and organizations that develop and modify software.

The *PMBOK® Guide* defines quality as delivered performance: "the degree to which a set of inherent characteristics fulfill requirements." The definition from software engineering is similar: "the degree to which a software product satisfies stated and implied needs when used under specified conditions" [2]. To paraphrase

Peter Drucker: "Quality of a software product or service is not what the developers put in. It is what the customer gets out and is willing to pay for" [24]. For example, software used to determine the whereabouts of one's friends may not need the same qualities of timeliness, accuracy, and precision as software used to guide interplanetary trajectories. Quality concerns receive increased emphasis for software that has an impact on the health, safety, and welfare of the general public, and for protection of software and data related to personal or business proprietary information.

Quality requirements may be unstated initially or they may be vague and ambiguous. As discussed in Section 5 of this *Software Extension*, software engineers and IT business analysts elicit needs from customers, the software users, and other stakeholders. IEEE Standard 830 [19] provides an extensive list of the types of requirements that should be considered but are sometimes overlooked. Whether known initially or whether they emerge during a software project, the software product should provide an acceptable level of quality for users and other stakeholders.

Quality attributes of software include, but are not limited to safety, security, reliability, availability, performance, ease of use, and ease of modification. Section 1.9 of this *Software Extension* lists quality attributes that are important for software users (e.g., efficiency, safety, security, reliability, availability) and quality attributes that are important to software developers and maintainers (e.g., maintainability is important to those who provide sustainment services). The ISO/IEC 25000 series of standards [25] provides extensive lists of software quality attributes that are aligned with different stakeholder needs.

For reasons of objectivity in evaluating quality, the *PMBOK® Guide* recommends independent quality audits. Independence of SQA and SQC can be obtained by establishing a different line of reporting for external SQA and SQC. Internal SQA is accomplished by individual introspection and by retrospective meetings of team members. For internal SQC, software team members other than the ones who produced a software component perform peer reviews and tests.

Mature organizations and teams foster collaboration between external SQA-SQC and the software development team to avoid the adversarial relationship that sometimes occurs. For small projects and organizations, SQA and SQC personnel may be members of the software development team, provided a degree of independence is maintained (i.e., someone is designated to be responsible for SQA and no one performs final tests of their own code). While larger organizations may mandate an organizational separation of external SQA and SQC personnel from development activities (i.e., to permit SQA and SQC personnel to audit, investigate, and recommend changes based on issues that arise or newly identified opportunities), collaborative exploration of quality issues is easily achieved within cross-functional product teams. On the other hand, when external SQA and SQC personnel are assigned from independent functional groups, and are not included in cross-functional teams, collaborative exploration of quality issues may be lost and SQA and SQC personnel may become adversaries to software developers.

The user role in determining whether software has acceptable quality may be played by different persons, depending on the project's context. In a commercial software product company, the user may be represented by the product manager or documented in one or more fictional persona that provides the knowledge, needs, and tasks of a typical user. In an IT enterprise project, the user may be an authorized subject matter expert in the business processes the software will serve. For a software project conducted under contract, the accepting authority of the acquiring organization may represent the user. It is important for software project managers to

8

ensure that the project team understands that the *user* is the person or persons who defines what "quality" and "fit for use" mean in order to satisfy user needs. However, the project manager needs to recognize that the users may not be able to indicate what they really want and need prior to using the software. For this reason, a project manager should rely on the expertise of business analysts, requirements engineers, and others who can elicit quality expectations.

Software quality has been a fundamental issue from the early days of developing algorithms to perform mathematical calculations quickly and accurately, to the present day demands for safety-critical, enterprise-wide, and commercial software. Beyond the basic pass/fail questions of whether the software runs and returns a usable result (sometimes called a software smoke test), the quality attributes for a particular software product may include elements from a very long list, which includes attributes that range from accessibility, adaptability, analyzability, availability, compatibility, and complexity, to survivability, testability, understandability, and usability (the well-known "ilities" of software).

The complexities of software quality have led to a number of quality models such as those in ISO/IEC 25000 and the other standards referenced in this section of the *Software Extension*. Software quality models include process quality, internal and external product quality, quality in use, data quality, and quality of the software code; the latter is appraised by inspections or "static" testing, and by exercising the software in "dynamic" testing.

From the perspective of project quality, a project manager considers: Is the work organized to produce quality software? Are the processes efficient and effective in achieving the project and product goals, and also in building a strong, cohesive team for ongoing work? What methods and tools are used and are they used effectively?

The internal quality model looks at the software as an open "white box," where software evaluators can directly examine the code and the accompanying artifacts, such as design documents, even as they are being developed. Automated software tools are available to perform many aspects of white-box examination. They include static and dynamic testing tools that check for code coverage by the test cases, adherence to coding standards, uninitialized variables, and many other types of coding errors.

The external quality model treats the software as a "black box" where software evaluators determine how the software behaves by observing input-output behavior, measuring the software's performance, examining how it performs its functions and achieves its quality requirements, and observing the conditions under which it fails. External quality assessment is typically accomplished by functional black box testing, which is usually performed by external SQC and may be observed by a representative of the intended user community. Black box testing is based on the requirements and not on the internal aspects of the software code.

Even when software passes predefined evaluations of internal and external quality, users may still think it lacks quality. The *quality in use* perspective looks at the impact of the product on users and other stakeholders when it is used for specified purposes in a specific environment and context. *Usability* is defined as the extent to which a product or system can be used by specified users to achieve specified goals with efficiency, effectiveness, and satisfaction in a specified context of use [26]. Characteristics of quality in use include (a) effectiveness (gets the job done); (b) satisfaction (usefulness, trust, pleasure in use, comfort); and (c) freedom from risk (economic risk mitigation, health and safety risk mitigation, and environmental risk mitigation).

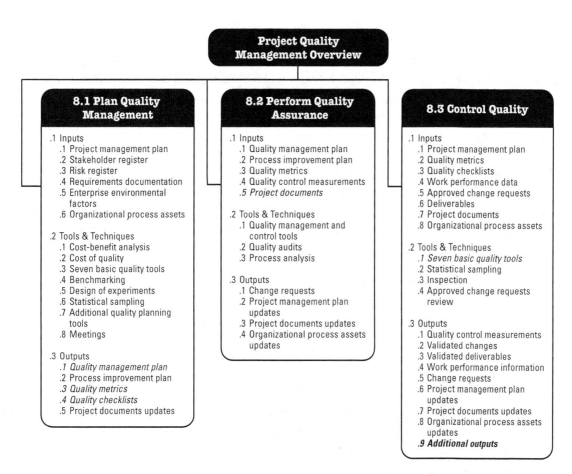

Figure 8-1. Software Project Quality Management Overview

A *data quality model* deals with how structured data is acquired, manipulated, and used in a computing system to satisfy user's needs; it includes data that can be shared within the same computing system or across different computing systems. Some examples of data quality characteristics are consistency, currency, completeness, precision, accuracy, and integrity of data.

Figure 8-1 provides an overview of Software Project Quality Management

8.1 Plan Quality Management

Most of the methods, tools, and techniques for planning quality management in Section 8.1 of the *PMBOK® Guide* are equally applicable to planning quality management for software projects. This section presents considerations that are unique to or especially important when planning quality management for software projects.

Plan Quality Management for both project and product is an inseparable element of project planning in general. Determining the scope and goals of the project and establishing the life cycle processes to be used leads to decisions about how to integrate quality assurance and quality control into the overall software development process. Balancing the tradeoffs between software features, quality attributes, schedule, cost, and criticality of the software determines how much emphasis will be given to software quality during the project. Defining what is acceptable quality to meet the users' needs determines when the product is ready for release and when the project can be closed. Explicit attention to process improvement can lead to midcourse changes in projects, as well as produce benefits for future projects within the organization.

A significant part of planning software project quality management activities is determining which of the software quality attributes are priorities for a particular project, and how the attributes are specified in the software requirements. Defining what quality attributes will be built into the product, and how the attributes will be measured by SQA and SQC activities, such as audits, reviews, and testing significantly affects the scope and resources required to successfully plan and execute a software project.

ISO/IEC/IEEE Standard 15026 for Systems and software engineering – Systems and Software Assurance [27], is a multi-part standard that provides a comprehensive framework for developing the appropriate assurance case(s) to guide software development projects where one or more critical properties need to be achieved.

Testing provides a good example of how quality management activities span the three key processes of software quality management (planning, performing, controlling): *test planning* is a component of Plan Quality Management, *analyze defect data* is a component of Perform Quality Assurance, and *test execution* is part of Control Quality. But planning for SQA and SQC is more than designating a small group of auditors and testers who are budgeted proportionately to the developer team and scheduled to pick out defects at the end of a project. Since it is less expensive to "build a little, test a little" than to spend months developing and integrating a complex system that fails verification and validation testing, SQA and SQC need to be performed by everyone on the team, through continuing peer reviews, walkthroughs, inspections, automated regression tests, and analyses. SQA and SQC are best planned to occur as part of requirements specification, architecture and data design, and software construction, as well as through configuration management and formal testing.

Adaptive software project life cycles that rely on frequent iterations to produce working, tested, and deliverable software are well suited for planning an integrated approach to SQA and SQC. For predictive software project life cycles that consist of distinct development phases, SQA and SQC are planned as distinct processes.

8.1.1 Plan Quality Management: Inputs

The inputs for planning quality management in Section 8.1.1 of the *PMBOK® Guide* are applicable for software projects. The following considerations also apply to the inputs for planning software project quality management.

In addition to the quality planning inputs identified in the *PMBOK® Guide*, software project managers typically place emphasis on identifying the stakeholders and the product requirements, as well as using quality statistics from previous projects.

In general, software projects fail because the software product does not meet user expectations of functionality and quality when developed within the constraints of schedule, budget, and available resources. The software project manager is responsible for ensuring that all stakeholders understand failure to meet users' quality expectations will result in project and product failure. In addition to the end users and their managers, other stakeholders are those who will affect or be affected by the software product, either while it is under development or during operation after it is delivered. For example, the stakeholders of an enterprise resource planning (ERP) system include IT operations staff who are responsible for sustaining the ERP system; their concerns will include the interoperability, performance, robustness, and documentation of the software. In addition to users and those responsible for product sustainment, members of the project team and external SQA and SQC are also product stakeholders (see Section 13 of this *Software Extension* for stakeholder management considerations). A stakeholder register provides an input for planning software quality management.

Quality requirements are an element of the overall product requirements; they are (or should be) established when the functional requirements are established. In companies that produce software products for commercial sale, the quality requirements are usually included in the market requirements document. IT projects may simply use a features/backlog list. When applicable, the project manager needs to make sure that the quality requirements are included. Quality requirements for contracted software (i.e., bespoke software) are typically included as an element of the statement of work.

Customers and users may not be able to precisely state performance requirements and other nonfunctional quality requirements. A software project manager may need to engage product managers, business analysts, requirements engineers, and other appropriate stakeholders in the elicitation of nonfunctional requirements to determine which quality attributes are most important to the customer and users. Requirements for software product quality may also include regulatory requirements (e.g., for life-critical systems). In contracting, quality requirements may be imposed on component providers and suppliers of custom-built or customized software components.

Inputs for planning the management of software process quality typically include quality analyses from past projects or from previous increments of the current product. Inputs for planning software quality management can be associated with quality analyses performed at the story, feature, iteration, or release level (e.g., to provide a basis for determining whether code reviews, testing, and other types of evaluations were executed as anticipated and whether they were successful); defect find/fix rates can be examined (to determine whether the numbers are rising or falling); time spent on fixing defects can be examined (to determine whether they are adversely impacting planned feature development and whether reviews and testing are yielding the expected results); and previous lists of known problems and deferred defects can be investigated by severity and by feature or module (to determine whether there are error-prone modules in the software).

The following inputs from Section 8.1.1 of the *PMBOK® Guide* are also applicable inputs for planning software project quality management.

8.1.1.1 Project Management Plan

See Section 8.1.1.1 of the *PMBOK® Guide*.

8.1.1.2 Stakeholder Register

See Section 8.1.1.2 of the *PMBOK® Guide*.

8.1.1.3 Risk Register

See Section 8.1.1.3 of the *PMBOK® Guide.*

8.1.1.4 Requirements Documentation

See Section 8.1.1.4 of the *PMBOK® Guide.*

8.1.1.5 Enterprise Environmental Factors

See Section 8.1.1.5 of the *PMBOK® Guide.*

8.1.1.6 Organizational Process Assets

See Section 8.1.1.6 of the *PMBOK® Guide.*

8.1.2 Plan Quality Management: Tools and Techniques

The tools and techniques for planning quality management in Section 8.1.2 of the *PMBOK® Guide* are applicable for software projects. In addition to the tools and techniques listed below, the following considerations also apply to tools and techniques for planning software project quality management.

Planning for software quality management includes confirming user needs and quality requirements, performing cost-benefit and cost-of-quality analyses, developing a testing strategy, and selecting a defect management and quality control approach. Some comments follow:

- **Planning for software quality.** The customer and users may not have experience in defining their quality expectations as testable requirements; therefore, the project team needs to be adept in eliciting the needed information. This often requires ongoing validation from the users that the software will meet their needs, using techniques such as prototypes, mock-ups, and other simulations.

- **Cost-benefit analysis (CBA).** For most software projects, there are trade-offs among the various levels of product quality, the amount of functionality delivered, and the time and effort required to deliver a quality product. An example of CBA is comparing the cost of testing and rework for different levels of defect removal. Determining an acceptable level of released defects may involve comparative benchmark evaluation of the relevant quality attributes in the major competitors' products. While it is natural for the project team to want to correct all problems detected, a software project manager typically does not plan for a significantly higher amount of defect correction than is warranted by user expectations. For example, depending on the context of the user and user environment, there may be no need to correct a defect that would be difficult to correct and that will rarely be encountered and for which there is a user work-around.

- **Cost of quality (COQ).** Cost of quality for software includes costs of the following SQC activities:
  - ○ *Appraisal:* cost of finding software defects,
  - ○ *Internal:* cost to fix defects discovered during software development or modification,
  - ○ *External:* cost to fix software defects reported by users, and
  - ○ *Prevention:* cost of reducing or eliminating the root causes of software defects.

Appraisal techniques for software include testing and demonstration of working software plus reviews and inspections of software work products (requirements, design, code, test plans, documentation).

For software, the cost of quality is not just the cost of correcting the code, but the larger costs associated with the effort to verify the change and validate its effectiveness, to communicate the change to all affected parties, and to change the work products or processes that use or are impacted by the software product. This cost is greatly increased once the software is in use and patches are applied or new versions are released.

Software quality planning includes developing a testing policy or testing strategy. In software, a "design of experiments" approach is captured in the testing strategy, and reflected in test plans and scenarios, and the level of test coverage to be achieved. Even relatively simple software may have thousands of potential branches through the code, which could be exercised with a nearly infinite range and extent of valid and invalid inputs. This would require an unacceptable amount of time to exhaustively test the software so a level of test coverage should be specified. In addition, it may be necessary to test the software with previously developed modules in various combinations. A testing strategy that will have a high likelihood of exposing serious defects should be planned.

Test planning also takes into account the need for corrective rework, data refresh, and retest, because rarely does one cycle of testing produce completely acceptable results. Since it is almost never possible, too time-consuming, or not cost effective to test everything, part of planning software quality management is choosing the test strategy, so that the most valuable and predictive tests are planned. Risk-based test strategy applies design, development and test resources to the areas with the most impact on successful delivery and use of the software.

A goal of planning quality management for a predictive life cycle software project is to arrange the sequence of work activities to obtain feedback from testing and reviews as early as possible by developing the final software product as a series of testable software increments. Software architects and software designers can help in identifying opportunities to build the software in a manner that provides feedback from evaluating successive increments of working software.

When using adaptive software project life cycles, different levels of testing happen at different points. Story-level testing involves validation of business rules and code quality relevant to small increments of software as the team develops them. Feature-level testing provides more detailed feedback concerning quality attributes. Verifying the increments with given inputs and outputs during a development cycle helps to find defects quickly and reduces the cost of testing later in the project.

Functional testing (including feature-level testing) includes integration testing across software components as well as quality-in-use testing. Good practice is to validate the product as early and as often as possible using real

8

or simulated customer databases and environments. Good practice includes coordinating work across the project so functional and feature testing can be performed throughout the project, rather than late in the project. The risks of major defects being identified late in the project is reduced when functional and feature testing are being performed throughout the project.

A software project manager also needs to plan for processes and procedures to identify, categorize, measure, and treat defects. Defect measures need to be defined in the planning software quality management. Software defects are generally categorized by severity (how many users will be affected and how badly). IEEE Standard 1044 – Classification for Software Anomalies [28] provides guidance in establishing defect classifications that are meaningful for software projects. Typically, the acceptable level of defects is specified by the planned kind of release (beta, general availability, customized). It is typical to allow none of the highest category defects to be released, but the percentage of second and third level defects often depends on the type of release and the users' expectations. Release criteria are project-specific and may involve a level of uncertainty.

Defects can be balanced against risk considerations (see Section 11 of this *Software Extension*). Software in the safety-critical domain usually has very high levels of release criteria. For non-safety-critical software, users may prefer early functionality that includes some bugs. Other software products, such as static web pages, cause very little risk to safety, but could affect the developer's reputation when poorly done. Risk management techniques are important in developing a testing strategy and assessing the impact of defects not discovered until after a software release.

The tools and techniques for planning quality management in Section 8.1.2 of the *PMBOK® Guide* are applicable to planning quality management for software projects.

8.1.2.1 Cost-Benefit Analysis

See Section 8.1.2.1 of the *PMBOK® Guide*.

8.1.2.2 Cost of Quality (COQ)

See Section 8.1.2.2 of the *PMBOK® Guide*.

8.1.2.3 Seven Basic Quality Tools

See Section 8.1.2.3 of the *PMBOK® Guide* and Section 8.3.2.1 of this *Software Extension*.

8.1.2.4 Benchmarking

See Section 8.1.2.4 of the *PMBOK® Guide*.

8.1.2.5 Design of Experiments

See Section 8.1.2.5 of the *PMBOK® Guide*.

8.1.2.6 Statistical Sampling

See Section 8.1.2.6 of the *PMBOK® Guide*.

8.1.2.7 Additional Quality Planning Tools

See Section 8.1.2.7 of the *PMBOK® Guide*.

8.1.2.8 Meetings

See Section 8.1.2.8 of the *PMBOK® Guide*.

8.1.3 Plan Quality Management: Outputs

The outputs from planning quality management in Section 8.1.3 of the *PMBOK® Guide* are applicable outputs for software projects. The following modifications also apply to the outputs for planning software project quality management.

8.1.3.1 Quality Management Plan

See Section 8.1.3.1 of the *PMBOK® Guide*.

In addition, a software quality management plan should address configuration management topics, including: (a) version control of source code, object code, and other work products, and (b) control of a definitive media library for approved versions of electronic files and approved product baselines. Practices such as continuous integration, closed-loop change processes, and iteration retrospectives are typically specified in a software project quality management plan. IEEE Standard 730 – Software Quality Assurance Plans [29] contains content to be included in a quality management plan, including detailed requirements for software quality assurance plans.

8.1.3.2 Process Improvement Plan

See Section 8.1.3.2 of the *PMBOK® Guide*.

8.1.3.3 Quality Metrics

See Section 8.1.3.3 of the *PMBOK® Guide*.

In addition, a software quality management plan may also contain the quality measurement plan, including elements such as software size measures, software quality measures, and acceptance thresholds. Software measures may be based on lines of code, but those measures vary with different programming languages and depend on the coding style more than the quality of the software. Lengthier code that is well commented and factored into functional modules may be easier to maintain than highly compressed code, resulting in a lower overall cost of quality. On the other hand, lengthier code may indicate lack of careful thinking about functionality and quality during software development.

Software functionality is measured by the number of requirements, function points, features, user stories, and/ or use cases implemented in the software rather than counting lines of code. Software quality measures may include churn in baselined requirements, percent of new requirements added, ratios of defect found to defects fixed, amount of software code changed, and trends in these measures. Additional quality measures may be added to address specific quality attributes, such as performance, throughput, resistance to security penetrations, or usability of the software and associated documentation.

The measurement plan, quality management plan, or project management plan may also define how project efficiency and effectiveness, and thus project quality, will be measured. The most basic measures, suitable for all types of software projects, are elapsed time and expended effort (e.g., days and staff-days) per function, feature, story, or use case. The resulting measures of productivity and production rate help in planning how rapidly software can be produced, including time and effort to correct known defects. These indicators provide inputs for Project Time Management (Section 6 of this *Software Extension*) and Project Cost Management (Section 7 of this *Software Extension*).

8.1.3.4 Quality Checklists

See Section 8.1.3.4 of the *PMBOK® Guide*.

Checklists are reminders to complete all steps in a procedure such as conducting a software test, either to train developers who are being introduced to new tools and techniques or to remind experienced developers to not inadvertently skip steps. In software projects, checklists cover the steps necessary to complete an inspection review, to successful complete an integration build, or to check code in and out of a repository. Checklists are one of the easiest and most effective ways to ensure consistency and accuracy in performing repetitive tasks and to ensure that the tasks are being carried out in the same manner, no matter who performs the tasks.

8.1.3.5 Project Documents Updates

See Section 8.1.3.5 of the *PMBOK® Guide*.

8.2 Perform Quality Assurance

Most of the methods, tools, and techniques for Perform Quality Assurance in Section 8.2 of the *PMBOK® Guide* are applicable to performing quality assurance for software projects. This section presents considerations that are unique to or especially important when performing quality assurance for software projects.

The *PMBOK® Guide* states that Perform Quality Assurance is the process of auditing the quality requirements and the results from quality control measurements to ensure that appropriate quality standards and guidelines are used. In software project management, software quality assurance (SQA) involves a broad view of the entire project to ensure that processes are being performed as documented and are producing acceptable results. In this *Software Extension* to the *PMBOK® Guide*, (SQA) is defined as a set of activities that define and assess the adequacy of the software processes used to develop and modify software products. SQA provides evidence for a statement of confidence that the software processes will (or will not) produce software products that conform to their requirements and will satisfy users' needs.

SQA thus covers more than audits of requirements and the results of software quality measurements. SQA comprises a full set of planned and systematic activities that can be demonstrated to provide confidence that a product or service will fulfill its requirements for quality. SQA uses the classic tools of audits and review of both internal and external SQC activities, including demonstrations, inspections, analyses, and testing (often divided into verification testing and validation testing). Both SQA and SQC personnel may be involved in analysis of defects and other problems and making recommendations for improvement.

IEEE standards that may be useful include IEEE Standard 829 – Software and System Test Documentation [30]; IEEE Standard 1008 – Unit Testing [31]; and IEEE Standard 1012 – System and Software Verification and Validation [32].

8.2.1 Perform Quality Assurance: Inputs

The inputs for performing quality assurance in Section 8.2.1 of the *PMBOK® Guide* are applicable to performing quality assurance for software projects.

8.2.1.1 Quality Management Plan

See Section 8.2.1.1 of the *PMBOK® Guide*.

8.2.1.2 Process Improvement Plan

See Section 8.2.1.2 of the *PMBOK® Guide*.

8.2.1.3 Quality Metrics

See Section 8.2.1.3 of the *PMBOK® Guide*.

8.2.1.4 Quality Control Measurements

See Section 8.2.1.4 of the *PMBOK® Guide*.

8.2.1.5 Project Documents

See Section 8.2.1.5 of the *PMBOK® Guide*.

Additional considerations for project documents that provide inputs for performing software project and product quality assurance include the following: the release plan and test plan, project or organizational procedures, project records and test result records, and reports from design and code reviews, inspections, and audits. Automated tools for requirements management, software configuration management, release management, and problem management are common sources of records for SQA reviews and audits. For some software projects, there may be documented records demonstrating that the planned efforts occurred. In other cases, those who are responsible for quality assurance may personally witness various procedures to satisfy themselves that the process being audited is working as planned. On small projects, it may be the project manager who performs this task internally and the product manager who performs it externally.

For predictive software projects, SQA personnel (both internal and external) participate during requirements analysis to define acceptance criteria and test plan details prior to the start of software development. The test plans themselves become part of the requirements communicated to the software development team. Other inputs for SQA are various analytical simulations that predict the most likely number of defects to be expected in the code, based on previous test results, the complexity of the software, and the experience of the software development team. The results are inputs to performing SQA and are used to check the validity of test results.

For software projects that use adaptive life cycles, the details of test plans, including specific acceptance criteria are progressively elaborated along with the requirements. Feature-level criteria are developed as part of analysis and design of the features. Detailed story-level acceptance criteria are defined as part of making the requirements backlog ready for the development team. This means that the SQA team is continuously involved with the development team from analysis to acceptance of the deliverable increments of software.

Additional inputs for performing software quality assurance may also include work performance data, such as work effort and elapsed time and cost to date, because these inputs can be compared to the project's plans in order to measure the variance between plans and actual results. By doing this type of comparison at frequent intervals, SQA personnel and the project manager are able to determine where changes may be necessary to processes or to or schedules and/or resources. Thus, the quality of planning is improved throughout the project.

8.2.2 Perform Quality Assurance: Tools and Techniques

The tools and techniques for performing quality assurance in Section 8.2.2 of the *PMBOK® Guide* are applicable tools and techniques for performing quality assurance for software projects. Additional considerations include the following.

For predictive software project life cycles, external SQA personnel who are independent of the development process typically conduct SQA activities. In other words, developers do not perform acceptance testing on their own work and those responsible for performing acceptance testing and other SQA activities do not report directly to the development project manager. For predictive software projects, SQA budgets are usually not controlled by the development project manager.

For a safety-critical project, an external group sometimes conducts SQA to ensure that the project and product meet the organization's and customer's policies and standards during the software project life cycle. These activities verify the extent to which the effectiveness of the quality control methods and activities are being met and quality objectives are being achieved.

Quality auditors compare actual processes to documented processes by observation and inspection of records. As described in Section 8.2 of the *PMBOK® Guide*, QA personnel audit the results from quality control measurements to assess whether or not the quality requirements are being met. Quality auditors may discover a lack of documentation or erroneous documentation that needs to be updated. In this case, the software project manager assures that action is taken to correct the discrepancies. While adaptive life cycle teams emphasize the preference for working, deliverable software over documentation, some level of documentation is necessary to meet internal and external quality requirements. Quality auditors ensure that project teams are meeting the necessary level of working, deliverable software and the supporting documentation.

SQA also examines the volatility of software product requirements. Frequent changes to requirements can be a warning that there are serious problems in the project. This may indicate that the system boundaries are not well defined, or that affordability constraints need to be addressed by adjusting the scope of product features. Note, however, that emerging requirements or derived requirements are not classified as symptoms of volatility. These are refinements. A software development project team may begin work on a set of requirements or features that are sufficiently well understood even when other requirements or features are still unknown or changing, or the project team may produce a prototype to allow users to determine whether the approach will fulfill their functional and quality expectations.

External SQA is often involved in identifying areas for process improvement. Process analysis is a foundational element of process improvement by identifying bottlenecks, process delays, and sources of error. Tools such as flowcharts and process flow diagrams, as well as state diagrams, can be used as process improvement tools to document process flows and process state transitions. For example, the various states that a defect passes through from first being reported until being resolved may be depicted in a flow diagram or a state-transition diagram.

Training is covered in Section 10 of this *Software Extension* (Human Resources); however, training may also be regarded as a quality assurance technique, particularly training required for individual software and team software processes.

8.2.2.1 Quality Management and Control Tools

See Section 8.2.2.1 of the *PMBOK® Guide*.

8.2.2.2 Quality Audits

See Section 8.2.2.2 of the *PMBOK® Guide*.

8.2.2.3 Process Analysis

See Section 8.2.2.3 of the *PMBOK® Guide*.

8.2.3 Perform Quality Assurance: Outputs

The outputs for performing quality assurance in Section 8.2.3 of the *PMBOK® Guide* are applicable outputs from performing quality assurance for software projects, with the indicated extension of Section 8.2.3.4.

8.2.3.1 Change Requests

See Section 8.2.3.1 of the *PMBOK® Guide*.

8.2.3.2 Project Management Plan Updates

See Section 8.2.3.2 of the *PMBOK® Guide*.

8.2.3.3 Project Documents Updates

See Section 8.2.3.3 of the *PMBOK® Guide*.

8.2.3.4 Organizational Process Assets Updates

See Section 8.2.3.4 of the *PMBOK® Guide*.

As described in Section 8.2.3 of the *PMBOK® Guide*, the outputs of the Quality Assurance process are audit reports and change requests that provide inputs to the Perform Integrated Change Control process (see Section 4.5 of the *PMBOK® Guide* and of this *Software Extension*). Audit reports and change requests may also show the need for changes in software project planning. These changes will be reflected in the software project team's process and product work activities.

The cost of corrective rework for software is often a significant percentage of the total cost of developing a software product. Understanding the sources and cost of corrective rework can result in updates to organizational process assets for software projects to reduce corrective rework.

Investment in quality improvement to prevent (or reduce) technical debt is closely related to the cost of quality. Failure to find and fix defects early in a software project life cycle and deferring the fixing of known defects create technical debts that are repaid later by the cost incurred for corrective rework. Accumulation of technical debt is sometimes referred to as "mortgaging the future" because the interest rate on the mortgage can be excessive for predictive software projects when defects are not discovered or corrected near the point of injection. These defects become exponentially more expensive to fix the longer they persist. It is not uncommon in such projects that a requirements defect not found until systems testing may cost, in time and effort, 100 times more to fix than it would cost to find and fix it during a requirements review. Techniques such as prototyping, inspections, reviews, and incremental development can control technical debt. Development and use of these techniques may result in updates to organizational process assets.

Adaptive software projects use the techniques of prototyping, inspections, reviews, and incremental development to minimize technical debt. In addition, adaptive software projects use frequent internal demonstrations of the evolving product to identify and quickly correct defects throughout the development process without incurring significant costs.

8.3 Control Quality

Section 8.3 of the *PMBOK® Guide* states that Control Quality is the process of monitoring and recording results from executing quality activities to assess performance and recommend necessary changes. Software quality control (SQC) is a system of technical activities used to measure and control the quality of the development processes and the quality of the product as it is being developed; and to report the quality measurement results throughout the lifetime of a software project.

For purposes of this *Software Extension*, "measure, control, and report" involve comparing work products to requirements (including agreements, policies, standards, plans, requirements, and expectations). SQC often relies on statistical methods such as control charts and Pareto diagrams to analyze software defects and the associated rework used to correct the defects. This analysis may generate feedback for process improvement.

The most effective method of controlling and improving software quality is to focus on early detection and removal of software defects using continuous verification and validation techniques (e.g., reviews, inspections, testing, and demonstration of product increments), and to focus on changing the software development process to reduce or prevent defects. A large part of quality control for software products has historically relied on a predictive approach of post-development techniques, including staged levels of software testing and analysis of the detected defects. Adaptive software project life cycles integrate testing and demonstration of working, deliverable software on repetitive cycles throughout the software development process.

Quality control is integrated into adaptive software project life cycles by the inclusion of testing, demonstrations, and a retrospective review on each iteration cycle. A retrospective review is used to assess the results of the completed iteration and to plan for improvements in successive iterations. Internal SQC activities are conducted by the project team using techniques such as pair programming, peer reviews, functional testing, and demonstrations of working software within the development team. External SQC personnel sometimes conduct feature-level and release-level testing.

Retrospectives can sometimes result in finger pointing or may occur at times when the developers are feeling rushed due to insufficient time to complete the features in the features backlog set. An important way to overcome frustration is to make sure that the software developers are involved in selecting the feature set and specifying the acceptance criteria, so that they understand the goals and will ensure that planning for the next iteration incorporates the needed process changes. This approach contributes to team learning and builds continuous improvement into the project iterations.

8.3.1 Control Quality: Inputs

The inputs for controlling quality in Section 8.3.1 of the *PMBOK® Guide* are applicable inputs for controlling quality for software projects. As described in the *PMBOK® Guide*, inputs to software quality control include management plans and checklists. Another significant input is the measurement plan for the prioritized quality attributes as defined in the release criteria. Project records, especially testing and configuration management records, are essential inputs and are typically maintained in controlled repositories.

8.3.1.1 Project Management Plan

See Section 8.3.1.1 of the *PMBOK® Guide*.

8.3.1.2 Quality Metrics

See Section 8.3.1.2 of the *PMBOK® Guide*.

8.3.1.3 Quality Checklists

See Section 8.3.1.3 of the *PMBOK® Guide*.

8.3.1.4 Work Performance Data

See Section 8.3.1.4 of the *PMBOK® Guide*.

8.3.1.5 Approved Change Requests

See Section 8.3.1.5 of the *PMBOK® Guide*.

8.3.1.6 Deliverables

See Section 8.3.1.6 of the *PMBOK® Guide*.

8.3.1.7 Project Documents

See Section 8.3.1.7 of the *PMBOK® Guide*.

8.3.1.8 Organizational Process Assets

See Section 8.3.1.8 of the *PMBOK® Guide*.

8.3.2 Control Quality: Tools and Techniques

The tools and techniques for controlling quality in Section 8.3.2 of the *PMBOK® Guide* are applicable for controlling quality for software projects. Additional considerations include the following.

Along with the items listed in the *PMBOK® Guide*, tools and techniques for software quality control (SQC) include reviews, testing, and the version control elements of configuration management. Reviews take many forms, including walkthroughs and inspections of requirements, design, and code, plus reviews of other work products, such as user manuals and installation instructions. Static analysis and dynamic testing tools are also used. Reviews may involve use of tools that check for common programming mistakes, such as uninitialized variables. Defects are corrected when they are found, thereby controlling the quality of the work products.

Walkthroughs and inspections applied early in the development process (i.e., to requirements and design documentation) are most effective for controlling software quality. Frequent testing of product increments is another technique that supports software quality control. Testing and demonstration of internal software builds may be conducted on a daily or even hourly basis during the construction phase of a predictive life cycle software project or during an internal iteration cycle of an adaptive life cycle software project. Of the QC tools and techniques identified in the *PMBOK® Guide*, inspection is one of the most effective ways to identify software defects and omissions in software and documentation [15, pages 298–293 and Appendix 7B].

Usability evaluations, in the form of demonstrations and walkthroughs, are cost-effective techniques for finding defects and discrepancies that might require reworking the software. Video-recorded usability testing with user representatives, using a "think-aloud" approach, is also useful for finding defects and discrepancies well before a release to end-users.

Test-driven development has long proven to be useful in controlling the quality of software. In this approach, test cases are written *before* writing any software code, and the test cases are run to demonstrate that the tests will fail. Then the new code is added, and the test cases are run again to demonstrate that they no longer fail. Tools are commonly used to automate such testing. In addition, desk exercises of walking through the code can be used.

Software testing includes unit testing of code modules, integration and verification testing, validation and acceptance testing, and regression testing. Often, development teams build scaffolding (temporary modules) to support early testing by simulating inputs and outputs from parts of the software that have not yet been constructed. This allows integration or regression testing to be performed at early stages of software development. Testing can also focus on specific quality attributes, such as performance, load, security, or usability. User observation, (formalized as usability testing), and user surveys measure quality-in-use characteristics, such as users' satisfaction or users' efficiency in performing work tasks.

Testing tools and automated scripts can repeatedly execute tests in a consistent manner with little or no manual intervention, automatically collect and store the test results, compare test results to previous results or expectations, and refresh the test data for another round of testing. Testing tools can provide time for the test team to focus on issues such as the design of tests and analysis of the results.

8

For some domains and kinds of software, model-driven development (MDD) can be used to improve software quality by automatically generating code skeletons from specifications expressed in suitable notations. This reduces the amount of error-prone coding. Model-driven development involves generating substantial parts of software from "models" written in languages such as unified modeling language (UML) and/or domain-specific languages.

Configuration management (CM) also plays a significant role in controlling quality during software development. CM provides routine and consistent checks to ensure the integrity, correctness, and completeness of each software build, often based on execution of prepared scripts. Enforced configuration control avoids the problems that arise when more than one developer works on the same module of code at the same time. Several tools working together usually automate configuration management. Control of different versions of each source file document, script, and the "configurations" (i.e., sets of these items that belong together) is accomplished using configuration management tools. These tools can also manage the different ways that components are put together to create different end products in a software product line or software product family.

CM tools can also be used to track the defects and other issues related to the software, plus the resolution of these issues. Some CM tools are available as free open-source products and some are commercial products. IEEE Standard 828 – Configuration Management in Systems and Software Engineering [33] provides guidance on all aspects of configuration control for systems and software.

SQC can also be used to identify record, analyze, and treat software defects. Software defects may be classified for severity (i.e., the impact on the user), urgency (i.e., the importance to users, often designated as "priority"), root cause of the defect, or location of the defect in the software code. In addition, defect find/fix data provides a statistical basis for assessing the level of stability or instability of a software system at a point in time.

8.3.2.1 Seven Basic Quality Tools

See Section 8.3.2.1 of the *PMBOK® Guide*.

SQC uses most of the quality tools described in Section 8.3.2.1 of the *PMBOK® Guide*; in particular, control charts, run charts, Pareto charts, and histograms. These charts help the software manager to visualize data and discern patterns and causes. In particular, they can be applied to the analysis of defect patterns in software, thus providing the basis to identify areas for preventative improvements.

Run charts and control charts are two of the most commonly used tools for quality control of software projects and products. A run chart is a control chart without upper and lower control limits; it is often used to track defects over time. The numbers of defects found each week (or day) is plotted along a time axis. A run chart shows trends, such as declining numbers of defects found as the product gains stability. A control chart is a run chart with upper and lower control limits that can be specified using statistical techniques or rules of thumb. An upper control limit of 5 may be specified for the number of serious defects found during software inspections. Exceeding the control limit on two successive inspections could trigger an investigation to determine corrective action to improve quality control processes. A lower control limit of 2 might be specified. Finding fewer than 2 serious defects during two successive inspections would trigger an investigation to determine whether the inspection process needs improvement or whether the software is of exceptional quality. In the latter case, the methods or techniques that resulted in superior quality might be propagated throughout the project and the organization.

Pareto charts can be used to show the number of defects in different software components. Components that have high numbers of defects (error-prone components) may require a design or code review by senior members of the team to determine the root cause of the problems. Pareto charts are also used to graph data from software configuration management. Software components that are changing excessively may indicate a dangerous kind of code volatility, for example, a situation in which each defect "fix" breaks some other part of the code.

Histograms are useful in identifying process failures. For example, an investigation may be necessary when software builds are failing frequently over time. By keeping track of reasons why the builds fail, the changes that need to be made can be identified. In the case of software build failure, it is may be determined that the build process hasn't been correctly automated or that the checklist for manual builds is incomplete or incorrect. Similarly, when regression tests fail repeatedly, the cause may be that a "fix" broke something else, earlier fixes were defective, or possibly that the wrong code was included.

8.3.2.2 Statistical Sampling

See Section 8.3.2.2 of the *PMBOK® Guide*.

8.3.2.3 Inspection

See Section 8.3.2.3 of the *PMBOK® Guide*.

8.3.2.4 Approved Change Requests Review

See Section 8.3.2.4 of the *PMBOK® Guide*.

8.3.3 Control Quality: Outputs

The following outputs for controlling quality in Section 8.3.3 of the *PMBOK® Guide* are applicable outputs for controlling quality for software projects.

8.3.3.1 Quality Control Measurements

See Section 8.3.3.1 of the *PMBOK® Guide*.

8.3.3.2 Validated Changes

See Section 8.3.3.2 of the *PMBOK® Guide*.

8.3.3.3 Verified Deliverables

See Section 8.3.3.3 of the *PMBOK® Guide*.

8.3.3.4 Work Performance Information

See Section 8.3.3.4 of the *PMBOK® Guide*.

8.3.3.5 Change Requests

See Section 8.3.3.5 of the *PMBOK® Guide*.

8.3.3.6 Project Management Plan Updates

See Section 8.3.3.6 of the *PMBOK® Guide*.

8.3.3.7 Project Documents Updates

See Section 8.3.3.7 of the *PMBOK® Guide*.

8.3.3.8 Organizational Process Assets Updates

See Section 8.3.3.8 of the *PMBOK® Guide*.

8.3.3.9 Additional Outputs

Additional outputs for controlling the quality of software projects and products include:

- Measurements of the quality attributes specified in the quality management plan and the release criteria.
- Changes to software and other artifacts validated by testing or inspection.
- Deliverables validated by testing or inspection to conform to the scope identified at the start of the project or iteration.
- Identification of gaps between planned and actual performance and reasons for the gaps.
- Updated checklists, test procedures, and other process assets.
- Lessons learned by means of the project lessons learned or iteration retrospective, along with the team's recommendations for changes in the process or product and the resultant change requests.
- Updates to the project management plans (e.g., schedule, resources, configuration management, test planning).

PROJECT HUMAN RESOURCE MANAGEMENT

Most of the material in Section 9 of the *PMBOK® Guide* is applicable to human resource management for software projects. This section of the *Software Extension to the PMBOK® Guide* presents additional considerations for managing software project human resources.

As stated in the *PMBOK® Guide*, Project Human Resource Management includes the processes that organize, manage, and lead the project team. The *PMBOK® Guide* provides general advice for human resource management that is suitable for a variety of project environments. It covers how to acquire appropriate project resources, develop them, and manage them from a domain-independent viewpoint. It can be applied to machinists, construction workers, or researchers.

However, because of the need to provide universal guidance applicable to all kinds of projects, the *PMBOK® Guide* does not focus on domain-specific guidance for knowledge workers, including software developers who collaborate to solve novel problems with incomplete information. This *Software Extension* focuses on managing human resources for software projects. The knowledge worker recommendations of authors such as Peter Drucker and Don Reinertson are also appropriate in these situations [34].

Software project team members typically possess technical knowledge and skills superior to those of their project managers as related to the software product. Therefore, to be most effective, project managers need to find ways to leverage the knowledge and skills of software project team members. Successful software project managers typically put less emphasis on directing the work and more on facilitating the efficiency and effectiveness of project teams. This subtle, but crucial shift dramatically changes the way teams are created, developed, and managed. It effectively changes the approach from Plan Human Resource Management to "Manage Project Team(s)."

Also, since software teams spend a large proportion of their time collaborating, discussing ideas, and making joint decisions, the "fit" of each team member within the team is extremely important. Rather than hiring a competent programmer who does good work in isolation, a programmer who can easily and effectively interact with the members of the software team may be a better choice than a competent programmer who does good work in isolation. It is desirable to have team members engaged in the selection process of other team members. This influences the "Acquire Project Team" process for a software project (see Section 9.2 of this *Software Extension*).

Software project teams often build novel solutions using new technology; therefore, they may not know the solution during initiation and planning of the project. Instead, they innovatively solve problems, iterate on proofs of concepts, and improve their processes as they develop the software product. This approach is most effective for self-empowered teams who self-diagnose, engage in introspection and retrospective meetings, and continuously improve. The process of instilling and promoting these concepts is common among successful software project managers; the concepts influence the way project managers develop and manage software project teams.

These considerations are described in the following sections of this *Software Extension*.

Figure 9-1 provides an overview of Software Project Human Resource Management; it is an adaptation of Figure 9-1 in the *PMBOK® Guide*.

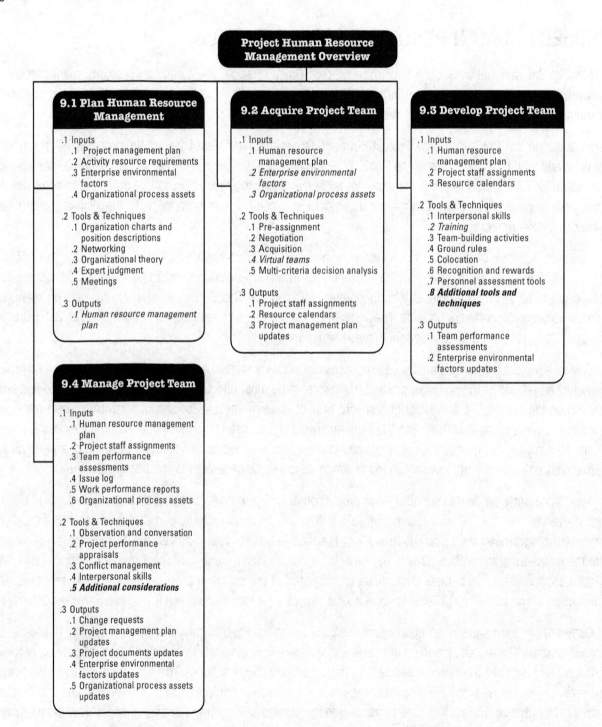

Figure 9-1. Software Project Human Resource Management Overview

9.1 Plan Human Resource Management

The Plan Human Resource Management process involves identifying and documenting project roles and responsibilities, required skills, and reporting relationships, and creating a staffing management plan. The inputs, tools and techniques, and outputs in Section 9.1 of the *PMBOK® Guide* are applicable to planning human resource management for software projects with the indicated extensions.

9.1.1 Plan Human Resource Management: Inputs

The inputs for planning human resource management in the *PMBOK® Guide* are applicable to planning human resource management for software projects.

9.1.1.1 Project Management Plan

See Section 9.1.1.1 of the *PMBOK® Guide*.

9.1.1.2 Activity Resource Requirements

See Section 9.1.1.2 of the *PMBOK® Guide*.

9.1.1.3 Enterprise Environmental Factors

See Section 9.1.1.3 of the *PMBOK® Guide*.

9.1.1.4 Organizational Process Assets

See Section 9.1.1.4 of the *PMBOK® Guide*.

9

9.1.2 Plan Human Resource Management: Tools and Techniques

The tools and techniques for planning human resource management in the *PMBOK® Guide* are applicable tools and techniques for planning human resource management for software projects.

9.1.2.1 Organization Charts and Position Descriptions

See Section 9.1.2.1 of the *PMBOK® Guide*.

9.1.2.2 Networking

See Section 9.1.2.2 of the *PMBOK® Guide*.

9.1.2.3 Organizational Theory

See Section 9.1.2.3 of the *PMBOK® Guide*.

9.1.2.4 Expert Judgment

See Section 9.1.2.4 of the *PMBOK® Guide*.

9.1.2.5 Meetings

See Section 9.1.2.5 of the *PMBOK® Guide*.

9.1.3 Plan Human Resource Management: Outputs

The one output for planning human resource management in the *PMBOK® Guide* is an applicable output for planning human resource management for software projects with the indicated extension.

9.1.3.1 Human Resource Management Plan

See Section 9.1.3.1 of the *PMBOK® Guide*.

For software projects, planning human resource management occurs with the recognition of some software project truisms and characteristics.

Software projects require collaboration and information sharing to innovatively solve problems and build new products. Team members are motivated by opportunities to expand their skills, solve interesting problems, build innovative software, and use effective software tools. Failing to recognize the motivational factors of software developers when planning human resource management can create many problems later in a software project.

Software teams perform better with less of a command-and-control structure and more of a facilitation approach to project management [35]. Instead of planning to give detailed task lists to team members, effective software project managers plan on presenting work as questions to be answered or problems to be solved and allow team members to organize internally to meet these challenges. This provides a more stimulating and rewarding environment for software team members and also defers design and construction decisions by keeping solutions open to creative approaches that may not have been envisioned during the initiation and planning phases of the software project.

A commonly used approach to managing software projects is for the project manager to adopt a servant leadership role, which enables empowered teams. Team members are encouraged to wear many hats and contribute regardless of their formal title, which balances the workload and enables completion of the tasks required for project success.

In recognition of the professionalism generally seen among project team members, project managers are encouraged to take a Theory Y view of team members rather than a Theory X approach [36].

McGregor's Theory X asserts that employees are inherently lazy and will avoid work whenever they can. Theory X managers believe that workers need to be closely supervised and comprehensive systems of controls should be developed and enforced. In contrast, Theory Y posits that employees are ambitious and self-motivated. They enjoy creative problem solving, but their talents are underused in most organizations. Theory Y managers communicate openly with team members, minimize the difference between superior-subordinate relationships, and create a comfortable environment in which subordinates can develop and use their talents and abilities. This climate includes shared decision making so that subordinates have a say in decisions that influence them and their work products [37].

When planning Software Project Human Management, effective software project managers modify their management style for the characteristics of software project team members, try to avoid command and control structures, and promote the problem-solving motivational factors that drive software professionals. Also, software project managers plan for cross-functional teams that have all the skills available among the team members that are needed to develop the software product.

9.2 Acquire Project Team

The inputs, tools and techniques, and outputs for acquiring a project team in Section 9.2 of the *PMBOK® Guide* are applicable to acquiring a software project team.

9.2.1 Acquire Project Team: Inputs

The inputs for acquiring a project team in the *PMBOK® Guide* are applicable to acquiring a project team for software projects, with the following extensions.

9.2.1.1 Human Resource Management Plan

See Section 9.2.1.1 of the *PMBOK® Guide.*

9.2.1.2 Enterprise Environmental Factors

See Section 9.2.1.2 of the *PMBOK® Guide.*

Special considerations may apply for software developers when setting up a physical work environment. Collaborative software workers require facilities for interaction and sharing, but also require individual physical space and a quiet environment at times. Computing facilities, lighting, and other ergonomic issues are important for software developers.

9.2.1.3 Organizational Process Assets

See Section 9.2.1.3 of the *PMBOK® Guide.*

In addition, software organizations sometimes acquire software project team members by hiring contract personnel to perform various project duties. Contract personnel may be members of the software development team or they may be hired to perform specialized tasks such as traceability or testing. These contracted personnel do not always have allegiance to the organization or the project and may not adapt readily to the corporate culture of the organization.

9.2.2 Acquire Project Team: Tools and Techniques

The tools and techniques for acquiring a project team in Section 9.2.2 of the *PMBOK® Guide* are applicable to acquiring a software project team. In addition, the following considerations address some particular aspects of acquiring a software project team.

Since software project team members share and manipulate information rather than tangible materials, team stability and dedicated team members are important attributes that reduce reiteration of the goals, the agreed-to approach, and the mechanisms for determining project status, which occurs when there is turnover in the team. Software project teams work best within strong matrix and projectized environments, where a dedicated team can work on a single project with few interruptions. Team members work together most effectively when they are colocated and face-to-face communications can occur on a continuous, ongoing basis.

The goal of acquiring software project team members is to create stable, colocated teams that have all of the skills needed to conduct the project. Silo teams with matrix reporting structures are less likely to be committed to shared project goals since some of their allegiance will be to their host group. When colocation is not possible, stable cross-functional teams in different time zones are preferable to silo teams.

When acquiring new team members, the involvement of present team members, in addition to the project manager and human resources personnel, increases the likelihood of building a cohesive, integrated team. Human resource and management personnel do the normal front-end screening of candidates to weed out unsuitable or unskilled applicants. The acceptable candidates are then invited for peer interviews where team members assess the candidate to determine whether the candidate will be a good fit for the team, and whether the candidate will make the team stronger or weaker. Care should be taken to ensure that new team members will bring diversity of viewpoints and fresh thinking to the team.

Different software groups, (e.g., the software developers, testers, and the SQA and SQC staff) will evaluate different characteristics of the candidate. Everyone wins when engaging the team in the interview process. The project team wins because they have already met and endorsed the prospective candidate. Candidates win because they get to meet their potential peers, learn what the organization and project are about, and are better able to assess the corporate culture. The project manager wins because the team members, who have the technical knowledge, will ask the appropriate technical questions. Finally, all subgroups within the project win by learning what characteristics are important to other subgroups within the project, thereby increasing their awareness and maturity.

The following tools and techniques for acquiring a project team in Section 9.2.2 of the *PMBOK® Guide* are applicable to acquiring a software project team.

9.2.2.1 Pre-assignment

See Section 9.2.2.1 of the *PMBOK® Guide*.

9.2.2.2 Negotiation

See Section 9.2.2.2 of the *PMBOK® Guide*.

9.2.2.3 Acquisition

See Section 9.2.2.3 of the *PMBOK® Guide*.

9.2.2.4 Virtual Teams

See Section 9.2.2.4 of the *PMBOK® Guide*.

Important factors when establishing virtual software teams include cross-cultural orientation and awareness, readily accessible repositories for work products, a configuration management infrastructure and, to the extent possible, in-person interaction on a periodic basis.

9.2.2.5 Multi-Criteria Decision Analysis

See Section 9.2.2.5 of the *PMBOK® Guide*.

9.2.3 Acquire Project Team: Outputs

The outputs for acquiring a project team in Section 9.2.3 of the *PMBOK® Guide* are applicable outputs for acquiring project teams for software projects.

9.2.3.1 Project Staff Assignments

See Section 9.2.3.1 of the *PMBOK® Guide*.

9.2.3.2 Resource Calendars

See Section 9.2.3.2 of the *PMBOK® Guide*.

9.2.3.3 Project Management Plan Updates

See Section 9.2.3.3 of the *PMBOK® Guide*.

9.3 Develop Project Team

The inputs, tools and techniques, and outputs for developing a project team in Section 9.3 of the *PMBOK® Guide* are applicable to developing a software project team.

Develop Project Team for a software project is concerned with improving the competencies, team interactions, and overall team environment to enhance project performance. For software projects this is a nested, recurring pattern that happens continuously on cycles of exploration and feedback that typically occur on hourly, daily, weekly, biweekly, and monthly iteration cycles.

9.3.1 Develop Project Team: Inputs

The inputs for developing a project team in Section 9.3.1 of the *PMBOK® Guide* are applicable inputs for developing a project team for software projects.

9.3.1.1 Human Resource Management Plan

See Section 9.3.1.1 of the *PMBOK® Guide*.

9.3.1.2 Project Staff Assignments

See Section 9.3.1.2 of the *PMBOK® Guide*.

9.3.1.3 Resource Calendars

See Section 9.3.1.3 of the *PMBOK® Guide*.

9.3.2 Develop Project Team: Tools and Techniques

The tools and techniques for acquiring a project team in Section 9.3.2 of the *PMBOK® Guide* are applicable to acquiring a project team for software projects, with the modification and addition included in this section of the *Software Extension*.

9.3.2.1 Interpersonal Skills

See Section 9.3.2.1 of the *PMBOK® Guide*.

9.3.2.2 Training

See Section 9.3.2.2 of the *PMBOK® Guide*.

A balance between training required for the current software project and training that enhances individual or team competency is needed, and this may be useful in future projects.

9.3.2.3 Team-Building Activities

See Section 9.3.2.3 of the *PMBOK® Guide*.

9.3.2.4 Ground Rules

See Section 9.3.2.4 of the *PMBOK® Guide*.

9.3.2.5 Colocation

See Section 9.3.2.5 of the *PMBOK® Guide*.

9.3.2.6 Recognition and Rewards

See Section 9.3.2.6 of the *PMBOK® Guide*.

9.3.2.7 Personnel Assessment Tools

See Section 9.3.2.7 of the *PMBOK® Guide*.

9

9.3.2.8 Additional Tools and Techniques

The following tools and techniques address some additional tools and techniques for developing a software project team.

- **Pair Programming.** The practice of pair programming, where two software developers share a programming task, can assist greatly with skills improvement and learning of good practices. Often, team members of dissimilar skill levels are paired and pair members are rotated frequently in order to maximize learning opportunities. This also has the benefit of sharing project information and technical knowledge throughout the team, thus reducing the dependency on key individuals for their knowledge and skills. In the event that a team member leaves the project, the impact is not as significant because there are others who understand the topic.

- **Test-Driven Development.** The practice of test-driven development (TDD) also helps improve team competencies through short feedback cycles of experimental learning. TDD or "red, green, refactor" refers to the steps of writing a test (that fails), then writing code until the test passes, then refactoring the code for clarity; this process may occur many times each day. By encouraging developers to think about how code will be tested before writing code, business purpose and usability are considered frequently, which enhances software quality and user acceptance. However, the main benefit is for the team members, who will increase their understanding and skills through rapid cycles of exploration, test, and feedback. These concepts, as they are reinforced in adaptive life cycle software projects, are illustrated in Figure 9-2.

- **Colocation.** Software project teams coalesce and become more productive when they are stable and colocated. It takes time for teams to progress through the Tuckman stages of forming, storming, norming, and finally to performing to optimize team output [38]. Swapping people in and out of a team triggers the storming and norming phases again as new team members find their place in the team and the team adjusts to them.

   Part of the storming and norming process for software project team members is learning how to deal with team conflict, negotiating, gaining commitment for decisions, and ultimately developing a sense of shared accountability for project outcomes. These are complex issues that impact all projects when skilled people need to collaborate on building novel solutions; they are particularly important issues for software project team members. Getting skilled people to work together and harness constructive disagreement and rigorously test decisions is a primary goal of software team development and a key skill of an effective software project manager.

   Colocation of team members helps this process and allows direct face-to-face communication. Colocation is not always possible, but given a choice of two teams—one experienced but dispersed and one less experienced but local—the local team is often the best choice for a software project.

   Colocation also facilitates open unfiltered debate. Without the barriers of video conferencing, email, and telephone, it is much easier to get to the heart of an issue when in direct communication. Empowered teams and shared decision-making help to build commitment.

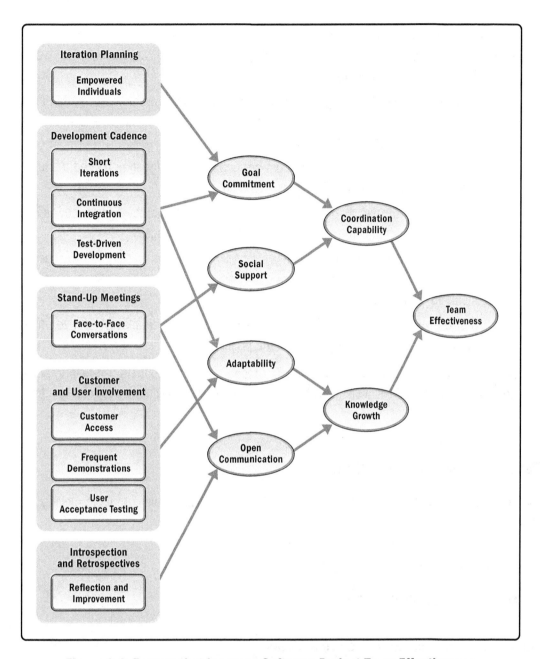

Figure 9-2. Factors that Increase Software Project Team Effectiveness

Iteration planning meetings, daily stand-up meetings, introspection, and retrospective meetings at the ends of iteration cycles reinforce and reiterate team member work commitments and team accountability for results.

Self-organizing teams schedule their own work and take ownership for problems and solutions wherever possible. For some teams, this may come naturally; for others, it can be a big transition that requires training and encouragement by project managers and senior management.

- **Developing Trust.** The challenges software teams face in working together and learning to trust one another, thrash out issues, make decisions, and commit to shared responsibility are well described in *The Five Dysfunctions of a Team* [39]:

    o **Absence of trust.** Unwillingness to express mistakes and weaknesses within the group. Team members need to be open about mistakes and accepting of mistakes and weaknesses in others in order to build a foundation of trust.

    o **Fear of conflict.** Teams that lack trust are unable to engage in unfiltered debate. Instead they resort to veiled discussions and guarded comments.

    o **Lack of commitment.** Without passionate debate, team members rarely buy-in to or commit to decisions though they may feign agreement during meetings.

    o **Avoidance of accountability.** Because of lack of commitment and buy-in, most people will hesitate to constructively confront their peers on actions and behaviors that seem counterproductive to the good of the team and the project.

    o **Inattention to results.** Failure to hold team members accountable leads to putting individual goals (or department goals) ahead of the project.

These dysfunctions are ever-present risks for software teams. Project managers can help to build a culture of trust and acceptance by sharing their mistakes with the team and demonstrating that it is OK to admit to mistakes provided they are corrected.

9.3.3 Develop Project Team: Outputs

The outputs from Develop Project Team in the *PMBOK® Guide* are applicable outputs for developing a software project team.

9.3.3.1 Team Performance Assessments

See Section 9.3.3.1 of the *PMBOK® Guide*.

9.3.3.2 Enterprise Environmental Factors Updates

See Section 9.3.3.2 of the *PMBOK® Guide*.

9.4 Manage Project Team

The inputs, tools and techniques, and outputs in Section 9.4 of the *PMBOK® Guide* are applicable to managing a software project team, with the extension included in this *Software Extension*.

9.4.1 Manage Project Team: Inputs

The inputs for managing a project team in the *PMBOK® Guide* are applicable inputs for managing a software project team.

9.4.1.1 Human Resource Management Plan

See Section 9.4.1.1 of the *PMBOK® Guide*.

9.4.1.2 Project Staff Assignments

See Section 9.4.1.2 of the *PMBOK® Guide*.

9.4.1.3 Team Performance Assessments

See Section 9.4.1.3 of the *PMBOK® Guide*.

9.4.1.4 Issue Log

See Section 9.4.1.4 of the *PMBOK® Guide*.

9.4.1.5 Work Performance Reports

See Section 9.4.1.5 of the *PMBOK® Guide*.

9.4.1.6 Organizational Process Assets

See Section 9.4.1.6 of the *PMBOK® Guide*.

9.4.2 Manage Project Team: Tools and Techniques

The tools and techniques for managing a project team in Section 9.4.2 of the *PMBOK® Guide* are applicable tools and techniques for managing a software project team.

9.4.2.1 Observation and Conversation

See Section 9.4.2.1 of the *PMBOK® Guide*.

9.4.2.2 Project Performance Appraisals

See Section 9.4.2.2 of the *PMBOK® Guide*.

9.4.2.3 Conflict Management

See Section 9.4.2.3 of the *PMBOK® Guide.*

9.4.2.4 Interpersonal Skills

See Section 9.4.2.4 of the *PMBOK® Guide.*

9.4.2.5 Additional Considerations

The following considerations address some additional aspects of managing a software project team.

Tracking performance of individual team members on a software project is a delicate issue. It is important to assess individual performance, interactions with colleagues, and development of skills. At the same time, care should be taken to not publicize measured performance at the individual level because many factors affect individual performance on a software project. For example, a talented project member may exhibit decreased productivity when working on the most complex part of the product, having been assigned to the difficult part because of the project member's skills. In addition, publicizing individual performance can result in self-centered behavior and provides little reward for collaborating with and helping other team members.

For these reasons, it is desirable to track performance at the team level; team members will have incentives to help colleagues in order to boost the team's overall productivity. For this reason, velocity (the production rate per iteration) is measured at the team level and not at the level of individuals.

Project managers who engage one-on-one with individual team members can learn each member's career development goals. Developing individual skills and roles of team members and finding opportunities for them to use these skills on the project greatly improves individual commitment and satisfaction. Team members become more aligned and committed to the project goals when they see how their personal goals are linked to project goals.

Because many software projects work on short iteration cycles, new roles can be tried for an iterative cycle or two before adopting or abandoning a new role. The opportunity to try new roles is appreciated by team members as being proactive to their needs without being disruptive to the project.

Periodic intervals for experimentation with new and different team roles is also advantageous to the project manager who rapidly obtains feedback on self-directed team adjustments. Iterative approaches provide short-time periods for experimentation and feedback to team members, which most people find to be rewarding.

Feedback is obtained by demonstrating increments of working software after which retrospective team meetings are held. These two events (demonstrations and retrospectives) provide valuable feedback to the project team members, project manager, and customer. A demonstration provides feedback on what the customer thinks of the new work, information is gained on how the project is (or is not) meeting its goals, and retrospectives plus introspection aids in adjusting and improving the development processes.

Resolving conflicts among team members also needs careful balance. Most team conflicts are indicators of a trusting environment where it is acceptable to present dissenting views. Passionate debate over technical issues builds commitment to outcomes; conflict is only an issue when it extends beyond business and technical issues and becomes personal.

Because of the intangible and malleable nature of software, there is rarely only one way to solve a problem, so debate and discussion over approaches is normal and healthy as long as the discussions do not escalate beyond what the team can solve or overflow into personal conflict. Should this occur, the approaches to conflict management recommended in Section 9.4.2.3 of the *PMBOK® Guide* can be used.

9.4.3 Manage Software Project Team: Outputs

The outputs for managing a project team in Section 9.4.3 of the *PMBOK® Guide* are applicable outputs for managing a software project team.

9.4.3.1 Change Requests

See Section 9.4.3.1 of the *PMBOK® Guide*.

9.4.3.2 Project Management Plan Updates

See Section 9.4.3.2 of the *PMBOK® Guide*.

9.4.3.3 Project Documents Updates

See Section 9.4.3.3 of the *PMBOK® Guide*.

9.4.3.4 Enterprise Environmental Factors Updates

See Section 9.4.3.4 of the *PMBOK® Guide*.

9.4.3.5 Organizational Process Assets Updates

See Section 9.4.3.5 of the *PMBOK® Guide*.

10

PROJECT COMMUNICATIONS MANAGEMENT

Most of the material in Section 10 of the *PMBOK® Guide* is applicable to communications management for software projects. This section of the *Software Extension to the PMBOK® Guide* presents additional considerations for managing software project communications.

According to Section 10 of the *PMBOK® Guide*, Project Communications Management includes the processes that are required to ensure timely and appropriate planning, collection, creation, distribution, storage, retrieval, management, control, monitoring, and the ultimate disposition of project information. This section of the *Software Extension to the PMBOK® Guide* addresses project communication for software projects by addressing issues that are important for managing software project communication and that merit guidance beyond that provided in the *PMBOK® Guide*.

The role of project communication is a primary consideration for software projects, because software is developed by teams of individuals who engage in closely coordinated, intellectual problem-solving activities. With no physical product to reference, effective communication is paramount for keeping team members productively engaged and stakeholders informed. Software teams reduce complexity and enhance communication through a combination of communication approaches that include visual displays, colocation (when possible), and an emphasis on face-to-face communication.

Figure 10-1 provides an overview of Software Project Communication Management; it is an adaptation of Figure 10-1 in the *PMBOK® Guide*.

10.1 Plan Communications Management

The inputs, tools and techniques, and outputs in Section 10.1 of the *PMBOK® Guide* are applicable to planning communications management for software projects, with the following additional considerations.

Software projects often exhibit high rates of change to accommodate changing and emerging requirements and shifting priorities. Frequent and productive communication among team members is important and can be achieved through planning meetings, daily stand-up meetings, frequent demonstrations of progress, and retrospective meetings. These approaches are typically, but not exclusively, applied to software projects that use adaptive project life cycles. Adaptive life cycles and the related communication techniques used may create confusion among stakeholders who are not familiar with them. In this case, the software project managers should plan extra time to explain the project life cycle processes. Meetings should be planned to ensure that all stakeholders understand project operations, team and other stakeholder communication protocols, and stakeholder involvement in the communication processes.

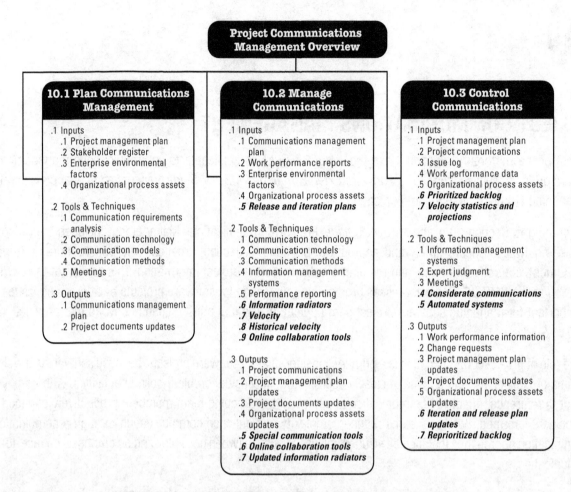

Figure 10-1 Project Communications Management Overview

Face-to-face (FTF) communication allows two-way dialogs; issues and questions can be addressed immediately, and emotion is readily conveyed. For example, while discussing a topic, when a person nods their head or otherwise indicates understanding or agreement with the speaker, further explanation can be curtailed, and the discussion can be directed to other topics. Because of the higher bandwidth, opportunities for questions and answers, and lower communication costs, face-to-face communication is the preferred means of communication for software development projects, whenever possible. It is easy to productively use face-to-face communication for colocated teams. Audio and video conferencing can be used to simulate face-to-face interactions when team members are geographically distributed.

To facilitate communication, the preferred solution for a large project is to break up a large team into multiple smaller teams that can leverage face-to-face communication and tacit knowledge within each of the smaller teams, and with well-defined communication channels among the teams.

The following equation can be used to calculate the number of communication paths, P, among a collection of project teams, where n is the number of members in a team and N is the number of teams. An assumption is made that each member of each project team communicates with all other members of their team, and one member of each project team communicates with one member of each of the other project teams.

$$P = \text{SUM}([n(n-1)/2]) + [N(N-1)/2]$$

For a single team ($N = 1$) the number of communications paths is $P = n(n-1)/2$; that is, communication paths within a project team increase on the order of the square of the number of team members.

Note, also, that a single team of 10 members has 45 communication paths, whereas two teams of 5 have 21 communication paths. Of course, the single point of contact for each team with the other team (i.e., the team leader) should have sufficient bandwidth to ensure effective communication between the two teams and among multiple teams when there are more than two project teams.

10.1.1 Plan Communications Management: Inputs

The inputs in Section 10.1.1 of the *PMBOK® Guide* are applicable for planning software project communications. The following additional observation is also applicable.

Adaptive life cycles for software projects often include iteration plans and release plans for the iterations that produce demonstrable increments of working, deliverable software. These plans communicate the agreed-upon product content for the next iteration cycle and the content of the next iterative release (where a release may be used for a customer demonstration or for internal review by the project team). These plans provide an important input for planning software project communications.

10.1.1.1 Project Management Plan

See Section 10.1.1.1 of the *PMBOK® Guide*.

10.1.1.2 Stakeholder Register

See Section 10.1.1.2 of the *PMBOK® Guide*.

10.1.1.3 Enterprise Environmental Factors

See Section 10.1.1.3 of the *PMBOK® Guide*.

10.1.1.4 Organizational Process Assets

See Section 10.1.1.4 of the *PMBOK® Guide*.

10.1.2 Plan Communications Management: Tools and Techniques

The tools and techniques in Section 10.1.2 of the *PMBOK® Guide* are applicable for planning software project communications.

10.1.2.1 Communication Requirements Analysis

See Section 10.1.2.1 of the *PMBOK® Guide*.

10.1.2.2 Communication Technology

See Section 10.1.2.2 of the *PMBOK® Guide*.

10.1.2.3 Communication Models

See Section 10.1.2.3 of the *PMBOK® Guide*.

10.1.2.4 Communication Methods

See Section 10.1.2.4 of the *PMBOK® Guide*.

10.1.2.5 Meetings

See Section 10.1.2.5 of the *PMBOK® Guide*.

10.1.3 Plan Communications Management: Outputs

The outputs in Section 10.1.3 of the *PMBOK® Guide* are applicable for planning software communications, with the indicated extensions.

10.1.3.1 Communications Management Plan

See Section 10.1.3.1 of the *PMBOK® Guide*.

10.1.3.2 Project Documents Updates

See Section 10.1.3.2 of the *PMBOK® Guide*.

Additionally, when planning communications management for a software project, it is important that the characteristics of software and knowledge work are recognized and incorporated. These include:

- Software projects are often novel undertakings for their customers and host organizations; therefore, communication may be needed to explain the tools and techniques that will be used when managing the project, especially for managing ambiguity during the initiating and planning processes of a software development project.

- Software project life cycles are often complex, therefore significant communication may be needed to explain the development process that will be used and the roles that various stakeholders will play.

- Software projects often experience high rates of change as the project evolves and product requirements emerge, so it is important that frequent communications are provided to keep stakeholders up to date. Communication mechanisms may include planning meetings, demonstrations of the evolving software product, and retrospective meetings.

- Geographically dispersed teams often undertake software projects; in these cases, electronic communication tools such as VOIP (voice over internet protocol), instant messaging, video conferencing, and project websites are often utilized.

- Both push (publish) and pull (subscribe) communication mechanisms are used to accommodate the high rate of information exchange often seen in software projects.

Adaptive life cycles for software projects address these characteristics of project communication by frequently demonstrating the evolving features and functionality and regularly delivering functionality into the users' environment, when desired, to provide higher project visibility for key stakeholders. A major attribute of adaptive life cycles is the elimination of long periods of internal project activity, which make it difficult for external stakeholders to understand what is happening.

Adaptive life cycle techniques facilitate the planning of software project communication because project information is a byproduct of the development processes (this is a major feature of adaptive software project life cycles). However, reliance on face-to-face interaction requires participation by the appropriate project stakeholders (customer, users, users' representatives, and others). Stakeholder attendance at planning meetings and iterative demonstrations of the evolving product is crucial. Other communication techniques will be required when face-to-face communication is not possible.

Also, ongoing engagement of and communication with stakeholders is important throughout the entire project life cycle because requirements, assumptions, and constraints often change as a software project evolves. It is also important to ensure that project stakeholders receive the information they need during planning meetings, product demonstrations, and project retrospectives. Stakeholders should be encouraged to actively participate in these meetings. Stakeholders should be asked what information they need, and it should be provided as expediently as possible.

10.2 Manage Communications

The inputs, tools and techniques, and outputs in Section 10.2 of the *PMBOK® Guide* are applicable to managing software project communications.

10.2.1 Manage Communications: Inputs

The inputs in Section 10.2.1 of the *PMBOK® Guide* are applicable inputs for managing software project communications. In addition, the input in Section 10.2.1.5 of this *Software Extension* applies to managing software project communications.

10.2.1.1 Communications Management Plan

See Section 10.2.1.1 of the *PMBOK® Guide*.

10.2.1.2 Work Performance Reports

See Section 10.2.1.2 of the *PMBOK® Guide*.

10.2.1.3 Enterprise Environmental Factors

See Section 10.2.1.3 of the *PMBOK® Guide*.

10.2.1.4 Organizational Process Assets

See Section 10.2.1.4 of the *PMBOK® Guide*.

10.2.1.5 Release and Iteration Plans

As stated in Section 10.1.1 of this *Software Extension*, adaptive life cycles for software projects typically include iteration and release plans. These plans provide an important input for managing software project communications.

10.2.2 Manage Communications: Tools and Techniques

The tools and techniques in Section 10.2.2 of the *PMBOK® Guide* are applicable tools and techniques for managing software project communications. In addition, Sections 10.2.2.6 to 10.2.2.9 provide extensions that are applicable to managing software project communications.

Because of the potential for high rates of change and the lack of a tangible, evolving product, tools and techniques for managing communications on software projects are especially important. Project information can be provided by means of push and pull mechanisms. Information such as status reports should be pushed out to stakeholders on a regular basis (perhaps weekly). Information can be published in a repository so that stakeholders can pull the desired information at the desired level of detail, as needed or desired.

10.2.2.1 Communication Technology

See Section 10.2.2.1 of the *PMBOK® Guide*.

10.2.2.2 Communication Models

See Section 10.2.2.2 of the *PMBOK® Guide*.

10.2.2.3 Communication Methods

See Section 10.2.2.3 of the *PMBOK® Guide*.

10.2.2.4 Information Management Systems

See Section 10.2.2.4 of the *PMBOK® Guide*.

10.2.2.5 Performance Reporting

See Section 10.2.2.5 of the *PMBOK® Guide*.

10.2.2.6 Information Radiators

Information radiators are large, graphic displays of software project status used to communicate project information. They are frequently updated and located where the project team and others can easily see them. Common kinds of information radiators include task boards, burnup and burndown graphs, defect reports, status of rework, and so forth.

A storyboard is a kind of information radiator for a software project. Sticky notes that describe project tasks are placed on a white board. The columns of a storyboard can be used to display items such as stories, tasks in progress, tasks completed, and story bugs (defects). The rows show the progress work items across the columns. A storyboard is depicted in Figure 10-2.

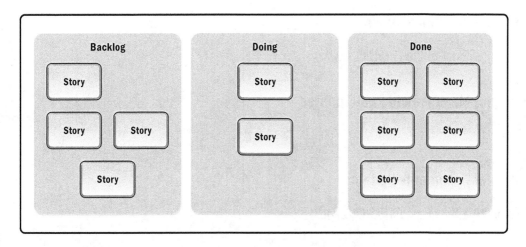

Figure 10-2. Depiction of a Storyboard

10.2.2.7 Velocity

Velocity is a measure of output produced by a software project team during an iteration cycle (i.e., the ratio of amount of product developed to effort consumed). Velocity is an indicator of team capacity and a measure of productivity and progress. Velocity can be measured using story points or features points developed per person-day of effort consumed.

10.2.2.8 Historical Velocity

Historical velocity (also known as "yesterday's weather") describes the team's velocity during recent, previous iterations. It reflects the fully loaded capability of the team's resources including the impacts of defects found and fixed and other work demands. Using yesterday's weather is a reliable way of estimating the team's current iteration capacity.

Yesterday's weather uses recent performance as an indicator for likely future performance. For example, if a team completed 30 story points last week, then forecasting 30 story points as an estimate for progress this week is probably more valid than using the 45 story points per week, which was estimated at the beginning of the project.

10.2.2.9 Online Collaboration Tools

Online collaboration tools can be used so that those who are remote from the team can participate in meetings, share documents and work in progress, visit the project website, and view project information such as information radiators and yesterday's weather.

10.2.3 Manage Communications: Outputs

The outputs in Section 10.2.3 of the *PMBOK® Guide* are applicable outputs for managing software project communications. In addition, the outputs in Sections 10.2.3.5 to 10.2.3.7 of this *Software Extension* are applicable to managing software project communications.

10.2.3.1 Project Communications

See Section 10.2.3.1 of the *PMBOK® Guide*.

10.2.3.2 Project Management Plan Updates

See Section 10.2.3.2 of the *PMBOK® Guide*.

10.2.3.3 Project Documents Updates

See Section 10.2.3.3 of the *PMBOK® Guide*.

10.2.3.4 Organizational Process Assets Updates

See Section 10.2.3.4 of the *PMBOK® Guide*.

10.2.3.5 Special Communication Tools

Software projects that use adaptive life cycles often use special communications tools to specify and measure scope, schedule, budget, progress, and risks. These communication tools may include product backlogs, release maps, cumulative flow diagrams, and risk burndown charts. These terms are defined in the Glossary.

10.2.3.6 Online Collaboration Tools

Software projects often use online collaboration tools to share and communicate project status. These tools allow geographically dispersed members to access project information. Online collaboration tools are also continuously available to project groups that may be located in different time zones. Online collaboration tools can provide a rich environment for storing documents, images, videos of product demonstrations, and threaded discussion forums.

10.2.3.7 Updated Information Radiators

A software project's information radiators may include a burndown chart, a parking lot diagram, and/or a cumulative-flow diagram; they are frequently updated to reflect the latest available information. A burndown chart and a parking lot diagram are illustrated in Figures 10-3 and 10-4. A cumulative-flow diagram is illustrated in Figure 6-5 of this *Software Extension*.

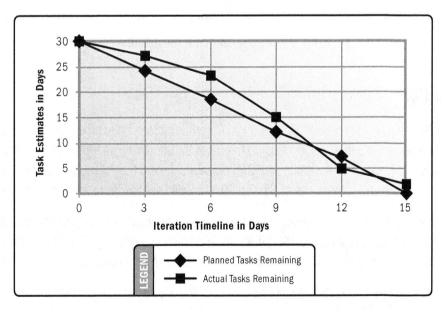

Figure 10-3. Burndown Chart for Software Project Iteration

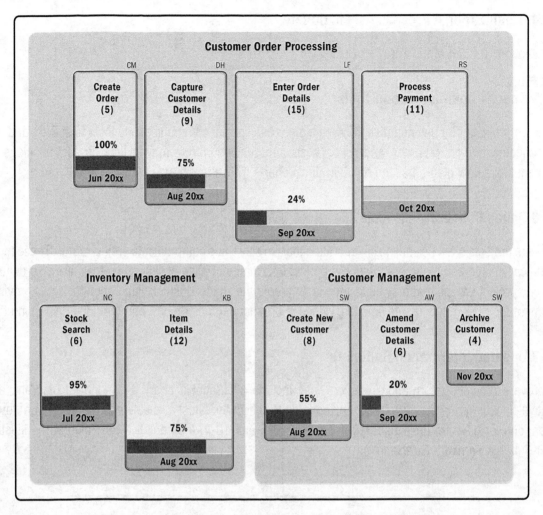

Figure 10-4. A Parking Lot Diagram for a Software Project

10.3 Control Communications

According to Section 10.3 of the *PMBOK® Guide*, Control Communications is the process of monitoring and controlling communications throughout the entire project life cycle to ensure the information needs of project stakeholders are met. The techniques presented in Section 10.3 of the *PMBOK® Guide* are generally applicable to controlling communications in software projects. The following extensions to Section 10.3 are also applicable to software projects.

Controlling communications for a software project involves (a) providing insight into the development progress as issues arise and are resolved, and (b) providing different information needed by different stakeholders. Commonly reported and useful metrics include measures of cost, schedule, product volume, defects, and progress.

Good metrics are simple and relevant to the end goal of delivering an acceptable product within the constraints of requirements, schedule, budget, resources, technology, and other relevant factors. Software project measures should be byproducts of the processes used; it should not require an inordinate effort to produce them.

For predictive software project life cycles, the following measures can be used: milestones achieved and missed, status of change requests and the risk register, status of software construction and testing, status of increments planned and developed, and issues identified and resolved by software quality assurance and software quality control personnel.

For adaptive software project life cycles, the content of the evolving software product is the primary measure of progress. Iterations of the life cycle add increments to the evolving product. Newly added content, in combination with existing content, is tested and demonstrated at the end of the iterations. The demonstrations, in combination with the prioritized features in the product backlog (prioritized by business value), provide a measure of value-adding work that remains to be done. For adaptive life cycles, metrics such as stories developed (and tested) compared to stories remaining, meet the criteria of being simple to produce and relevant to the end goal.

Adaptive reporting tools such as cumulative flow diagrams, burnup/burndown graphs, and parking lot diagrams also provide valuable project information.

10.3.1 Control Communications: Inputs

The inputs in Section 10.3.1 of the *PMBOK® Guide* are applicable inputs for controlling software project communications. In addition, the inputs in 10.3.1.6 and 10.3.1.7 of this *Software Extension* are applicable for controlling software project communications.

10.3.1.1 Project Management Plan

See Section 10.3.1.1 of the *PMBOK® Guide*.

10.3.1.2 Project Communications

See Section 10.3.1.2 of the *PMBOK® Guide*.

10.3.1.3 Issue Log

See Section 10.3.1.3 of the *PMBOK® Guide*.

10.3.1.4 Work Performance Data

See Section 10.3.1.4 of the *PMBOK® Guide*.

10.3.1.5 Organizational Process Assets

See Section 10.3.1.5 of the *PMBOK® Guide*.

10.3.1.6 Prioritized Backlog

For adaptive software project life cycles, the prioritized product backlog plays a key role in controlling communications. It is the primary method used to communicate the agreed-upon work and the sequence of upcoming development. The backlog can be communicated using an online tool, a spreadsheet, or a stack of task cards.

10.3.1.7 Velocity Statistics and Projections

For adaptive life cycles, current velocity information and historical trends are used to determine the rate at which work was completed in previous iterations. This information is essential for estimating the amount of work that can be completed in subsequent iterations. Figure 10-5 illustrates a typical velocity chart for a software project.

10.3.2 Control Communications: Tools and Techniques

The tools and techniques in Section 10.3.2 of the *PMBOK® Guide* are applicable for managing software project communications. In addition, the tools and techniques in Sections 10.3.2.4 and 10.3.2.5 of this *Software Extension* are applicable to controlling software project communications.

10.3.2.1 Information Management Systems

See Section 10.3.2.1 of the *PMBOK® Guide*.

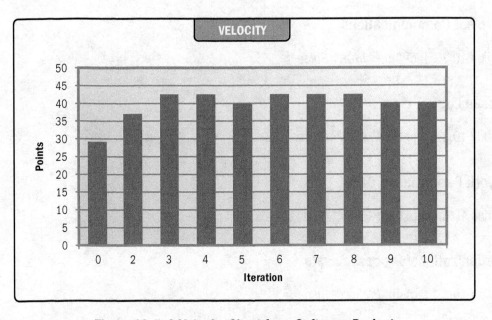

Figure 10-5. A Velocity Chart for a Software Project

10.3.2.2 Expert Judgment

See Section 10.3.2.2 of the *PMBOK® Guide*.

10.3.2.3 Meetings

See Section 10.3.2.3 of the *PMBOK® Guide*.

10.3.2.4 Considerate Communications

Software development requires concentrated thought in a quiet setting. It is often reported that it takes about 20 minutes to enter a productive state that can be disrupted by a phone call or a minute or two of conversation [37]. This presents a dilemma for software developers; on the one hand they need to get to a state of flow, but on the other hand, they need a colocated team environment with high bandwidth and face-to-face communications for resolving issues and obtaining rapid feedback.

When possible, one approach is to arrange a work area that includes quiet rooms for working and a common work area for discussing issues with team members. Another approach is the use of quiet hours that provide the quiet atmosphere of a library. During specified quiet hours, phones are disabled and no visitors or meetings are scheduled.

The use of electronic messaging may also be used to minimize the impact on concentration while still allowing communication. Regardless of the approach used, communications control should support the concentrated effort required for creative work.

10.3.2.5 Automated Systems

Systems that automatically collect project status can be used to improve communications efficiencies. These systems, often used to control communication in software projects, include Wiki sites, project websites, and collaboration-based internet or intranet sites.

10.3.3 Control Communications: Outputs

The outputs in Section 10.3.3 of the *PMBOK® Guide* are applicable for controlling software project communications. In addition, the outputs listed in Sections 10.3.3.6 and 10.3.3.7 of this *Software Extension* are also applicable.

10.3.3.1 Work Performance Information

See Section 10.3.3.1 of the *PMBOK® Guide*.

10.3.3.2 Change Requests

See Section 10.3.3.2 of the *PMBOK® Guide*.

10.3.3.3 Project Management Plan Updates

See Section 10.3.3.3 of the *PMBOK® Guide*.

10.3.3.4 Project Documents Updates

See Section 10.3.3.4 of the *PMBOK® Guide*.

10.3.3.5 Organizational Process Assets Updates

See Section 10.3.3.5 of the *PMBOK® Guide*.

10.3.3.6 Iteration and Release Plan Updates

An iteration plan confirms the project team's commitment to the work to be done and the software to be delivered at the end of the next iteration. A release plan describes when demonstrable, working software will be available (for demonstration or for release into the users' environment) and what features and functionality will be included. For adaptive life cycle software projects, it is important to distribute and explain updates to iteration and release plans because they may change frequently.

10.3.3.7 Reprioritized Backlog

When using adaptive life cycles for software projects, the customer has the opportunity to reprioritize the backlog of features to be developed throughout the project life cycle. The backlog of features to be developed implies the remaining work to be done and the current priorities. The backlog also shows the planned sequence of development and the schedule forecast, which can be developed using velocity averaged over recent iterative development cycles. The backlog of product features and remaining work, along with estimates of scheduled feature delivery, are important elements of project communication that help to control customer/user/product owner expectations and eliminate unpleasant surprises.

©2013 Project Management Institute. *Software Extension to the PMBOK® Guide Fifth Edition*

11

PROJECT RISK MANAGEMENT

Most of the material in Section 11 of the *PMBOK® Guide* is applicable to risk management for software projects. This section of the *Software Extension to the PMBOK® Guide* presents additional considerations for managing software project risk.

According to Section 11 of the *PMBOK® Guide*, Project Risk Management includes the processes of conducting risk management planning, identification, analysis, response planning, and controlling risk on a project. The objectives of Project Risk Management are to increase the probability and impact of positive events and decrease the probability and impact of negative events in the project. This section of the *Software Extension to the PMBOK® Guide* addresses risk management for software projects by describing risks and risk mitigation strategies that are important for managing software projects, and which merit attention beyond that provided in the *PMBOK® Guide*.

As defined in the Glossary to this *Software Extension*, risk is an uncertain event or condition that, if it occurs, has a positive or negative effect on a project's objectives. In ISO Guide 73:2009 – Risk Management: Vocabulary [40], risk is defined as the "combination of the probability of an event and its consequence." This widely used definition is applied in the principal software engineering standard for risk management: ISO/IEC/IEEE 16085 – Systems and software engineering—Life cycle processes—Risk management [41].

Each software development project has different uncertainties, risks, and opportunities because each software project is a unique combination of requirements, design, and construction, resulting in a distinct software product. Software project risks and software technical risks affect every stakeholder. Therefore, almost every one of the 47 processes in the *PMBOK® Guide* and this *Software Extension* is concerned with managing risks. Software risk management aims to improve the probability of achieving the project goals; software opportunity management aims to exceed the project goals. Opportunity management is commonly practiced in software project management, especially in adaptive projects that have the opportunity to rapidly respond to customer-requested changes, apply new technology, or accept additional resources. The risk management process is "a continuous process for systematically identifying, analyzing, treating, and monitoring risk throughout the life cycle of a product or service" [41].

Software project risk management and opportunity management for software projects includes planning, identifying, and analyzing software project risks and opportunities; performing software project qualitative and quantitative risk and opportunity analyses; planning risk and opportunity responses; and monitoring and controlling project risks and opportunities. Commonly occurring risks for software projects include technical, schedule, cost, quality (e.g., security, safety, availability), team dynamics, and customer/stakeholder risk factors. Risk treatments include accepting, avoiding, transferring, or mitigating risk. Mitigating risk can occur by either immediate action or tracking and deferred action, when warranted.

While this section primarily addresses software development project risk management, the techniques and approaches are also applicable to delivery of software as a service. In that case, the primary risk is a break in service continuity, that is, the inability to continually deliver services at agreed-upon levels.

Most of the material in Section 11 of the *PMBOK® Guide* is directly applicable to managing risk for predictive life cycle software projects; therefore, this section of the *Software Extension* focuses primarily on risk management for adaptive life cycle software projects.

Figure 11-1 provides an overview of Software Project Risk Management.

11.1 Plan Risk Management

The inputs, tools and techniques, and outputs for planning risk management in Section 11.1 of the *PMBOK® Guide* are applicable to planning risk management for software projects with the following additions and clarifications.

11.1.1 Plan Risk Management: Inputs

The inputs for planning risk management in Section 11.1.1 of the *PMBOK® Guide* are applicable inputs for planning software project risk management.

11.1.1.1 Project Management Plan

See Section 11.1.1.1 of the *PMBOK® Guide*.

11.1.1.2 Project Charter

See Section 11.1.1.2 of the *PMBOK® Guide*.

11.1.1.3 Stakeholder Register

See Section 11.1.1.3 of the *PMBOK® Guide*.

11.1.1.4 Enterprise Environmental Factors

See Section 11.1.1.4 of the *PMBOK® Guide*.

11.1.1.5 Organizational Process Assets

See Section 11.1.1.5 of the *PMBOK® Guide*.

The following considerations are also applicable. Software risk planning occurs repeatedly, beginning with an initial formal or informal risk-benefit analysis and a decision to initiate or not initiate the project. For large, formal software projects, projects in regulated environments, and projects involving safety-critical software, a documented risk management plan is essential. Most projects have less formal risk management procedures or follow an overall enterprise risk management plan. While all team members should be responsible for identifying

Project Risk Management Overview

11.1 Plan Risk Management

.1 Inputs
  .1 Project management plan
  .2 Project charter
  .3 Stakeholder register
  .4 Enterprise environmental factors
  .5 Organizational process assets

.2 Tools & Techniques
  .1 Analytical techniques
  .2 Expert judgment
  .3 Meetings
  .4 Additional considerations

.3 Outputs
  .1 Risk management plan

11.4 Perform Quantitative Risk Analysis

.1 Inputs
  .1 Risk management plan
  .2 Cost management plan
  .3 Schedule management plan
  .4 Risk register
  .5 Enterprise environmental factors
  .6 Organizational process assets

.2 Tools & Techniques
  .1 Data gathering and representation techniques
  .2 Quantitative risk analysis and modeling techniques
  .3 Expert judgment

.3 Outputs
  .1 Project documents updates

11.2 Identify Risks

.1 Inputs
  .1 Risk management plan
  .2 Cost management plan
  .3 Schedule management plan
  .4 Quality management plan
  .5 Human resource management plan
  .6 Scope baseline
  .7 Activity cost estimates
  .8 Activity duration estimates
  .9 Stakeholder register
  .10 Project documents
  .11 Procurement documents
  .12 Enterprise environmental factors
  .13 Organizational process assets
  .14 Risk taxonomies

.2 Tools & Techniques
  .1 Documentation reviews
  .2 Information gathering techniques
  .3 Checklist analysis
  .4 Assumptions analysis
  .5 Diagramming techniques
  .6 SWOT analysis
  .7 Expert judgment
  .8 Retrospective meetings

.3 Outputs
  .1 Risk register

11.5 Plan Risk Responses

.1 Inputs
  .1 Risk management plan
  .2 Risk register

.2 Tools & Techniques
  .1 Strategies for negative risks or threats
  .2 Strategies for positive risks or opportunities
  .3 Contingent response strategies
  .4 Expert judgment
  .5 Additional considerations

.3 Outputs
  .1 Project management plan updates
  .2 Project documents updates
  .3 Additional considerations

11.3 Perform Qualitative Risk Analysis

.1 Inputs
  .1 Risk management plan
  .2 Scope baseline
  .3 Risk register
  .4 Enterprise environmental factors
  .5 Organizational process assets

.2 Tools & Techniques
  .1 Risk probability and impact assessment
  .2 Probability and impact matrix
  .3 Risk data quality assessment
  .4 Risk categorization
  .5 Risk urgency assessment
  .6 Expert judgment
  .7 Additional considerations

.3 Outputs
  .1 Project documents updates

11.6 Control Risks

.1 Inputs
  .1 Project management plan
  .2 Risk register
  .3 Work performance data
  .4 Work performance reports

.2 Tools & Techniques
  .1 Risk reassessment
  .2 Risk audits
  .3 Variance and trend analysis
  .4 Technical performance measurement
  .5 Reserve analysis
  .6 Meetings

.3 Outputs
  .1 Work performance information
  .2 Change requests
  .3 Project management plan updates
  .4 Project documents updates
  .5 Organizational process assets updates

11

Figure 11-1. Software Project Risk Management Overview

and communicating risks, there should be a designated risk management leader. Specialized domain knowledge may make risks more apparent to some team members than to others.

Risk management planning is an element of project planning and is reflected in a software project plan at many levels, including risk management activities, data gathering, monitoring, decisions and assessments, and changes to work plans. Depending upon the nature of risks, the life cycle model and processes may be adjusted. Each of the assumptions and constraints used to develop the project plan should be examined for risk.

Projects can take a proactive risk-driven approach, prioritizing high-risk items and tackling them early in the project while there is time to try alternative approaches and to improve on initial efforts. Thus, risks relating to software requirements and architecture are typically handled earlier in the project life cycle. By proactively undertaking high-risk work early, the software project team can reduce the overall impact to the project. By deferring high-risk work, problems may result and the probability of rework or a revised approach is much higher while the time remaining to recover from problems is short. Simply put, it is more efficient and effective to resolve risks earlier than later.

11.1.2 Plan Risk Management: Tools and Techniques

The tools and techniques for planning risk management in Section 11.1.2 of the *PMBOK® Guide* are applicable tools and techniques for planning software project risk management with the additional considerations in Section 11.1.2.4 of this *Software Extension*.

11.1.2.1 Analytical Techniques

See Section 11.1.2.1 of the *PMBOK® Guide*.

11.1.2.2 Expert Judgment

See Section 11.1.2.2 of the *PMBOK® Guide*.

11.1.2.3 Meetings

See Section 11.1.2.3 of the *PMBOK® Guide*.

11.1.2.4 Additional Considerations

Adaptive life cycle software projects pull requirements and user stories from a backlog that may undergo frequent reprioritization; this permits risk management actions as early as possible in the project life cycle, minimizing delayed and compounded effects. Also, since integration and regression testing is built into each iterative cycle, the probability of untested high-risk elements in the product towards the end of the project is greatly reduced. All software project managers and teams, regardless of life cycle, can choose to address high-risk activities first. However, adaptive projects have additional flexibility for risk management because the software project team can pull high-risk stories and features forward from the backlog.

Adaptive life cycle projects allow for frequent reassessment of risks and reprioritization at the end of each iteration, which can take advantage of newly identified opportunities to add features or take action to mitigate newly identified risks. The project team can add risk avoidance and risk reduction actions into the backlog and choose to proactively attack the risks before they have an impact on the project. The team should think of risk avoidance and risk mitigation as part of the value proposition for the adaptive planning cycle.

11.1.3 Plan Risk Management: Outputs

The output for planning risk management in Section 11.1.3 of the *PMBOK® Guide* is an applicable output for planning software project risk management, with the following extensions.

11.1.3.1 Risk Management Plan

See Section 11.1.3.1 of the *PMBOK® Guide*.

In addition, when planning for the next iteration of an adaptive life cycle, the project team typically balances delivering business value with risk reduction. Sometimes the team may select a next feature to be implemented that has the best return on investment. Sometimes they will undertake an action to avoid or mitigate risk since the impact of the risk occurring would be greater than the ROI value of the next feature in the product feature set, as depicted in Figure 11-2.

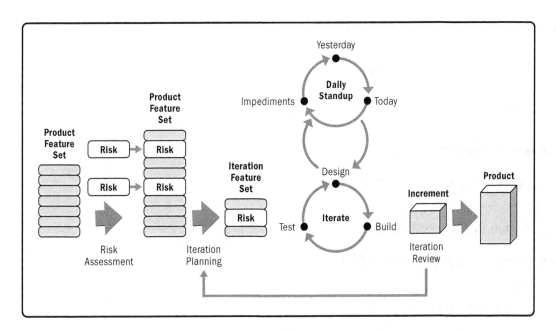

Figure 11-2. Business and Risk Reduction Activities Prioritized in the Product Feature Set

The software project manager needs to ensure that risk management procedures, frequency of reporting cycles, and a risk register are established at the beginning of the project. The risk register can be as simple as a spreadsheet or whiteboard with annotated note cards or stories attached. For large projects and critical software products, specialized software tools aid in managing the outputs from planning risk management.

11.2 Identify Risks

The inputs, tools and techniques, and outputs for identifying risks in Section 11.2 of the *PMBOK® Guide* are applicable for identifying risks for software projects.

11.2.1 Identify Risks: Inputs

The inputs for identifying project risk in Section 11.2.1 of the *PMBOK® Guide* are applicable for identifying software project risks with the additional considerations in Section 11.2.1.14 in this *Software Extension*.

11.2.1.1 Risk Management Plan

See Section 11.2.1.1 of the *PMBOK® Guide*.

11.2.1.2 Cost Management Plan

See Section 11.2.1.2 of the *PMBOK® Guide*.

11.2.1.3 Schedule Management Plan

See Section 11.2.1.3 of the *PMBOK® Guide*.

11.2.1.4 Quality Management Plan

See Section 11.2.1.4 of the *PMBOK® Guide*.

11.2.1.5 Human Resource Management Plan

See Section 11.2.1.5 of the *PMBOK® Guide*.

11.2.1.6 Scope Baseline

See Section 11.2.1.6 of the *PMBOK® Guide*.

11.2.1.7 Activity Cost Estimates

See Section 11.2.1.7 of the *PMBOK® Guide.*

11.2.1.8 Activity Duration Estimates

See Section 11.2.1.8 of the *PMBOK® Guide.*

11.2.1.9 Stakeholder Register

See Section 11.2.1.9 of the *PMBOK® Guide.*

11.2.1.10 Project Documents

See Section 11.2.1.10 of the *PMBOK® Guide.*

11.2.1.11 Procurement Documents

See Section 11.2.1.11 of the *PMBOK® Guide.*

11.2.1.12 Enterprise Environmental Factors

See Section 11.2.1.12 of the *PMBOK® Guide.*

11.2.1.13 Organizational Process Assets

See Section 11.2.1.13 of the *PMBOK® Guide.*

11.2.1.14 Risk Taxonomies

While every software project manager and team needs to identify risk factors, it is helpful to be aware of the more common types of risks for software projects. The Software Engineering Institute (SEI) has published several three-level risk taxonomies, notably for operational risk and development project risk. These taxonomies break down risks by class, for example, program constraints, product engineering, and development environment; then by element, such as requirements within product engineering; and then by attribute, such as stability or formality of requirements. Table 11-1 is a simple first-level risk breakdown structure, with examples of common software project risks.

Table 11-1 First-Level Risk Breakdown

Project Risk	Description
Technical	Software does not work as required: excessive defects; software does not scale to capacity or performance requirements; undefined or misunderstood requirements; late integration of software modules reveals errors during late testing; software does not fulfill customer expectations and needs; software is not easily usable by end users; excessive rework or refactoring due to unstable requirements, requirements inflation, or changes in scenarios; choice of new development platforms, languages, or tools with limited staff availability, software becomes corrupted due to inadequate configuration management of baseline, development work, and test versions; technology changes and upgrades during the project; external dependency on another project's ability to deliver usable, timely input.
Safety	Developed system has defects that can cause injury, death, or environmental destruction.
Security	Developed system integrity inconsistent with required software criticality (likelihood of severe consequences from malfunction); developers unfamiliar with probable security threats to the software; inadequate system design for access control, protection of personal or proprietary data at rest and in transit, and defense of system against malware and hacking; reuse of code with undetermined pedigree; disaster or security breach affects the development or production infrastructure.
Team	Inexperienced in the tools, organizational processes, development method, or customer business requirements; understaffed (staff not yet on board or pulled for other projects); staff burnout; staff turnover; communication and coordination issues within the team or with stakeholders due to dispersed or virtual team or cultural differences; new staff pulling attention of experienced staff; multiple developers working on the same code branch.
Schedule	Baseline schedule is inconsistent with actual velocity; project won't finish essential or required features on time for scheduled release; scope creep impacts completion of original goals; delays in development lead to pressure to abbreviate testing; project completion measurements are not reflective of effective status (replying on SLOC or percent complete estimates); plans don't address initial architecture and data design or documentation or integration testing; test schedule allows time for only one run, ignoring the probability of retest.
Costs	Inaccurate estimates of labor rates and productivity/velocity, actual costs beyond available funding, unable to meet affordability challenge.
Customer and Stakeholders	Unavailability of business process data, unavailability of technical data on systems being replaced or interfaced, unavailability of acceptance criteria (or market needs analysis), unavailability of customer or user representatives for requirements/feature prioritization, user testing, and system acceptance.

11.2.2 Identify Risks: Tools and Techniques

The tools and techniques in Section 11.2.2 of the *PMBOK® Guide* for identifying risks are applicable to identifying risks for software projects, with the following additions and clarifications.

11.2.2.1 Documentation Reviews

See Section 11.2.2.1 of the *PMBOK® Guide*.

11.2.2.2 Information Gathering Techniques

See Section 11.2.2.2 of the *PMBOK® Guide*.

11.2.2.3 Checklist Analysis

See Section 11.2.2.3 of the *PMBOK® Guide*.

11.2.2.4 Assumptions Analysis

See Section 11.2.2.4 of the *PMBOK® Guide*.

11.2.2.5 Diagramming Techniques

See Section 11.2.2.5 of the *PMBOK® Guide*.

11.2.2.6 SWOT Analysis

See Section 11.2.2.6 of the *PMBOK® Guide*.

11.2.2.7 Expert Judgment

See Section 11.2.2.7 of the *PMBOK® Guide*.

11.2.2.8 Retrospective Meetings

During retrospective meetings, project teams evaluate the evolving system, review areas that may be lagging behind, and discuss areas with problems and concerns regarding the remaining work to be done. In doing so, project risks may be identified.

11.2.3 Identify Risks: Outputs

The risk register output in Section 11.2.3.1 of the *PMBOK® Guide* is an applicable output for identifying risks for software projects.

11.2.3.1 Risk Register

See Section 11.2.3.1 of the *PMBOK® Guide*.

11.3 Perform Qualitative Risk Analysis

The inputs, tools and techniques, and outputs in Section 11.3 of the *PMBOK® Guide* for performing qualitative risk analysis are applicable to performing qualitative risk analysis for software projects, with the following additions and clarifications.

It is human nature to focus on the more immediate risks, but advanced risk management is used to also identify and control the longer-term risks. Software product development needs to be sustainable, from various viewpoints: financial, team continuity, the software design framework, and the quality of code for future changes. Risk analysis should also look for immediate and sustained opportunities.

11.3.1 Perform Qualitative Risk Analysis: Inputs

The inputs for performing qualitative risk analysis in Section 11.3.1 of the *PMBOK® Guide* are applicable to performing qualitative risk analysis for software projects with the following additional considerations.

Additional inputs for performing qualitative risk analysis for software projects include: (a) criticality of the software product (its impact on its users and the operational environment), (b) the effect should a risk interfere with the completion and successful delivery of the software product, and (c) the overall effect on the producing organization (that is, a "bet the company" project or an optional enhancement to a mature product).

11.3.1.1 Risk Management Plan

See Section 11.3.1.1 of the *PMBOK® Guide*.

11.3.1.2 Scope Baseline

See Section 11.3.1.2 of the *PMBOK® Guide*.

11.3.1.3 Risk Register

See Section 11.3.1.3 of the *PMBOK® Guide*.

11.3.1.4 Enterprise Environmental Factors

See Section 11.3.1.4 of the *PMBOK® Guide*.

11.3.1.5 Organizational Process Assets

See Section 11.3.1.5 of the *PMBOK® Guide*.

11.3.2 Perform Qualitative Risk Analysis: Tools and Techniques

The tools and techniques for performing qualitative risk analysis in Section 11.3.2 of the *PMBOK® Guide* are applicable to performing qualitative risk analysis for software projects with the additional considerations in Section 11.3.2.7 of this *Software Extension*.

11.3.2.1 Risk Probability and Impact Assessment

See Section 11.3.2.1 of the *PMBOK® Guide*.

11.3.2.2 Probability and Impact Matrix

See Section 11.3.2.2 of the *PMBOK® Guide*.

11.3.2.3 Risk Data Quality Assessment

See Section 11.3.2.3 of the *PMBOK® Guide*.

11.3.2.4 Risk Categorization

See Section 11.3.2.4 of the *PMBOK® Guide*.

11.3.2.5 Risk Urgency Assessment

See Section 11.3.2.5 of the *PMBOK® Guide*.

11.3.2.6 Expert Judgment

See Section 11.3.2.6 of the *PMBOK® Guide*.

11.3.2.7 Additional Considerations

The following considerations also apply. Qualitative analyses of risk are, by definition, difficult or impossible to quantify and are usually based on subjective and limited experience. Accurately estimating the quantitative probability of a risk requires a statistically significant experience base of similar projects (similar in complexity, criticality, infrastructure and tools, team experience, and organizational process resources). In practice, only very large organizations are able to accumulate experience bases and, for competitive reasons, are reluctant to share it with external stakeholders and other organizations. Often, experience concerning the rate of work completion (i.e., velocity) is not available until the project is well underway when there is less time to exert corrective measures.

Additional causal analysis (e.g. asking "why" repeatedly) can help identify root causes of identified risks. Qualitative risk analysis benefits from recent experience (e.g., for similar infrastructure and team members accustomed to working together). The analysis may be distorted by the impact of recent work (i.e., the tendency to emphasize the most recent experience rather than the long-term average). A risk that became a problem on a previous project may be considered likely to occur in the next project unless corrective action has been taken to reduce the probability of occurrence or impact if it should occur; the problems encountered in previous projects may be considered to be thoroughly nullified by lessons learned and mitigations applied, so that the probability of recurrence is considered to be minimal. However, the precautionary mitigations may impose extraordinary costs in monitoring and control, such as increasing testing, scheduling a large number of project reviews and executive presentations, and imposing heavy documentation requirements, which in themselves create the risk of excessive cost and noncompetitive business processes.

Qualitative ratings of risks for software projects can be based on subjective values such as low, medium, high, or very high for both probability and potential impact, as illustrated in Table 11-2. A low-risk exposure might correspond to a small schedule delay or cost overrun or a minor quality issue; a medium value to a more significant value of a project or product parameter, a high value to a major issue; and a very high value to a potentially catastrophic situation.

For adaptive life cycle projects, a risk exposure matrix can be used to prioritize features for inclusion in the next iterative cycle by focusing on the features that will have the largest risk/return value for the business or the end users, as illustrated in Figure 11-2. This is similar to opportunity analysis, stated in risk management terms.

11.3.3 Perform Qualitative Risk Analysis: Outputs

The output for performing qualitative risk analysis in Section 11.3.3 of the *PMBOK® Guide* is applicable to performing qualitative risk analysis for software projects.

11.3.3.1 Project Documents Updates

See Section 11.3.3.1 of the *PMBOK® Guide*.

Table 11-2. A Typical Qualitative Risk Exposure Matrix

Impact Probability	Low	Medium	High	Very High
Low	Low	Medium	High	Medium
Medium	Low	High	High	High
High	Medium	High	Very High	Very High
Very High	Medium	High	Very High	Extreme

11.4 Perform Quantitative Risk Analysis

The inputs, tools and techniques, and outputs for performing quantitative risk analysis in Section 11.4 of the *PMBOK® Guide* are applicable to performing quantitative risk analysis for software projects.

Quantitative techniques are often used on major software projects, such as competitive software acquisitions or enterprise initiatives. The time and expertise required for extensive quantitative risk analysis may not be justified for simpler projects.

Quantitative analysis may be used to prioritize (a) unmitigated risks in the product backlog, and (b) risk avoidance and risk mitigation activities. A software project technical risk has a cost impact, and a risk mitigation or risk transfer option has a quantifiable cost, such as the cost of procuring software in comparison to the labor cost of building the software—these can be translated into monetary units. Similarly, human resource and business risks can be estimated in monetary terms. Of course, not all risks have avoidance or mitigation steps that can be scheduled into a software project. Some risks may have to be accepted (e.g., the project is delayed while waiting for a procured component), but those risks that can be proactively addressed can be prioritized in the adaptive project's backlog.

Quantitative risk analysis has several practical limitations. It is not possible to estimate the probability and impact of all potential problems (risks). For example, consider the risk of developing software that makes it easy for hackers to access private user data. There is no cost until after the project is ended when the software is being used in the operational environment. At that time, a security breach could result in fines, legal fees, and remediation costs to the users for credit monitoring, litigation costs, and loss of future business. The expenses are potentially large and serious, but not easily quantified at the time of risk analysis during software development.

For software projects, risk identification and risk analysis attempt to focus on the most probable and highest-impact risks rather than the cumulative impact of a succession of minor risks. Also, the impact of some risks may be hard to quantify as far as direct costs to the project or organization. The precision of the monetary value may not be great, but the point of quantitative risk analysis for software projects is usually to take action based on relative scorings rather than precise numbers. The goal is to reach consensus with the software project stakeholders on justifiable numbers to use as a basis for prioritization, not to report costs on a balance sheet.

The objectivity and relevance of a quantitative risk analysis ultimately depends on qualitative judgment, the availability of an experience base, and the objectivity of the experts estimating the best, most likely and worst-case points.

11.4.1 Perform Quantitative Risk Analysis: Inputs

The inputs in Section 11.4.1 of the *PMBOK® Guide* for performing quantitative risk analysis are applicable to performing quantitative risk analysis for software projects.

11.4.1.1 Risk Management Plan

See Section 11.4.1.1 of the *PMBOK® Guide*.

11.4.1.2 Cost Management Plan

See Section 11.4.1.2 of the *PMBOK® Guide*.

11.4.1.3 Schedule Management Plan

See Section 11.4.1.3 of the *PMBOK® Guide*.

11.4.1.4 Risk Register

See Section 11.4.1.4 of the *PMBOK® Guide*.

11.4.1.5 Enterprise Environmental Factors

See Section 11.4.1.5 of the *PMBOK® Guide*.

11.4.1.6 Organizational Process Assets

See Section 11.4.1.6 of the *PMBOK® Guide*.

11.4.2 Perform Quantitative Risk Analysis: Tools and Techniques

The tools and techniques in Section 11.4.2 of the *PMBOK® Guide* for performing quantitative risk analysis are applicable to performing quantitative risk analysis for software projects with the following extensions to Data Gathering and Representation Techniques (11.4.2.1) and Quantitative Risk Analysis and Modeling Techniques (11.4.2.2).

11.4.2.1 Data Gathering and Representation Techniques

See Section 11.4.2.1 of the *PMBOK® Guide*.

In addition, quantitative ratings of risk exposure can be based on numeric values, as illustrated in Table 11-3. The entries in Table 11-3 are the products of the corresponding values of probability and normalized impacts; this

Table 11-3. A Typical Quantitative Risk Exposure Matrix

Impact	25	50	75	100
Probability				
0.25	6.25	12.5	18.75	25
0.5	12.5	25	37.5	50
0.75	18.75	37.5	56.25	75
0.95	23.75	47.5	71.25	95

product is called the risk exposure. A project manager or assigned risk manager may assign both an unmitigated risk exposure and a mitigated risk exposure, along with the cost of risk mitigation. Risk leverage factors (the difference between unmitigated and mitigated risk exposures divided by the cost of risk mitigation) can be used to evaluate the effectiveness of various risk reduction strategies. See also Figure 11-11 in the *PMBOK® Guide*.

Risk exposure (probability × impact) can be used to calculate monetary value as follows:

Risk expected monetary value = Risk probability (0.0 – 1.0) × Risk impact (in monetary units)

A software project thus has a quantitative value (cost or benefit) for each risk mitigation activity in comparison to the cost and value of new work. For example, assume there is a risk of having an inadequate reporting tool in place (assume $0 future cost for the existing tool), which could be completely mitigated by buying and using a high-performance reporting engine that costs $10,000 to buy, implement, and run. If the project estimates that there is a 50% chance of needing this tool, then the evaluated cost (or economic value) of purchasing the new tool is $5,000 (0.5 × $10,000).

On the other hand, even though the existing tool has a zero cost for use, suppose that the cost of staff time over the same period to collect and analyze data and compile reports is estimated to be $25,000 and, based on experience, there is again a 50% chance that reports will not be usable or ready on time. The cost of continuing with the existing tool is $12,500; therefore, purchasing the new tool is the better value.

Using this approach, a software project manager can rank project risks to produce a prioritized list of risks ordered by expected monetary value, which can be used to prioritize the value of requirements in terms of risk. These activities support meaningful discussions with the software project sponsors. In Figure 11-3, the second

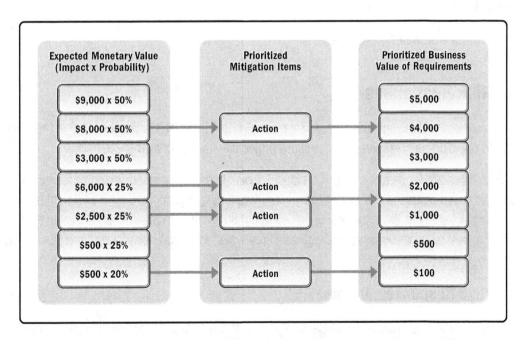

Figure 11-3. Comparative Priorities of Risk Treatment and Business Value

risk from the top has an expected monetary value of 0.5 × $8000 or $4000. Therefore, when it comes to selecting requirements (features) for an upcoming iteration, the risk mitigation action associated with risk #2 ranks similar to the functional requirements value for risk #2. In other words, this risk mitigation work is of equal value to the organization as the addition of a new software feature.

11.4.2.2 Quantitative Risk Analysis and Modeling Techniques

See Section 11.4.2.2 of the *PMBOK® Guide*.

The following consideration also applies. Quantitative simulations may identify the need for more extensive risk mitigation, and for applying schedule and budget contingency reserves. Monte Carlo simulations can be used to compute project outcomes at various levels of probability and to indicate the probability of obtaining the "most likely" estimate (see Figures 11-14 and 11-18 of the *PMBOK® Guide*).

11.4.2.3 Expert Judgment

See Section 11.4.2.3 of the *PMBOK® Guide*. See also Section 11.3.2.6 of this *Software Extension*.

11.4.3 Perform Quantitative Risk Analysis: Outputs

The output in Section 11.4.3 of the *PMBOK® Guide* for performing quantitative risk analysis is an applicable output from performing quantitative risk analysis for software projects.

11.4.3.1 Project Documents Updates

See Section 11.4.3.1 of the *PMBOK® Guide*.

11.5 Plan Risk Responses

The inputs, tools and techniques, and outputs for planning risk responses in Section 11.5 of the *PMBOK® Guide* are applicable to planning risk responses for software projects, with the following extensions.

Planning risk responses for software projects includes evaluating risk treatment alternatives and selecting them. A project manager can evaluate the risk exposure of an untreated risk, the exposure after treatment (the *residual risk*), and the cost of the risk treatment. When the cost of the risk treatment is high compared to the impact of the risk, accepting the risk may be the best response. Accepted risks remain on a watch list or in a risk register for ongoing monitoring.

11.5.1 Plan Risk Responses: Inputs

The inputs for planning risk responses in Section 11.5.1 of the *PMBOK® Guide* are applicable to planning risk responses for software projects.

11.5.1.1 Risk Management Plan

See Section 11.5.1.1 of the *PMBOK® Guide*.

11.5.1.2 Risk Register

See Section 11.5.1.2 of the *PMBOK® Guide*.

11.5.2 Plan Risk Responses: Tools and Techniques

The tools and techniques for planning risk responses in Section 11.5.2 of the *PMBOK® Guide* are applicable for software projects with the additional considerations in Section 11.5.2.5 of this *Software Extension*.

11.5.2.1 Strategies for Negative Risks or Threats

See Section 11.5.2.1 of the *PMBOK® Guide*.

11.5.2.2 Strategies for Positive Risks or Opportunities

See Section 11.5.2.2 of the *PMBOK® Guide*.

11.5.2.3 Contingent Response Strategies

See Section 11.5.2.3 of the *PMBOK® Guide*.

11.5.2.4 Expert Judgment

See Section 11.5.2.4 of the *PMBOK® Guide*.

11.5.2.5 Additional Considerations

In addition to the tools and techniques for planning risk responses in Section 11.5.2 of the *PMBOK® Guide*, risk-based testing assesses the probability of elements of the software being defective and the consequences of those defects. Where the probability and consequence are high, that element is tested more extensively. Where the probability and consequence are low, that element is either tested less extensively or not tested at all. This allows the limited testing resources to be focused on providing the highest benefit.

Risk leverage factors (RLF) may be calculated for various risks as an aid to planning software project risk responses by calculating the risk exposure of an untreated risk (RE_{ut} = probability × impact), risk exposure after treatment (RE_{at} = residual probability × impact) and including the cost of the risk treatment, RT_c, where all three factors are expressed in monetary terms:

$$RLF = [RE_{ut} - RE_{at}]/RT_c$$

Risk leverage factors for identified risks can be used to prioritize the application of limited risk treatment funds. Higher values of RLF indicate higher cost-return benefits.

11.5.3 Plan Risk Responses: Outputs

The outputs for planning risk responses in Section 11.5.3 of the *PMBOK® Guide* are applicable for software projects with the additional considerations in Section 11.5.3.3 of this *Software Extension*.

11.5.3.1 Project Management Plan Updates

See Section 11.5.3.1 of the *PMBOK® Guide*.

11.5.3.2 Project Documents Updates

See Section 11.5.3.2 of the *PMBOK® Guide*.

11.5.3.3 Additional Considerations

The following considerations also apply. Aside from acceptance and immediate response for quickly remedied risks, risk responses to avoid, transfer, or mitigate risk may require detailed planning to execute. The summary of risks maintained in the risk register should include the specific risk treatment planned, the monitoring schedule, threshold values that will trigger a risk response, who is responsible, affected stakeholders, cost and schedule for the risk treatment, and measures to evaluate the progress and effectiveness of the risk treatment. The impact of the risk treatment should also be noted; the risk treatment may itself introduce secondary risks, safety concerns, or environmental impacts.

Table 11-4 contains typical risk responses used to avoid, mitigate, or transfer risk for software projects. No special approaches need to be stated for accepting risk; often the risk is accepted until a more cost-effective way to mitigate or transfer the risk is identified.

Table 11-4 Typical Risk Responses for Software Projects

Project Risk	Description
Technical	*Avoid Risk:* Use proven development platform and language. Change the requirements. *Transfer:* Use commercially available tools and modules or reuse existing software modules rather than creating new designs (buy rather than build). *Mitigate:* Engage the constant involvement of customers and developers. Work in short iterations so that risk can be identified early and development for risk mitigation has time to make an impact. Train the team on new development methods; obtain project sponsor commitment to the changes. Conduct regression testing for changes to critical software that may impact downstream modules or overall performance.
Security	*Avoid Risk:* While there is no way to avoid all security risks and threats, use secure coding and access control techniques, and accredited architectures, follow security standards. *Transfer:* Obtain software kits and tools from recognized sources with a commitment to remediate security vulnerabilities. Recognized sources include the open source community as well as proprietary commercial software vendors. *Mitigate:* Train developers in secure coding. Engage intrusion detection and independent software penetration testers for software certificate.
Team	*Avoid Risk:* Use a dedicated, experienced manager and teams, and established organizational processes. *Transfer:* Use collaborative processes so there is no single point of failure; engage recruiting or contract labor providers to offer backup or surge staff. (Note that adding staff late in a project often slows the project further while the new staff come up to speed.) *Mitigate:* Balance staff between more expensive senior staff and less costly junior resources with coaching and training. Improve team communication methods to avoid duplicative work or rework.
Schedule	*Avoid Risk:* Review baseline schedule for accuracy in proportionate allocation of time to activities, resource loading and critical path. Allow time for planning and design before beginning large-scale development. *Transfer:* Involve customers in change control decisions at project checkpoints or sprint priorities and content. Get the team involved in planning and estimating. *Mitigate:* Start critical and higher-risk activities early in the schedule to allow time to prototype, test, iterate, integrate, and retest. Build reserve into the schedule. Get early feedback on variance from schedule and adjust iterative plans.
Costs	*Avoid Risk:* Estimate by function points completed and tested, rather than by SLOC or percent complete estimates. Use multiple cost-estimating techniques. *Transfer:* Offer change proposals to include the customer in the cost of unexpected issues or the benefit of cost-saving opportunities. *Mitigate:* Shift resources from less critical activities or de-scope lower priorities.
Customer and Stakeholders	*Avoid Risk:* Develop a project charter, contract, or work agreement to clarify roles and expected customer responsibilities. *Transfer:* Designate a customer representative to represent the voice of the user with multiple sponsoring organizations. *Mitigate:* Specify contingencies and assumptions in the absence of customer data. Conduct walkthroughs and prototypes to build customer acceptance.

11

11.6 Control Risks

The inputs, tools and techniques, and outputs for controlling risks in Section 11.6 of the *PMBOK® Guide* are applicable to controlling risks for software projects with the following additions and extensions.

Risk monitoring and control for software projects includes tracking identified risks, monitoring residual risks, executing risk treatment plans, and evaluating their effectiveness. On small software projects, monitoring and controlling risks are part of the project manager's duties. On large programs, another individual, often a quality assurance or planning specialist, is designated as the risk manager and is delegated the responsibility for recording new risks in the risk register and, in consultation with the project manager, ensures that risk mitigations are being implemented and completed by agreed-upon completion dates.

11.6.1 Control Risks: Inputs

The software project manager (or risk manager) typically schedules regular reviews of the impacts and probabilities of identified risks until those risks are closed out. Risk managers also capture experience data and lessons learned for use in future phases and other projects.

Organizations vary in their tolerance of risk. The *risk threshold* is the point at which the probability of a risk becomes large enough that it can no longer be accepted and needs further treatment. To determine when the risk threshold is reached, software projects use indicators such as technical performance measures (TPM) or more selectively, key performance indicators (KPI), which show how successfully a risk is being managed. For example, when the churn in requirements exceeds a defined percentage, or the number of defects per thousand lines of code (KLOC) discovered during testing passes a defined level, or the cost or schedule performance index (CPI or SPI) exceeds a prespecified limit, a risk threshold has been reached. This condition is called a *risk trigger* for the risk manager to initiate a contingency plan for risk treatment.

The inputs for controlling risks in Section 11.6.1 of the *PMBOK® Guide* are applicable to controlling risks for software projects, with the following addition to 11.6.1.4.

11.6.1.1 Project Management Plan

See Section 11.6.1.1 of the *PMBOK® Guide*.

11.6.1.2 Risk Register

See Section 11.6.1.2 of the *PMBOK® Guide*.

11.6.1.3 Work Performance Data

See Section 11.6.1.3 of the *PMBOK® Guide*.

11.6.1.4 Work Performance Reports

See Section 11.6.1.4 of the *PMBOK® Guide*.

In addition to the reports identified in Section 11.6.1.4 of the *PMBOK® Guide*, test reports are valuable for controlling project risks. Test results associated with defective code can be analyzed to expose design flaws and determine whether mitigating action is necessary.

11.6.2 Control Risks: Tools and Techniques

The tools and techniques for controlling risks in Section 11.6.2 of the *PMBOK® Guide* are applicable to controlling risks for software projects, with the following clarifications and additions.

11.6.2.1 Risk Reassessment

See Section 11.6.2.1 of the *PMBOK® Guide*.

11.6.2.2 Risk Audits

See Section 11.6.2.2 of the *PMBOK® Guide*.

11.6.2.3 Variance and Trend Analysis

See Section 11.6.2.3 of the *PMBOK® Guide*.

11.6.2.4 Technical Performance Measurement

See Section 11.6.2.4 of the *PMBOK® Guide*.

11.6.2.5 Reserve Analysis

See Section 11.6.2.5 of the *PMBOK® Guide*.

11.6.2.6 Meetings

See Section 11.6.2.6 of the *PMBOK® Guide*.

The following considerations also apply. Adaptive life cycle software projects incorporate many mechanisms for dealing with change (an easily reprioritized backlog, short iterations, daily stand-up meetings, frequent demonstrations of working, deliverable software, and retrospective meetings) that also lend themselves to proactive response to risks as follows:

- **Daily stand-up meetings.** From a risk management perspective, the purpose of daily stand-up meetings is for the team to identify new risks, issues, and signs of potential trouble, which if left unchecked could become real threats to the project. Daily stand-up meetings also overcome the risk that team members will not prioritize their time productively or will be unable to solve technical issues without coordination with other team members.

  Asking whether there are any issues or impediments blocking progress can surface new project risks for the development team because today's issues could become tomorrow's risks and problems. So it is important to pay attention to the issues being raised and enter any appropriate issues to the risk register and undertake the necessary risk assessment steps. Also, when the team reports "impediments to progress" at the daily stand-up meetings, these may be candidates for potential problems (i.e., risks), so the risk management plan should account for the iterative nature of review and identification of risks.

- **Retrospective meetings.** Retrospective meetings that regularly review the project for work that went well in addition to work that did not go well are good vehicles for identifying risk for a software project.

  Over the course of a project, adaptive software development teams use tools such as risk burndown graphs and risk profiles to illustrate the effectiveness of the risk-driven approach. The goal is to rapidly reduce risks on the project. During a retrospective meeting immediately following an iterative cycle, a team may close out risks that have been eliminated and reevaluate the likelihood of risks occurring or recurring during the next period.

- **Software prototype feedback.** Prototype evaluations reveal stakeholder concerns with the proposed solution, which can result in technical and schedule risks. Addressing the concerns will likely require updates to the release and iteration plans and reprioritization of risk mitigations.

- **Training.** Adaptive life cycles provide some techniques for good risk management but they do not insulate software projects from risks. Indeed, if an adaptive approach is new to an organization, then its introduction will be a risk; anything new represents a risk of misapplication, misunderstanding, confusion, and failure. Having an active project sponsor and informed stakeholder involvement; selecting a project manager, team leaders, and team members with experience using the adaptive approach; and scheduling time for team training are common techniques to overcome the risk of introducing new methods and processes.

11.6.3 Control Risks: Outputs

The outputs for controlling risks in Section 11.6.3 of the *PMBOK® Guide* are applicable outputs for controlling risks of software projects, with the following extension in Section 11.6.3.4 of this extension.

11.6.3.1 Work Performance Information

See Section 11.6.3.1 of the *PMBOK® Guide*.

11.6.3.2 Change Requests

See Section 11.6.3.2 of the *PMBOK® Guide*.

11.6.3.3 Project Management Plan Updates

See Section 11.6.3.3 of the *PMBOK® Guide*.

11.6.3.4 Project Documents Updates

See Section 11.6.3.4 of the *PMBOK® Guide*.

In addition, risk burndown charts, similar to progress burndown charts, can be used to track the number of risks identified, treated, and closed out; they can be displayed as visual charts for the project team. Information in a risk register can be summarized in a *risk profile.* According to ISO/IEC/IEEE Standard 16085 [41], the project risk profile includes the risk management context, a record of each risk's current and historical state and priority, and all of the risk action requests. The risk action state includes the probability, consequences, and risk threshold for the risk.

11

11.6.3.5 Organizational Process Assets Updates

See Section 11.6.3.5 of the *PMBOK® Guide*.

12

PROJECT PROCUREMENT MANAGEMENT

Most of the material in Section 12 of the *PMBOK® Guide* is applicable to procurement management for software projects. This section of the *Software Extension to the PMBOK® Guide* presents additional considerations for managing software project procurements.

The introduction to Section 12 of the *PMBOK® Guide* states: "Project Procurement Management includes the processes necessary to purchase or acquire products, services, or results needed from outside the project team. The organization can be either the buyer or seller of the products, services, or results of a project."

Large software organizations, like other engineering organizations, typically have a procurement department that deals with contracting issues related to the procurement of products and services. Small software organizations may not have a similar support function and, as a result, the software project manager may play an increased role in managing software project procurements.

Also, as indicated in the introductory paragraph of Section 12 of the *PMBOK® Guide*, an organization may be the seller of the products, services, or results of a project. In some cases, a software organization may be a prime contractor or a subcontractor (seller) to another organization or governmental agency. In these cases, some or all of the processes to be followed and the metrics to be reported by the software project manager may be elements of the statement of work for the project.

This section of the *Software Extension to the PMBOK® Guide* focuses on the considerations involved in procuring services for a software project or new software products, such as a procuring a custom-built software application or turnkey infrastructure. It addresses planning, conducting, controlling, and closing out software project procurements, primarily from the point of view of the acquiring software project manager. It also addresses the acquisition of commercially off-the-shelf software (COTS) for use in a software product. Licensing of software packages, obtaining rights to modify open source software, reuse of existing components, and the purchase of specialty services to build software are all elements of software procurement.

Services provided by software may also be procured. It is important to understand the exact nature of the services provided by the software; how they might evolve over time; and what control the acquirer retains over the data provided to be processed by the service, the results obtained, and any security obligations. These considerations are usually covered in a service level agreement (SLA). Often, the standard agreement issued by the provider may not meet the acquirer's (i.e., the software project's) specific needs.

Other procured services can include outsourcing of software development, assistance from software consultants and experts in software development processes, staff augmentation by contracted developers and testers, and provision of supporting services such as data migration and conversion, SQA, CM, and product documentation.

Because software requires frequent updates to meet changes in functional requirements, to address security threats, or provide infrastructure upgrades, it is rarely purchased without provision for ongoing maintenance. In some cases, the

12

software acquirer will obtain a license with specific terms and conditions that prevent access to the software source code; in these cases the acquirer will pay a fee for upgrades. When there is no initial purchase price, as with freeware or open source software, adaptation costs and the costs of versioning and maintenance are procurement considerations.

This section does not address the specialized work of procurement agents such as contract administrators and software buyers, nor does it address the legal and regulatory particulars of contracts and agreements for software, documentation, and other intellectual property, which vary from country to country. Figure 12-1 provides an overview of Software Project Procurement Management.

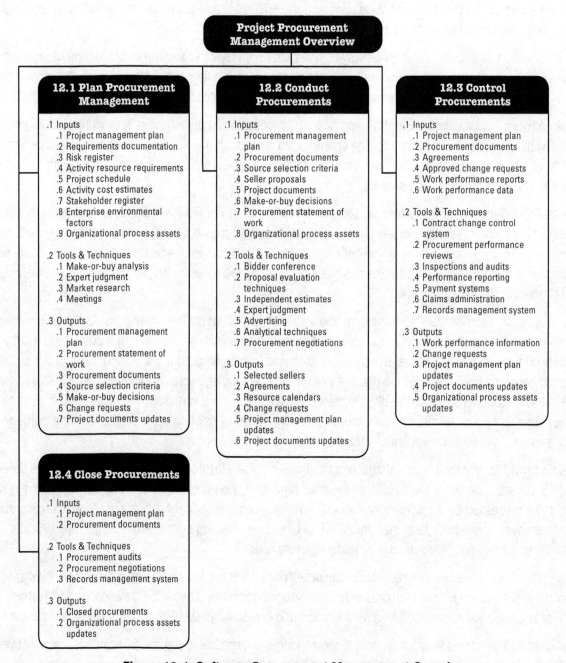

Figure 12-1. Software Procurement Management Overview

12.1 Plan Procurement Management

The inputs, tools and techniques, and outputs in Section 12.1 of the *PMBOK® Guide* are applicable for planning software procurement management.

12.1.1 Plan Procurement Management: Inputs

The inputs in Section 12.1.1 of the *PMBOK® Guide* are applicable for planning software procurement management.

12.1.1.1 Project Management Plan

See Section 12.1.1.1 of the *PMBOK® Guide*.

12.1.1.2 Requirements Documentation

See Section 12.1.1.2 of the *PMBOK® Guide*.

12.1.1.3 Risk Register

See Section 12.1.1.3 of the *PMBOK® Guide*.

12.1.1.4 Activity Resource Requirements

See Section 12.1.1.4 of the *PMBOK® Guide*.

12.1.1.5 Project Schedule

See Section 12.1.1.5 of the *PMBOK® Guide*.

12.1.1.6 Activity Cost Estimates

See Section 12.1.1.6 of the *PMBOK® Guide*.

12.1.1.7 Stakeholder Register

See Section 12.1.1.7 of the *PMBOK® Guide*.

12.1.1.8 Enterprise Environmental Factors

See Section 12.1.1.8 of the *PMBOK® Guide*.

12.1.1.9 Organizational Process Assets

See Section 12.1.1.9 of the *PMBOK® Guide*.

12

12.1.2 Plan Procurement Management: Tools and Techniques

The tools and techniques in Section 12.1.2 of the *PMBOK® Guide* are applicable for planning software procurement management, with the following modifications and extensions.

The first step in planning for software procurement is making the decision that a software product or service needs to be acquired. The organization may perform a business case analysis, trade study, or market survey of available capabilities, or conduct a needs assessment or a make-or-buy study to determine whether the best way to meet a resource need is to acquire a software product or service (see Section 12.1.2.1 of the *PMBOK® Guide*). It is a good practice to document the alternatives considered before proceeding with procurement and to communicate the procurement strategy to the project stakeholders.

- **Identifying suppliers**. Bidders' conferences with potential suppliers are often conducted as part of the initial market survey. Architectural and technical decisions may severely limit the options for potential suppliers, since the supplier should have experience with the intended software environment. Procuring infrastructure such as an operating system, middleware, or a common development environment will drive how custom software capabilities are created. Conversely, the architecture of the software product needs to provide the necessary organization, infrastructure, and interfaces to enable integration of special functionality, application support, or utility software that may be procured. Suppliers competent to handle these issues should be identified.

- **Statement of objective or statement of work.** The choice of how to specify requirements for procurement depends on the scope, impact, and audience affected by the software or service, as indicated in Figure 12-2.

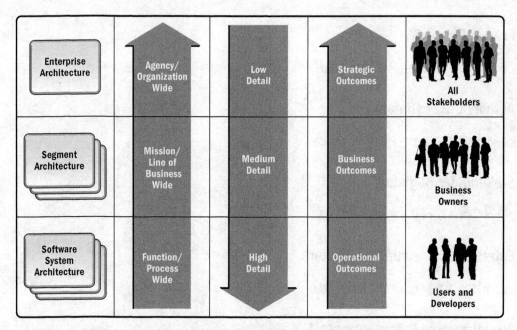

Figure 12-2. Level of Detail for Software/Service Acquisition Requirements

In all cases, the acquirer needs to specifically identify the required deliverables. A statement of objectives (SOO) is often used in performance-based contracting, where the acquirer indicates the results to be achieved, leaving the supplier to determine the processes, tools, and resources needed to deliver the service or product.

Detailed requirements statements for software procurements can be complex. Over-specification may lead to higher than necessary procurement costs when most of the needed features are available in one or more commercially available off-the-shelf software packages (COTS). However, without the essential features identified, the likelihood of the software meeting the needs is greatly reduced. Requirements may also include a list of the standards or specifications to which the system or service is required to conform. Lack of a detailed requirements statement at the onset of a project often leads to an adaptive strategy in which only a few outcomes or scenarios are specified to get an acquisition project started.

A statement of work (SOW) itemizes the details of the work to be performed in a software acquisition. A SOW for software procurement typically includes the scope of contractual obligations for the contracted (i.e., bespoke) software. It should include management requirements as well as technical requirements. Management requirements may include status reporting schedule, metrics to be reported, requests for participation in meetings and reviews, and early delivery of product subset capabilities, when desired. A SOW is often appropriate for time-and-effort support. (Section 12.1.3.2 of the *PMBOK® Guide* provides additional details concerning the Procurement SOW.)

- **Establishing proposal evaluation criteria.** Criteria for evaluating procurement proposals submitted by potential suppliers (i.e., bidders) should include the supplier's specific technical capabilities, management approach, experience, and cost factors. The evaluation criteria should explain how the various factors will be weighted and evaluated. Usually, cost is not the most important factor in selecting a software or service provider, and within the cost factors, the initial cost is less important than the total cost over the project or product life cycle.

  The acquiring project manager also needs to define the acceptance criteria or performance standard for the product or service to be provided. Acceptance criteria for custom software may include successful completion of acceptance testing by the users, or after installation and successful operation in the production environment.

- **Preparing terms and conditions.** Terms and conditions provide the details on how, where, and when the software product or service will be delivered. The supplier may have a preferred set of contract conditions related to cost, schedule, capabilities, maintenance, contract type, intellectual property rights, and data rights; the acquirer may also have a preferred set of contract conditions, which may be different from those of the supplier. Therefore, it is critical that the software project manager participate in the development of the terms and understand their impact.

  Determining the appropriate licensing approach (ownership of intellectual property and data rights) is critical in nearly all software procurements. Specifics as to who owns the product, noncompete clauses, warranties, and data management are a few of the issues to be resolved. It is important to objectively identify the acquirer's needs for licensing rights and to determine the appropriate kind of license. The acquirer may develop a licensing strategy for computer software and require the vendor to provide a

12

list of software products that have restrictions not explicitly stated in their commercial agreements. The licensing strategy should address four questions:

- o Who needs to use the product, to modify it, and to what extent?

- o What restrictions apply to accessing the supplied software by computer workstations and central processing units?

- o What restrictions apply to transferring and/or sharing the supplied software to other parts of the acquirer's organization?

- o Are there plans to incorporate the supplied software into the acquirer's products?

The acquiring project or organization should be aware of the license terms and conditions for open-source software. For example, some widely used open-source licenses require that any product developed using the software will be freely open source as well, or may be free for personal use but chargeable for commercial use. Such open-source license terms may be undesirable when the acquirer intends to own the derived software and to sell it as part of a product.

Terms and conditions should include the type of contract, payment schedule, and expected period of performance. Since the acquired product or service needs to arrive in time for the overall project schedule, the software project manager should understand and account for the schedule risk associated with delivery of custom-built (bespoke) software by allowing a significant margin in the time for acquired software to be integrated with project-developed software.

12.1.2.1 Make-or-Buy Analysis

See Section 12.1.2.1 of the *PMBOK® Guide*.

12.1.2.2 Expert Judgment

See Section 12.1.2.2 of the *PMBOK® Guide*.

12.1.2.3 Market Research

See Section 12.1.2.3 of the *PMBOK® Guide*.

12.1.2.4 Meetings

See Section 12.1.2.4 of the *PMBOK® Guide*.

12.1.3 Plan Procurement Management: Outputs

The outputs in Section 12.1.3 of the *PMBOK® Guide* are applicable outputs for planning software procurement management, as indicated below.

Once the decision is made to procure software or service, the organization needs a procurement strategy. Depending on the scope and criticality of the procurement, a formal plan and schedule milestones may be developed.

Outputs from planning software procurement management include: (a) a list of potential suppliers, (b) technical and managerial requirements, (c) a statement of objectives or statement of work, (d) evaluation criteria, (e) preferred terms and conditions, and (f) a request for proposals or request for tender.

A request for proposal (RFP) provides the necessary information to potential suppliers. It includes the technical requirements (SOO or SOW), the terms and conditions, the evaluation criteria for the proposal and the delivered software product, and instructions for bidders. The instructions explain what information should be included in the proposal, the anticipated procurement schedule, and the anticipated start date and period of performance. Instructions often specify a maximum length for the proposal and the required structure of the proposal, so responses can be more easily compared. Software proposal instructions commonly require that proposals contain information needed to evaluate a bidder's capabilities and stability, such as descriptions of related projects, customer references, information on the qualifications of key personnel and staff certifications, and descriptions of facilities and technical resources.

12.1.3.1 Procurement Management Plan

See Section 12.1.3.1 of the *PMBOK® Guide*.

12.1.3.2 Procurement Statement of Work

See Section 12.1.3.2 of the *PMBOK® Guide*.

12.1.3.3 Procurement Documents

See Section 12.1.3.3 of the *PMBOK® Guide*.

12.1.3.4 Source Selection Criteria

See Section 12.1.3.4 of the *PMBOK® Guide*.

12.1.3.5 Make-or-Buy Decisions

See Section 12.1.3.5 of the *PMBOK® Guide*.

12.1.3.6 Change Requests

See Section 12.1.3.6 of the *PMBOK® Guide*.

12.1.3.7 Project Documents Updates

See Section 12.1.3.7 of the *PMBOK® Guide*.

12.2 Conduct Procurements

Section 12.2 of the *PMBOK® Guide* indicates that the primary activities in software project procurement include providing the procurement package to potential suppliers and communicating with them, receiving and evaluating offers, making a preliminary selection of one or more suppliers, and negotiating the agreement with the selected supplier.

For commercially available software packages, price can be the primary determinant, but the lowest proposed price may not be the lowest cost should the seller prove to be unable to deliver the products, services, or results in a timely and technically acceptable manner. Evaluations of suppliers should consider the supplier's project management practices and organizational stability; the risk of supplier default should be evaluated. One way of controlling risk is to add a contract provision for placing the source code into escrow, in the event of a contract dispute or dissolution of the supplier's organization.

On reviewing the proposals, the acquirer may determine that the best choice for the project may be to modify the SOO or SOW. Changes between the RFP requirements and the final agreement may be negotiated to support such considerations as affordability, timely completion of a basic set of delivered software features, provision of named key personnel who be involved in performance of the work, reduced risk, alignment of the supplier's schedule with the project's master schedule, or additional tasks or functions and future upgrades. Negotiations may also address topics such as product acceptance, reporting, cost, usage, intellectual property rights, and data rights.

12.2.1 Conduct Procurements: Inputs

The inputs in Section 12.2.1 of the *PMBOK® Guide* are applicable inputs for conducting software procurements.

12.2.1.1 Procurement Management Plan

See Section 12.2.1.1 of the *PMBOK® Guide*.

12.2.1.2 Procurement Documents

See Section 12.2.1.2 of the *PMBOK® Guide*.

12.2.1.3 Source Selection Criteria

See Section 12.2.1.3 of the *PMBOK® Guide*.

12.2.1.4 Seller Proposals

See Section 12.2.1.4 of the *PMBOK® Guide*.

12.2.1.5 Project Documents

See Section 12.2.1.5 of the *PMBOK® Guide*.

12.2.1.6 Make-or-Buy Decisions

See Section 12.2.1.6 of the *PMBOK® Guide*.

12.2.1.7 Procurement Statement of Work

See Section 12.2.1.7 of the *PMBOK® Guide*.

12.2.1.8 Organizational Process Assets

See Section 12.2.1.8 of the *PMBOK® Guide*.

12.2.2 Conduct Procurements: Tools and Techniques

The tools and techniques in Section 12.2.2 of the *PMBOK® Guide* are applicable for conducting software procurements.

12.2.2.1 Bidder Conferences

See Section 12.2.2.1 of the *PMBOK® Guide*.

12.2.2.2 Proposal Evaluation Techniques

See Section 12.2.2.2 of the *PMBOK® Guide*.

12.2.2.3 Independent Estimates

See Section 12.2.2.3 of the *PMBOK® Guide*.

12.2.2.4 Expert Judgment

See Section 12.2.2.4 of the *PMBOK® Guide*.

12.2.2.5 Advertising

See Section 12.2.2.5 of the *PMBOK® Guide*.

12.2.2.6 Analytical Techniques

See Section 12.2.2.6 of the *PMBOK® Guide*.

12.2.2.7 Procurement Negotiations

See Section 12.2.2.7 of the *PMBOK® Guide*.

12.2.3 Conduct Procurements: Outputs

The outputs in Section 12.2.3 of the *PMBOK® Guide* are applicable outputs from conducting software procurements.

12.2.3.1 Selected Sellers

See Section 12.2.3.1 of the *PMBOK® Guide*.

12.2.3.2 Agreements

See Section 12.2.3.2 of the *PMBOK® Guide*.

12.2.3.3 Resource Calendars

See Section 12.2.3.3 of the *PMBOK® Guide*.

12.2.3.4 Change Requests

See Section 12.2.3.4 of the *PMBOK® Guide*.

12.2.3.5 Project Management Plan Updates

See Section 12.2.3.5 of the *PMBOK® Guide*.

12.2.3.6 Project Documents Updates

See Section 12.2.3.6 of the *PMBOK® Guide*.

12.3 Control Procurements

In addition to the issues addressed in Section 12.3 of the *PMBOK® Guide*, the following considerations apply to procurement of commercially off-the-shelf (COTS) and free open source software.

Because COTS and free open source software products often have frequent release cycles and security updates, staying current requires an ongoing expenditure of resources to install and maintain current versions.

It is also helpful to be aware of the likely evolution and life expectancy of a COTS or open source software product. The software provider may discontinue support of a product, and support from third parties or the open source community may vary or be unavailable.

12.3.1 Control Procurements: Inputs

The inputs in Section 12.3.1 of the *PMBOK® Guide* are applicable for controlling software procurements.

12.3.1.1 Project Management Plan

See Section 12.3.1.1 of the *PMBOK® Guide*.

12.3.1.2 Procurement Documents

See Section 12.3.1.2 of the *PMBOK® Guide*.

12.3.1.3 Agreements

See Section 12.3.1.3 of the *PMBOK® Guide*.

12.3.1.4 Approved Change Requests

See Section 12.3.1.4 of the *PMBOK® Guide*.

12.3.1.5 Work Performance Reports

See Section 12.3.1.5 of the *PMBOK® Guide*.

12.3.1.6 Work Performance Data

See Section 12.3.1.6 of the *PMBOK® Guide*.

12.3.2 Control Procurements: Tools and Techniques

The tools and techniques in Section 12.3.2 of the *PMBOK® Guide* are applicable for controlling software procurements.

12.3.2.1 Contract Change Control System

See Section 12.3.2.1 of the *PMBOK® Guide*.

12.3.2.2 Procurement Performance Reviews

See Section 12.3.2.2 of the *PMBOK® Guide*.

12.3.2.3 Inspections and Audits

See Section 12.3.2.3 of the *PMBOK® Guide*.

12.3.2.4 Performance Reporting

See Section 12.3.2.4 of the *PMBOK® Guide*.

12.3.2.5 Payment Systems

See Section 12.3.2.5 of the *PMBOK® Guide*.

12.3.2.6 Claims Administration

See Section 12.3.2.6 of the *PMBOK® Guide*.

12.3.2.7 Records Management System

See Section 12.3.2.7 of the *PMBOK® Guide*.

12.3.3 Control Procurements: Outputs

The outputs in Section 12.3.3 of the *PMBOK® Guide* are applicable for controlling software procurements.

12.3.3.1 Work Performance Information

See Section 12.3.3.1 of the *PMBOK® Guide*.

12.3.3.2 Change Requests

See Section 12.3.3.2 of the *PMBOK® Guide*.

12.3.3.3 Project Management Plan Updates

See Section 12.3.3.3 of the *PMBOK® Guide*.

12.3.3.4 Project Documents Updates

See Section 12.3.3.4 of the *PMBOK® Guide*.

12.3.3.5 Organizational Process Assets Updates

See Section 12.3.3.5 of the *PMBOK® Guide*.

12.4 Close Procurements

The considerations for closing software procurements in Section 12.4 of the *PMBOK® Guide* are applicable for closing software procurements, with the following extensions.

While a software procurement activity usually ends before the software project ends, the need for the acquired service or software product may continue. Closing one procurement activity may signal the need to open another for ongoing maintenance. Another consideration is long-term relevance of the technology and the ability of the supplier to support technical change over time. When a software project manager plans to integrate a COTS product or custom-built software into their product, the project manager needs to be aware that the technology used to develop the COTS product or custom-built software could adversely affect the ability to make product enhancements in the future.

12.4.1 Close Procurements: Inputs

The inputs in Section 12.4.1 of the *PMBOK® Guide* are applicable inputs for closing software procurements.

12.4.1.1 Project Management Plan

See Section 12.4.1.1 of the *PMBOK® Guide*

12.4.1.2 Procurement Documents

See Section 12.4.1.2 of the *PMBOK® Guide*

12.4.2 Close Procurements: Tools and Techniques

The tools and techniques in Section 12.4.2 of the *PMBOK® Guide* are applicable for closing software procurements.

12.4.2.1 Procurement Audits

See Section 12.4.2.1 of the *PMBOK® Guide*.

12.4.2.2 Procurement Negotiations

See Section 12.4.2.2 of the *PMBOK® Guide.*

12.4.2.3 Records Management System

See Section 12.4.2.3 of the *PMBOK® Guide.*

12.4.3 Close Procurements: Outputs

The outputs in Section 12.4.3 of the *PMBOK® Guide* are applicable outputs from closing software procurements.

12.4.3.1 Closed Procurements

See Section 12.4.3.1 of the *PMBOK® Guide.*

12.4.3.2 Organizational Process Assets Updates

See Section 12.4.3.2 of the *PMBOK® Guide.*

13

PROJECT STAKEHOLDER MANAGEMENT

Most of the material in Section 13 of the *PMBOK® Guide* is applicable to stakeholder management for software projects. This section of the *Software Extension to the PMBOK® Guide* presents additional considerations for managing software project stakeholders.

The introduction to Section 13 of the *PMBOK® Guide* states: "Project Stakeholder Management includes the processes required to identify all people or organizations impacted by the project, analyzing stakeholder expectations and impact on the project, and developing appropriate management strategies for effectively engaging stakeholders in project decisions and execution.

The introduction to Section 13 of the *PMBOK® Guide* also states that stakeholder satisfaction should be managed as a key project deliverable.

Figure 13-1 provides an overview of Software Project Stakeholder Management.

Stakeholder management is critical for achieving successful outcomes for software projects because software is an intangible product and is often novel. Software is difficult to visualize until it is demonstrated. In addition, there often exists a gulf of expectation between what a customer or product owner states and what the developer interprets. Misalignments among stakeholders represent a major risk for successful completion of software projects.

As illustrated in Figure 13-2, predictive life cycle software projects have high stakeholder involvement at the beginning of the project when plans and requirements are being developed and at key milestone reviews, such as requirement, design and test reviews, as well as at product acceptance. Predictive software projects can increase stakeholder involvement by constructing the software in increments that are periodically demonstrated. Adaptive life cycle software projects include frequent demonstrations of evolving increments of deliverable software for the customer and other stakeholders, thus maintaining product visibility and frequent stakeholder engagement throughout the duration of a software project.

13.1 Identify Stakeholders

The material in Section 13.1 of the *PMBOK® Guide* is applicable to identifying stakeholders for software projects.

Software project stakeholders can be internal or external to the organization, and may include software maintenance and IT support personnel. In identifying stakeholders, it is important to consider their geographic location, time zone, and cultural backgrounds.

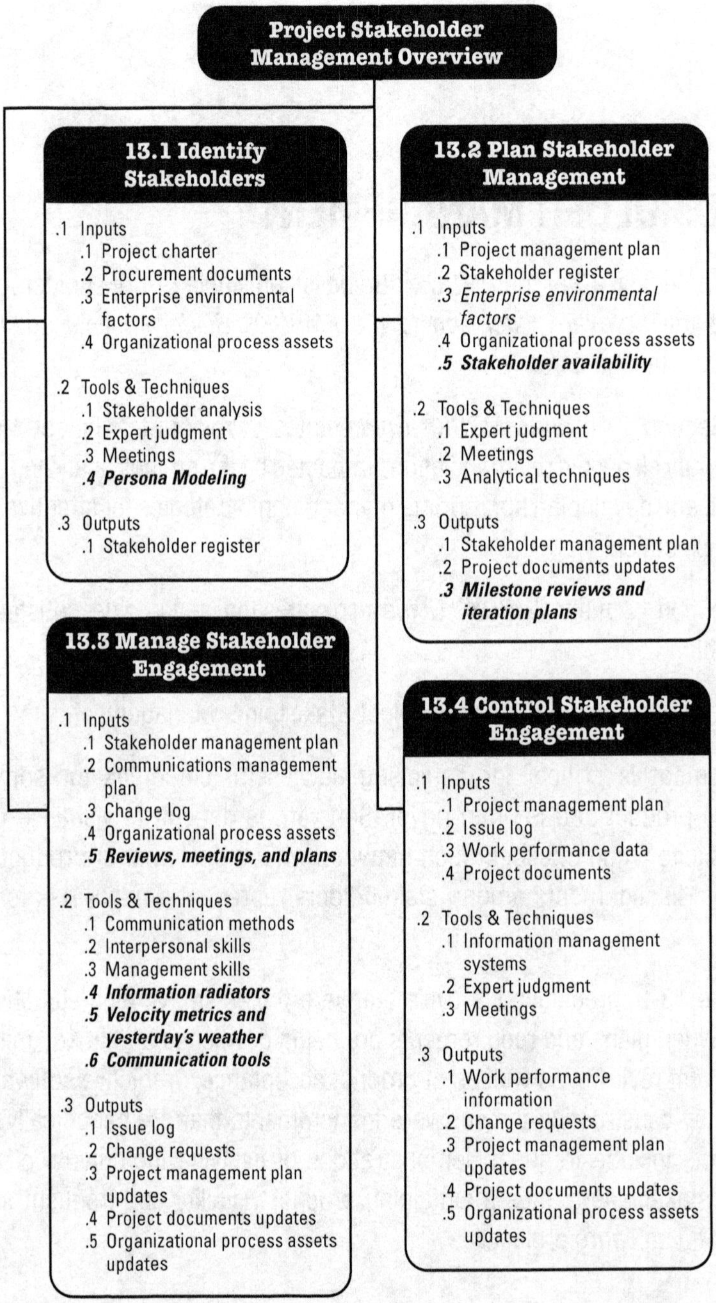

Project Stakeholder Management Overview

13.1 Identify Stakeholders

.1 Inputs
  .1 Project charter
  .2 Procurement documents
  .3 Enterprise environmental factors
  .4 Organizational process assets

.2 Tools & Techniques
  .1 Stakeholder analysis
  .2 Expert judgment
  .3 Meetings
  .4 Persona Modeling

.3 Outputs
  .1 Stakeholder register

13.2 Plan Stakeholder Management

.1 Inputs
  .1 Project management plan
  .2 Stakeholder register
  .3 Enterprise environmental factors
  .4 Organizational process assets
  .5 Stakeholder availability

.2 Tools & Techniques
  .1 Expert judgment
  .2 Meetings
  .3 Analytical techniques

.3 Outputs
  .1 Stakeholder management plan
  .2 Project documents updates
  .3 Milestone reviews and iteration plans

13.3 Manage Stakeholder Engagement

.1 Inputs
  .1 Stakeholder management plan
  .2 Communications management plan
  .3 Change log
  .4 Organizational process assets
  .5 Reviews, meetings, and plans

.2 Tools & Techniques
  .1 Communication methods
  .2 Interpersonal skills
  .3 Management skills
  .4 Information radiators
  .5 Velocity metrics and yesterday's weather
  .6 Communication tools

.3 Outputs
  .1 Issue log
  .2 Change requests
  .3 Project management plan updates
  .4 Project documents updates
  .5 Organizational process assets updates

13.4 Control Stakeholder Engagement

.1 Inputs
  .1 Project management plan
  .2 Issue log
  .3 Work performance data
  .4 Project documents

.2 Tools & Techniques
  .1 Information management systems
  .2 Expert judgment
  .3 Meetings

.3 Outputs
  .1 Work performance information
  .2 Change requests
  .3 Project management plan updates
  .4 Project documents updates
  .5 Organizational process assets updates

Figure 13-1. Software Project Stakeholder Management Overview

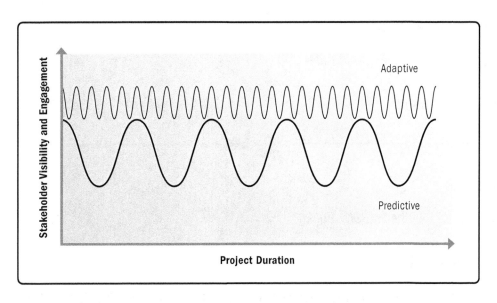

Figure 13-2. Product Visibility and Stakeholder Engagement

13.1.1 Identify Stakeholders: Inputs

The inputs in Section 13.1.1 of the *PMBOK® Guide* are applicable inputs for identifying software project stakeholders.

13.1.1.1 Project Charter

See Section 13.1.1.1 of the *PMBOK® Guide*.

13.1.1.2 Procurement Documents

See Section 13.1.1.2 of the *PMBOK® Guide*.

13.1.1.3 Enterprise Environmental Factors

See Section 13.1.1.3 of the *PMBOK® Guide*.

13.1.1.4 Organizational Process Assets

See Section 13.1.1.4 of the *PMBOK® Guide*.

13.1.2 Identify Stakeholders: Tools and Techniques

The tools and techniques in Section 13.1.2 of the *PMBOK® Guide* are applicable for identifying software project stakeholders. Section 13.1.2.4 provides an additional technique for identifying software project stakeholders.

13.1.2.1 Stakeholder Analysis

See Section 13.1.2.1 of the *PMBOK® Guide*.

13.1.2.2 Expert Judgment

See Section 13.1.2.2 of the *PMBOK® Guide*.

13.1.2.3 Meetings

See Section 13.1.2.3 of the *PMBOK® Guide*.

13.1.2.4 Persona Modeling

Software project teams sometimes use persona modeling to identify and analyze project stakeholders. Personas are summaries of key stakeholders and their interests. They have the following characteristics: an archetypal description, grounded in reality; goal-orientation; specific and relevant; and tangible and actionable. Personas are not replacements for requirements but instead augment and support prioritization of the requirements. Personas provide insight by providing focus, understanding, and empathy for the users of a system. Personas may be composites based on real people or research data; care should be taken to protect sensitive personal information. An example of persona modeling is illustrated in Figure 13-3.

Persona attributes may include goals, influencers, questions, and frustrations and pain points in addition to knowledge, activities, and interest. These attributes can be tailored to software projects to provide a basis for stakeholder analysis.

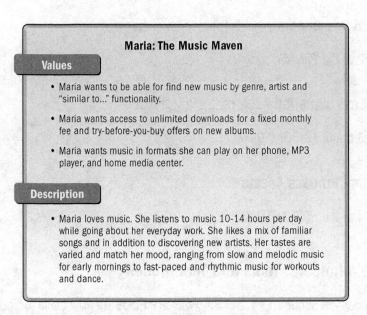

Figure 13-3. Persona Modeling

Persona modeling can be used as an aid to developing product requirements during the initiation and planning phases of a predictive life cycle software project and throughout the iteration cycles an adaptive life cycle software project.

Persona modeling supports better decision making by keeping a team focused on delivery of value-adding requirements and product features. Teams can shorten discussions by referencing personas that team members are familiar with to settle issues of needs, wants, and exclusions.

13.1.3 Identify Software Project Stakeholders: Outputs

The output in Section 13.1.3 of the *PMBOK® Guide*, is applicable for identifying software project stakeholders.

13.1.3.1 Stakeholder Register

See Section 13.1.3.1 of the *PMBOK® Guide*.

13.2 Plan Stakeholder Management

As stated in the introduction to Section 13 of the *PMBOK® Guide,* stakeholder management also focuses on continuous dialogue with stakeholders to meet their needs and expectations, addressing issues as they occur, and fostering appropriate stakeholder engagement in project decisions and activities.

For software projects, it is especially important to plan for frequent involvement of customers, product owners, and other key stakeholders to provide validation that the project is progressing towards the desired goal and that the evolving product is suitable, because software functionality and behavior are difficult to assess until demonstrated. The acronym IKIWISI (I'll Know It When I See It) is often used to describe this issue and highlights the need for frequent demonstrations to fine-tune required (and desired) functionality and behavior of the evolving software. Because of the opportunity for divergent expectations among external stakeholders and project team members, software project managers should plan for software demonstrations in timeframes of weeks rather than months whenever possible.

13.2.1 Plan Stakeholder Management: Inputs

The inputs in Section 13.2.1 of the *PMBOK® Guide* are applicable for planning stakeholder management for software projects, with the modification of Section 13.2.1.3 and the additional input for identifying software project stakeholders provided in 13.2.1.5.

13.2.1.1 Project Management Plan

See Section 13.2.1.1 of the *PMBOK® Guide*.

13.2.1.2 Stakeholder Register

See Section 13.2.1.2 of the *PMBOK® Guide*.

13.2.1.3 Enterprise Environmental Factors

Bureaucracy, office politics, and personal dynamics lead to inefficiencies in decision making and are unavoidable inputs to stakeholder management. Although these factors are present in all business situations, these issues are typically exposed early in software projects that use adaptive project life cycles because the project manager and the team members interact closely with project stakeholders. These issues may take longer to surface and resolve when using a predictive software project life cycle because interactions between the project and external stakeholders typically occur on a less frequent basis.

13.2.1.4 Organizational Process Assets

See Section 13.2.1.4 of the *PMBOK® Guide*.

13.2.1.5 Stakeholder Availability

Adaptive software projects typically plan for customer involvement on a daily, weekly, or monthly basis depending on the adaptive life cycle used. Software projects that have limited access to external stakeholders to view demonstrations of product increments and review progress will likely plan to produce product increments on a monthly basis. Projects with better access to stakeholders can plan to produce increments more frequently; perhaps on weekly or biweekly cycles. Other factors that may influence the frequency of increment production include sharing of resources with slow cadence projects and the software processes and tools used to release software to a test environment.

Predictive life cycle projects should plan for inputs from the customer and other stakeholders as frequently as possible. Although major milestones may be infrequent for a large predictive software project, technical interchange meetings can be arranged to discuss technical and managerial issues, review progress, view prototypes, and evaluate product increments more frequently.

13.2.2 Plan Stakeholder Management: Tools and Techniques

The tools and techniques in Section 13.2.2 of the *PMBOK® Guide* are applicable for planning software project stakeholder management.

13.2.2.1 Expert Judgment

See Section 13.2.2.1 of the *PMBOK® Guide*.

13.2.2.2 Meetings

See Section 13.2.2.2 of the *PMBOK® Guide*.

13.2.2.3 Analytical Techniques

See Section 13.2.2.3 of the *PMBOK® Guide*.

13.2.3 Plan Stakeholder Management: Outputs

The outputs in Section 13.2.3 of the *PMBOK® Guide* are applicable outputs for planning software project stakeholder management. In addition, Section 13.2.3.3 is applicable to planning software project stakeholder management.

13.2.3.1 Stakeholder Management Plan

See Section 13.2.3.1 of the *PMBOK® Guide*.

13.2.3.2 Project Documents Updates

See Section 13.2.3.2 of the *PMBOK® Guide*.

13.2.3.3 Milestone Reviews and Iteration Plans

For predictive life cycle software projects, plans for the number, frequency and kind of milestone reviews (and technical interchange meetings) that will involve project stakeholders should be included as an output of planning stakeholder management. For adaptive life cycle software projects, plans for the retrospective meetings and planning meetings that occur at the end of an iteration cycle and the start of the next one, which involves project stakeholders, should be included as an output of planning stakeholder management.

13.3 Manage Stakeholder Engagement

The inputs, tools and techniques, and outputs for managing stakeholder engagement in Section 13.3 of the *PMBOK® Guide* are applicable for managing software project stakeholders, with the following additional considerations.

In addition, software projects that develop new and unprecedented software products are, or should be, collaborative explorations towards functionally and financially acceptable solutions. This rarely happens by accident and, in most cases, stakeholder engagement is actively managed to ensure that project objectives are stated and met. For adaptive software project life cycles, this takes the form of scheduled demonstrations and user trials of working, deliverable software at the end of selected iterations that produce increments of product capability. For predictive software projects, active engagement of stakeholders involves milestone reviews and technical interchange meetings that can include evaluations of prototypes and demonstrations of product increments.

When receiving feedback from customers, users, and other stakeholders following their evaluation of a prototype or an increment of functionality, it may be tempting to interpret no comments as good news and not as silence concerning issues or problems. Rarely is "no news" from stakeholders considered to be good news, especially early in a software project. Lack of feedback is more likely a sign of insufficient stakeholder involvement. Efforts should be made to ensure that project stakeholders thoroughly evaluate milestone status, prototypes, and incremental versions of the product. When this does not occur, issues and desired changes may be discovered later in the project when the issues are more costly to fix, or it may be too late to incorporate requested changes while maintaining the delivery schedule.

13.3.1 Manage Stakeholder Engagement: Inputs

The inputs for managing project stakeholder engagement in Section 13.3.1 of the *PMBOK® Guide* are applicable for software projects. In addition, the input in Section 13.3.1.5 is applicable for software projects.

13.3.1.1 Stakeholder Management Plan

See Section 13.3.1.1 of the *PMBOK® Guide*.

13.3.1.2 Communications Management Plan

See Section 13.3.1.2 of the *PMBOK® Guide*.

13.3.1.3 Change Log

See Section 13.3.1.3 of the *PMBOK® Guide*.

13.3.1.4 Organizational Process Assets

See Section 13.3.1.4 of the *PMBOK® Guide*.

13.3.1.5 Reviews, Meetings, and Plans

Milestone reviews provide opportunities for stakeholder engagement in predictive life cycle software projects. Periodic technical interface meetings (TIMs) can also be held. For software projects that use adaptive life cycles, iteration plans provide an important input for managing software project stakeholder engagement. These plans provide an initial estimate of what will be included in each iterative demonstration or release of the software. Retrospective meetings during each release demonstration provide the opportunity to dynamically update iteration and release plans.

13.3.2 Manage Stakeholder Engagement: Tools and Techniques

The tools and techniques in Section 13.3.2 of the *PMBOK® Guide* are applicable for managing software project stakeholder engagement. Sections 13.3.2.4 and 13.3.2.5 of this *Software Extension* provide additional considerations software projects.

13.3.2.1 Communication Methods

See Section 13.3.2.1 of the *PMBOK® Guide.*

13.3.2.2 Interpersonal Skills

See Section 13.3.2.2 of the *PMBOK® Guide.*

13.3.2.3 Management Skills

See Section 13.3.2.3 of the *PMBOK® Guide.*

13.3.2.4 Information Radiators

As explained in Section 10 of this *Software Extension*, information radiators are large, graphical displays of the metrics used to report project status. They are frequently updated and located in view of the software project team and other project stakeholders. Commonly used graphs include task boards, burnup and burndown graphs, cumulative flow diagrams, and defect lists. Information radiators can diffuse internal politics and unhealthy competition with project-relevant information. See Section 10 of this *Software Extension* for examples of information radiators.

13.3.2.5 Velocity Metrics and Yesterday's Weather

See Sections 10.2.2.7 and 10.2.2.8 in this *Software Extension* (Velocity Statistics and Yesterday's Weather) for additional tools to manage software project stakeholder engagement.

13.3.2.6 Communication Tools

As discussed in Section 10 of this *Software Extension*, adaptive life cycle models for software projects use a set of communications tools for describing scope, schedule, progress, and risks. These tools include product backlogs, release maps, cumulative flow diagrams, and product burndown graphs, and risk burndown graphs. They provide outputs from managing software project stakeholder engagement.

Predictive software projects use techniques such as earned value reporting, CCB status reports, configuration management reports, and risk registers as tools for communicating project status.

13.3.3 Manage Stakeholder Engagement: Outputs

The outputs for managing stakeholder engagement in Section 13.3.3 of the *PMBOK® Guide* are applicable outputs from managing software project stakeholder engagement. In addition, the output in 13.3.3.6 is an applicable output from managing stakeholder engagement for software projects.

13.3.3.1 Issue Log

See Section 13.3.3.1 of the *PMBOK® Guide*.

13.3.3.2 Change Requests

See Section 13.3.3.2 of the *PMBOK® Guide*.

13.3.3.3 Project Management Plan Updates

See Section 13.3.3.3 of the *PMBOK® Guide*.

13.3.3.4 Project Documents Updates

See Section 13.3.3.4 of the *PMBOK® Guide*.

13.3.3.5 Organizational Process Assets Updates

See Section 13.3.3.5 of the *PMBOK® Guide*.

13.4 Control Stakeholder Engagement

The inputs, tools and techniques, and outputs for controlling project stakeholder engagement in Section 13.4 of the *PMBOK® Guide* are applicable for controlling software project stakeholder engagement. The following considerations also apply.

Controlling stakeholder engagement and expectations is arguably the single most important success factor for any software project manager. Techniques for controlling stakeholder engagement for predictive life cycle software projects include, but are not limited to: including the appropriate stakeholders in milestone reviews, technical interchange meetings, and demonstrations of product increments; using change control requests and change control procedures to handle requested changes; and involving the appropriate stakeholders in decisions on tradeoffs among requirements, schedule, budget, and technology, both initially and on an ongoing basis.

Techniques for managing adaptive life cycle software projects and controlling stakeholder engagement offer some unique challenges as well as unique opportunities. In particular, software project managers and the software team need to engage stakeholders for ongoing participation in the adaptive life cycle model. Customers and other stakeholders need to understand how the project will be managed and the expectations for their involvement. The particular adaptive life cycle that will be used should be explained to the customer and other stakeholders. The software project team also needs to know what is expected of them when interacting with external stakeholders. Obtaining enthusiastic engagement by external stakeholders and by inexperienced project team members can be challenging and time consuming.

For adaptive life cycle projects, it is important that the customer and other decision-making stakeholders understand that they are responsible for feature identification, feature prioritization, and sequencing of software development; that they control what gets worked on; and that they are to be provided with demonstrations of progress and product functionality, which will require their involvement and feedback.

13.4.1 Control Stakeholder Engagement: Inputs

The inputs for controlling project stakeholder engagement in Section 13.4.1 of the *PMBOK® Guide* are applicable for software projects.

13.4.1.1 Project Management Plan

See Section 13.4.1.1 of the *PMBOK® Guide*.

13.4.1.2 Issue Log

See Section 13.4.1.2 of the *PMBOK® Guide*.

13.4.1.3 Work Performance Data

See Section 13.4.1.3 of the *PMBOK® Guide*.

13.4.1.4 Project Documents

See Section 13.4.1.4 of the *PMBOK® Guide*.

13.4.2 Control Stakeholder Engagement: Tools and Techniques

The tools and techniques for controlling stakeholder engagement in Section 13.4.2 of the *PMBOK® Guide* are applicable to controlling software project stakeholder engagement.

13.4.2.1 Information Management Systems

See Section 13.4.2.1 of the *PMBOK® Guide*.

13.4.2.2 Expert Judgment

See Section 13.4.2.2 of the *PMBOK® Guide*.

13.4.2.3 Meetings

See Section 13.4.2.3 of the *PMBOK® Guide*.

13.4.3 Control Stakeholder Engagement: Outputs

The outputs for controlling stakeholder engagement in Section 13.4.3 of the *PMBOK® Guide* are applicable for controlling software project stakeholder engagement.

13.4.3.1 Work Performance Information

See Section 13.4.3.1 of the *PMBOK® Guide*.

13.4.3.2 Change Requests

See Section 13.4.3.2 of the *PMBOK® Guide*.

13.4.3.3 Project Management Plan Updates

See Section 13.4.3.3 of the *PMBOK® Guide*.

13.4.3.4 Project Documents Updates

See Section 13.4.3.4 of the *PMBOK® Guide*.

13.4.3.5 Organizational Process Assets Updates

See Section 13.4.3.5 of the *PMBOK® Guide*.

Appendix X1
Contributors and Reviewers of the *Software Extension to the PMBOK® Guide Fifth Edition*

X1.1 *Software Extension to the PMBOK® Guide Fifth Edition* Core Committee

The following individuals were members of the project Core Committee responsible for drafting the standard, including review and adjudication of reviewer recommendations.

Representing the IEEE Computer Society:

Richard E. ("Dick") Fairley, PhD, CSDP, (Committee Chair)
Philippe Kruchten, PhD, PEng
Kenneth E. Nidiffer, PhD, PMP
Annette Reilly, PhD, PMP
Richard Turner, DSc
Charlene ("Chuck") Walrad, MS, PhD
Kate Guillemette (Product Development Editor, IEEE Computer Society)

Representing the Project Management Institute:

Dennis Stevens, PMI-ACP, CSM, (Committee Vice Chair)
Jesse Fewell, PMP, CST
Mike Griffiths, PMP, PMI-ACP
Krupakar Reddy, PMP, PRINCE2 Practitioner
Cindy Shelton, PMP, PMI-ACP
Karl Best, CAPM, CStd, (PMI Standards Project Specialist)

X1.2 *Software Extension to the PMBOK® Guide Fifth Edition* Subject Matter Expert Reviewers

The following individuals were invited subject matter experts who reviewed the draft and provided recommendations through the SME Review.

Dottie Acton
Karl Andy Anderson, MA, PMP
Ramam Atmakuri, MSc, PMP
Jayaram BG, PMP, MSc
Peter Borsella, PMP, CST
Pieter Botman, PEng, SMIEEE
Mike Burrows, AKT, KCP
Steve Butler MBA PMP
Brenda Byers, ITCP, PMP
Chris Cartwright, MPM, PMP
Arjuna Rao Chavala, MTech, PMP
Jean-Marc Desharnais, MAP
Bob Dombroski, PMP
Mark Henley
Thomas Juli, PhD, PMP
Gargi Keeni
Susan K (Kathy) Land, CSDP
Timothy Lethbridge, PEng, CSDP
Dinesh Mohata, BE, ME
James W. Moore, CSDP, F-IEEE
Dan Rawsthorne
Guy Schleffer MBA PgMP
Udayabharathi Shrivastava
Steve Tockey, MSE, CSDP
Leonel Y. Utiyama, PMP
Ayerite Diepiriye Wayne, MCP, MCSD

X1.3 *Software Extension to the PMBOK® Guide Fifth Edition* Public Exposure Draft Reviewers

The following individuals were volunteers who reviewed the draft and provided recommendations through the Public Exposure Draft Review.

Adeel Ahmad, CAPM
Anuj Ahuja MBA, PMP
Phillip Akinwale
Mohammed Abdullah Al Mamoon, MBA, PMP
Haluk Altunel, PhD, PMP
Anthony P. Amalraj, MBA, PMP
Barnabas Seth Amarteifio, PMP, ITIL
Sorabh Bajaj
Cynthia Balusek, PMP
Krishna Mohan Bandi, PMP
Manuel F. Baquero V., MSc, PMP
Tracy Barnett, PMP
George A. Barnhart
Gianni Basaglia
Jens Berger
Stefan Bertschi, PhD
Arthur E. Bodiker PMP
Pieter Botman, PEng, SMIEEE
Miguel Angel Bureo, PMP
Kelly Bystry, MBA, PMP
Joseph Calinsky
Leonardo Carvalho
Vincent Chiew, PMP, PhD
Marcin Chomicz
Suhasini Cilamkoti
Andrew Coates, PMP
David A. Cohen, PMP, CIPP/US
Sergio Luis Conte, PhD, PMP
Edmundo Reyes Cuellar, CAPM
Teodor Darabaneanu, PMP, CSM
Suranjan Das
P.H. Manjula Deepal De Silva, BSc, PMP

Jason K. Dirnbauer, CAPM, ITIL
R. Bernadine Douglas, MS, PMP
Fedor Dzerzhinskiy, CSDP
Lesa Edwards, MBA, PMP
Gregory Enstrom
Daniel Fenton, PMP
Mohamed Ferawana, PMP, MEM
Daniel Finci, PMP, SCM
Kenneth R. Fisher, PMP, CSM
David Flad
Fam Woon Fong, PMI-RMP, PMP
Ali Forouzesh, PMP, OPM3cc
Jeff Furman, PMP, CTT+
Gerardo A Garavito F, PMP, PMI-ACP
Carl M. Gilbert, PMP, PMI-ACP
Jaswinderpal (Jesse) Gill, PMP
Theofanis Giotis
Garth Glynn, MA(Ed), MBCS
José Rafael Alcalá Gómez, MBA, PMP
Samuel López González de Murillo, PMP, MPM
Juan Carlos González, PMP, ITIL
Kouros Goodarzi, MSc, PMP
Anita Griner
Javier Guadarrama, PMP
Dyi-Shyan Guo, PhD,PMP
Jeffrey Harrell, MBA, PCP
Rahmat Bin Hashim, PMP
Guillermo Gomez Hernandez, CSM, ITILF
Brad Hill, MBA, PMP
Keith D. Hornbacher, MBA
Benjamin Howell, PMP

Gheorghe Hriscu, PMP, CGEIT
Vladimirs Ivanovs, IPMA assessor, ITIL Expert
Can Izgi, PMP
Rajesh Jadhav, PMI-RMP, PgMP
Rebecca Jahelka
Cari Jewell, PMP
Catherine M. Jordan, PMP
Orhan Kalayci, MSc, PMP
Shailesh Kalmegh, PMP, CSP
Katsuichi Kawamitsu, PMP, ITC
Suhail Khaled, PMP
Tarig Ahmed Khalid, PMP, CBAP
Ezz A. Khayyat, PMP
Ian Koenig, PMP
Suja G. Kurian, MS
Thomas M. Kurihara
Abhilash Kuzhikat, PMP, CISA
Arun Lal, PMP
Robert Laudensack, PMP, IPMA
Ronald Lear, Certified SCAMPI HMLA, (CMMI-DEV &
Deborah A. Lemmon, MSSE, PMP
Brian Levy
Yong Li, PMP, CISA
Dimitrios Litsikakis
Giovanni Macchia
Maxime Macron
Shankar Mahadevan, PMP, CIPM
Rama Krishna Mahankali, PMP, CSM
Konstantinos Maliakas, MSc, PMP
Sangu Mangkuppa

Roy Marra, BSc, PMP

Daniel Tadeu Martínez C.
Branco, MBA, PMP

Geevan George Mathew
PMP, CSM

Tanusree McCabe

Robert T. McCann, CSEP, CSDP

Russell A. Meermans, PMP

Yan Bello Méndez, PMP

Gloria J. Miller, MBA, PMP

Haitham K. M. Mokhtar, BSc,
PG Dip

Nathan Mourfield, MHA, PMP

Hemachandran Kutty Krishnan
Nair, PMP, MBA

Venugopal S. Nair, PMP

Abirami Narayanan, PMP

João Armênio Neto, MSc, PMP

Patrick Michael O'Connor, PMP,
PSM I

Venkateswar Panduranga
Oruganti, FIETE, PMP

Michelle Pallas, PMP, CIRM

Luke Panezich, PMP, CSM

Stéphane R. Parent,
PMI-SP, PMP

Homero Méndez Parra, BEE, PMP

Luiz Claudio Parzianello

Mary A. Pignatelli

Jose Angelo Pinto, PMP, OPM3
Certified Trainer

Albert Plunkett

Napoleón Posada, MBA, PMP

Pravin Prabhu, BE, PMP

Sazzad Rafique, PMP, CPHIMS

Manuel Ramírez V., PMP

Armando Rey Ramos

Christopher Richards

Bernard Roduit

Steve Roggenkamp, PE, PMP

Rafael Fernando Ronces Rosas,
PMP, ITIL

Kumar Sadasivan, PMP

Boopalan Saibaba, BE, PMP

Mercedes Martinez Sanz, PMP

Mohammad Sarwat, PMP, RMP

Tejas Sawat, MBA, CAPM

Vidya C. Sekhar, PMP, CISSP

G. Lakshmi Sekhar, BE, PMP

Gururaja Kudli Seshadri, PMP SVC)

Olby Shaju, PMP

C.P. Shameer

Stacey Shearn

Aditya (Shuk) Shukla,
PMI-ACP, PMP

Gustavo Silva

Anand Sivalingam

Maharajan Skandarajah, PMP

Klas Skogmar

Michael Smith

Ravishankar Srinivasan, PMP

Walter Sutterlin, PMP

Rafal Szperlak, PMP

Prashanth Tharakan, MS, PMP

Michael A. Thomas, MS, PMP

Steve Tockey, MSE, CSDP

Atul Tomar, PMP

Mukund Toro, PMP

Biagio Tramontana, Eng, PMP

Konstantin Trunin, PMP

Nikolas Turkowsky

Ebenezer Uy, CSCU

Ravi Valdivia

Sandro Valdivia, PMP

Evan Van Gelder, MBA, PMP

Tom Van Medegael, PMP

Vijay Vemana, MTech, PMP

Mangi Vishnoi, PMP, MAIPM

Poonam Vishnoi, PMGTI, AgileGTI

Atin Wadehra, MBA, PMP

Mark Waller

Daniel Walsh

Dale Walters, CISSP

Luke Waspe, BCom, PMP

Kevin R. Wegryn, MA, PMP

Mary Whitfield

Robin Yeman, PMI-ACP, PMP

X1.4 PMI Standards Member Advisory Group (MAG)

The following individuals are members of the PMI Standards Member Advisory Group, who provided direction to and final approval for the *Software Extension to the PMBOK® Guide Fifth Edition*.

Monique Aubry, PhD, MPM
Margareth Fabiola dos Santos Carneiro, PMP, MSc
Larry Goldsmith, MBA, PMP
Cynthia Snyder, MBA, PMP
Chris Stevens, PhD
Dave Violette, MPM, PMP

X1.5 PMI Consensus Body

The following individuals are members of the PMI Standards Consensus Body, who gave final approval for the *Software Extension to the PMBOK® Guide Fifth Edition*.

Monique Aubry, PhD, MPM
Robert E. Baker, PMP
Nigel Blampied, PE, PMP
Nathalie A. Bohbot, PMP
Dennis L. Bolles, PMP
Margareth Carneiro
Chris Cartwright, MPM, PMP
Charles T. Follin, PMP
Larry Goldsmith, MBA, PMP
Dana J. Goulston, PMP
Dorothy Kangas, PMP
Thomas M. Kurihara
Timothy A. MacFadyen, MBA, PMP
David Christopher Miles, CEng, OPM3
Mike Musial, PMP, CBM
Debbie O'Bray, CIM (Hons)
Nanette Patton, MSBA, PMP
Crispin ("Kik") Piney, BSc, PgMP
Michael Reed, PMP
Chris Richards, PMP
Jen L. Skrabak, MBA, PMP
Carol Steuer, PMP
Chris Stevens

Geree Streun, PMI-ACP, PMP
Matthew Tomlinson, PMP, PgMP
Dave Violette, MPM, PMP
Quynh Woodward, MBA, PMP
John Zlockie, MBA, PMP

X1.6 IEEE Computer Society Board of Governors

The following individuals are members of the IEEE Computer Society Board of Governors who reviewed and gave IEEE CS approval for the *Software Extension*.

Pierre Bourque
Elizabeth Burd
José-Ignacio Castillo-Velázquez
Thomas M. Conte
Ann DeMarle
Hakan Erdogmas
Dennis Frailey
Jean-Luc Gaudiot
Atsuhiro Goto
David Alan Grier
Harold Javid
Hironori Kasahara
Gargi Keeni
Phillip A. Laplante
Fabrizio Lombardi
Cecilia Metra
Dejan S. Milojičić
Paolo Montuschi
Nita Patel
Arnold N. Pears
Jane Chu Prey
Diomidis Spinellis
Charlene "Chuck" Walrad
John W. Walz
Stefano Zanero

X1.7 PMI Standards Harmonization Team

The following individuals are members of the PMI Standards Harmonization Team, who reviewed and provided direction on the harmonization of content between the *PMBOK® Guide* – Fifth Edition, *The Standard for Program Management* – Third Edition, *The Standard for Portfolio Management* – Third Edition, and the *Organizational Project Management Maturity Model (OPM3®)* – Third Edition.

Karl F. Best, CAPM, CStd
Steve Butler, MBA, PMP
Folake Dosunmu, PgMP, OPM3
Randy Holt, MBS, PMP, Chair
Dorothy L. Kangas, PMP
Joseph W. Kestel, PMP
M. Elaine Lazar, AStd, MA
Timothy MacFadyen
Vanina Mangano
David Christopher Miles CEng, OPM3-CC
Eric S. Norman, PMP, PgMP
Michael Reed, PMP
Chris Richards, PMP
Jen L. Skrabak, MBA, PMP
Carol Steuer, PMP
Bobbye S. Underwood, PMI-ACP, PMP
Dave Violette, MPM, PMP
Kristin Vitello, CAPM
Quynh Woodward, MBA, PMP
John Zlockie, MBA, PMP

X1.8 PMI Production Staff

Donn Greenberg, Manager, Publications
Roberta Storer, Product Editor
Barbara Walsh, Publications Production Supervisor

REFERENCES

[1] Project Management Institute. (2013). *A Guide to the Project Management Body of Knowledge (PMBOK® Guide) Fifth Edition.* Newtown Square, PA: Author.

[2] IEEE Standard 24765:2010. Systems and Software Engineering—Vocabulary. Available from http://www.computer.org/sevocab

[3] Project Management Institute. (2012). *PMI Lexicon of Project Management Terms.* Newtown Square, PA: Author. Also available from http://www.pmi.org/lexiconterms

[4] Project Management Institute. *Code of Ethics and Professional Conduct.* Available from http://www.pmi.org/codeofethics

[5] Software Engineering Code of Ethics and Professional Practice. Available from http://www.computer.org/cms/Computer.org/Publications/code-of-ethics.pdf

[6] Association of Information Technology Professionals (AITP) Code of Ethics and Standards of Conduct. Available from http://c.ymcdn.com/sites/www.aitp.org/resource/resmgr/forms/code_of_ethics.pdf

[7] American Society for Information Science and Technology (AIS&T) Professional Guidelines. Available from http://www.asis.org/AboutASIS/professional-guidelines.html

[8] Sackman, H., Erikson, W.J., & Grant, E. E. (1968). Exploratory Experimental Studies Comparing Online And Offline Programming Performance. *Communications of the ACM, 11*(1).

[9] DeMarco, T., & Lister, T. (2013). *Peopleware: Productive Projects and Teams* (3rd Ed.). New York: Dorset House.

[10] IEEE Standard 15288-2004. Adoption of ISO/IEC 15288:2002 Systems Engineering—System Life Cycle Processes.

[11] ISO/IEC/IEEE Standard 12207:2008. Systems and Software Engineering—Software Life Cycle Processes.

[12] SEI. (November 2010). Capability Maturity Model Integrated for Development (CMMI-DEV V1.3). Available from www.sei.cmu.edu/reports/10tr034.pdf

[13] SEI (date). Capability Maturity Model Integrated for Services (CMMI-SVC V1.3). Available from www.sei.cmu.edu/reports/10tr034.pdf

[14] SEI. (November 2010). CMMI for Acquisition (CMMI-ACQ V1.3). Available from www.sei.cmu.edu/reports/10tr032.pdf

[15] SEI (July 2009) People Capability Maturity Model (P-CMM) Version 2.0 (2nd ed). Available from http://www.sei.cmu.edu/reports/09tr003.pdf

[16] Fairley, R., (2009). *Managing and Leading Software Projects,* Wiley, Hoboken, NJ.

[17] Conway, M. (1968). How Do Committees Invent*? Datamation*, April 1968.

[18] ISO/IEC/IEEE 16326:2009. Systems and Software Engineering—Life Cycle Processes—Project Management.

[19] ISO/IEC/IEEE 29148:2011. Systems and Software Engineering—Life Cycle Processes—Requirements Engineering.

[20] IEEE Standard 830-1998. IEEE Recommended Practice for Software Requirements. Specifications.

[21] IEEE Standard 1362-1998. IEEE Guide for Information Technology—System Definition—Concept of Operations (ConOps) Document.

[22] Brooks, F. P., Jr. (1995.) *The Mythical Man-Month.* Anniversary Edition Reading, MA: Addison-Wesley.

[23] IEEE Standard 1028-2008. IEEE Standard for Software Reviews and Audits.

[24] Drucker, P. F. (1999). *Management Challenges for the 21st Century.* New York: HarperCollins Publishers.

[25] ISO/IEC 25000:2005. Software Engineering—Software Product Quality Requirements and Evaluation SQuaRE)—Guide to SQuaRE.

[26] ISO 9241-20:2008. Ergonomics of Human-System Interaction—Part 20: Accessibility Guidelines for Information/Communication Technology (ICT) Equipment and Services.

[27] IEEE Standard 15026-2-2011. Adoption of ISO/IEC TR 15026-2:2011 Systems and Software Engineering—Systems and Software Assurance—Part 2: Assurance Case.

[28] IEEE Standard 1044-2009. IEEE Standard Classification for Software Anomalies.

[29] IEEE Standard 730-2002. IEEE Guide for Software Quality Assurance Plans.

[30] IEEE Standard 829-2008. IEEE Standard for Software and System Test Documentation.

[31] IEEE Standard 1008-1987. IEEE Standard for Software Unit Testing.

[32] IEEE Standard 1012-2012. IEEE Standard for System and Software Verification and Validation.

[33] IEEE Standard 828-2012 IEEE Standard for Configuration Management in Systems and Software Engineering.

[34] Reinertson, D. G. (1997). *Managing The Design Factory*, New York: The Free Press.

[35] Glen, P., Maister, D. H., & Bennis, W. G. (2002). *Leading Geeks: How to Manage and Lead the People Who Deliver Technology.* San Francisco: Jossey-Bass.

[36] McGregor, D. (1960). *The Human Side of Enterprise*. New York: McGraw-Hill.

[37] DeMarco, T., Hruschka, P., Lister, T., McMenamin, S., Robertson, J., & Robertson, S. (2008). *Adrenaline Junkies and Template Zombies: Understanding Patterns of Project Behavior*. New York: Dorset House.

[38] Tuckman, B. (1965). Developmental Sequences in Small Groups. *Psychological Bulletin, 63,* pp. 384–399.

[39] Lencioni, P. M. (2002). *The Five Dysfunctions of a Team: A Leadership Fable*. San Francisco: Jossey-Bass, pp. 188–189.

[40] ISO Guide 73:2009, Risk Management: Vocabulary.

[41] IEEE Standard 16085-2006. IEEE/ISO/IEC 16085:2006 Systems and Software Engineering—Software Life Cycle Processes—Risk Management.

GLOSSARY

This glossary includes terms and definitions not already defined or used in a different sense from the definitions in the glossary of *A Guide to the Project Management Body of Knowledge – Fifth Edition (PMBOK® Guide) Glossary* or in ISO/IEC/IEEE Standard 24765 for Systems and Software Engineering – Vocabulary (SEVOCAB).

Activity-Oriented WBS. A work breakdown structure in which activities and tasks are denoted by verbs that indicate work to be accomplished. Each task name includes the work product or work products to be produced by that task.

Anchor Point. A milestone in software scheduling at which a major project life cycle transition occurs.

Backlog. A set of software features awaiting development in a subsequent iteration.

Burndown. An indicator of the work completed and an estimate of remaining work to be completed or remaining effort needed to complete a product development iteration cycle. Work is measured as all work done to deliver story points, stories, features, functions, function points, user stories, use cases, or requirements during a product development iteration. See also *burnup*.

Burndown Rate. The number of software story points, features, functions, user stories, use cases, or requirements completed per work unit (week or iteration). See *velocity*.

Burnup. An indicator of the number of story points, features, functions, user stories, use cases, or requirements completed and the work remaining or remaining effort needed to complete a product development iteration cycle. Work is measured as all work done to deliver story points, stories, features, functions, function points, user stories, use cases, or requirements during a product development iteration. See *burndown*.

Business Value. A concept that is unique to each organization and includes tangible and intangible elements. Through the effective use of project, program, and portfolio management disciplines, organizations will possess the ability to employ reliable, established processes to meet enterprise objectives and obtain greater business value from their investments.

Cadence. Frequency of performing a periodic activity, such as incremental product release.

Cumulative Flow Diagram (CFD). A chart indicating features completed over time, plus features in development, and those features in the backlog. Optionally, may indicate features at some intermediate milestones, such as features designed but not yet constructed.

Dark Matter. The work missed in the original project plan that is required to complete the deliverable product.

Epic. A high-level or complex user story to be refined into more detailed user stories.

Governance. The process of establishing and enforcing strategic goals and objectives, organizational policies, and performance parameters.

Ideal Time. A best-case estimate of the time needed for a developer or team to complete a task or deliver a feature.

Increment. A tested, deliverable version of a software product that provides new or modified capabilities.

Information Radiator. A large and frequently updated display of project information that is continually visible to the project team and other stakeholders. Examples of information radiators include burndown charts, cumulative flow diagrams, and parking lot diagrams.

Iteration. A systematic repetition of one or more software development activities.

Late Binding. The assignment of tasks to specific resources when the resources are available to start work, rather than when the project is planned.

Modeling. The activity of representing some elements of a process, device, or concept.

On-Demand Scheduling. A scheduling approach in which work is pulled from a backlog according to the perceived value to customers and is assigned as resources become available. See *late binding*.

Parking Lot Diagram. A displayed listing of incomplete tasks or user stories not yet being worked on, in progress, or completed. This listing may be grouped by function with the estimated priority and expected date to start, finish, or dispose of the items. See *information radiator*.

Production Rate. A measure of the amount of work completed per unit of time, such as user stories or features per week. Compare *burndown rate* and *velocity*.

Refactor. To restructure software code without altering its behavior for the purpose of improving quality attributes, easing future extension or adaptation, or adhering to an architectural style.

Release Map. A displayed forecast of when software features will be released and how they will be grouped into releases.

Retrospective Meeting. A team meeting at the end of an iteration cycle or at the end of a software project to reflect on what went well, what was learned, and what should be done differently next time.

Schedule as Independent Variable (SAIV). A date-certain scheduling method for a project with a specific end date, after which the value of a product declines precipitously or a penalty for noncompletion is applied.

Sequence Diagram. A Unified Modeling Language (UML) diagram that depicts time-sequential ordering of interactions, as in a use case scenario of interactions between an actor and some system elements. Can be used to depict sequential and concurrent data flow or process flow.

Software Quality Assurance (SQA). A set of activities that assess adherence to, and the adequacy of the software processes used to develop and modify software products. SQA also determines the degree to which the desired results from software quality control are being obtained.

Software Quality Control (SQC). A set of activities that measure, evaluate, and report on the quality of software project artifacts throughout the project life cycle.

Story Point. The relative measure of the effort needed to develop a user story, compared with what is considered a typical user story by the project team.

Tacit Knowledge. Undocumented information.

Tailoring. Adaptation of a software process by adding, modifying, and deleting process activities that are deemed inapplicable for the project.

Technical Debt. The deferred cost of work not done at an earlier point in the product life cycle.

Theme. User stories associated by a common factor, such as functionality, data source, or security level.

Time-Boxed. Having a prescribed duration limit for a project task.

User Story. A narrative description of a software requirement, function, feature, or quality attribute presented as a narrative of desired user interactions with a software system.

Velocity. The rate of current work unit completion measured as work units completed per fixed time period, such as story points, delivered features, functions, function points, user stories, use cases, or requirements completed in a given time period. Used as a measure of burndown rate or burnup rate.

Virtual Team. A team that is separated by geography or work schedules and that maintains electronic communication.

Workflow Board. In software development, a visual representation of work for developers who pull tasks from the task backlog; used for on-demand or resource-bound scheduling. Also known as kanban board.

Work Unit. A project task such as a constructing or testing a function point, user story, feature, or requirement.

Yesterday's Weather. A report of work performance in the most recent reporting period.

INDEX

A

Acceptance criteria, 95, 152
Acceptance testing, 157
Acquire Project Team, 163, 165–168
    inputs, 165–166
    outputs, 168
    tools and techniques, 166–167
Activity attributes, 95
Activity diagram, 94
Activity lists, 95
Activity-oriented work breakdown structures, 73
    decomposition in, 75
    product scope in, 75
    product structure in, 75, 76
    rolling wave elaboration of, 76–77
Adaptive life cycles, 17, 32–37
    activity sequencing, 97
    agility attributes in, 33
    change control in, 58–59
    communications in, 177, 181, 185
    cost estimating and, 126
    defining scope in, 71–73
    Direct and Manage Project Work processes in, 52
    documentation and, 153
    incremental product planning, 111
    integration and verification processes in, 49
    iteration attributes, 33, 34
    key elements, 35
    metrics, 187
    project manager activities in, 52
    release planning, 66
    requirements in, 67
    risk control, 211–212
    risk management planning, 194–195
    rolling wave planning for, 78
    schedule compression in, 111
    scope control, 83
    scope validation inputs, 80
    special communications tools, 185
    SQA and SQC activities in, 140, 144, 152, 155
    stakeholder involvement, 32, 229, 236, 238–239
    test planning in, 147
    time boxes in, 34
Agile methods, 17, 32–33
Agreements, 47
AIS&T. *See* American Society for Information Science and Technology
AITP. *See* Association of Information Technology Professionals
American Society for Information Science and Technology (AIS&T), 3
Analogous estimating, 128, 130
Analytical techniques, for cost management planning, 123
Analyze defect data, 144
Anchor points, 95
Application software, 1
Architectural constraints, 98
Association for Computing Machinery, 3
Association of Information Technology Professionals (AITP), 3
Automated communication systems, 189
Automated software testing, 142, 157

B

BABOK. *See* Business Analysis Body of Knowledge
Backlogs, 88
    communicating, 188
    feature, 35
    iteration, 35
    prioritized, 108, 188
    reprioritization, 112, 190, 194
Basel-III, 122
Bottom-up estimating, 129
Break-even point, 125
Brooks Law, 110

G

Government regulations, 125, 145
Group decision-making techniques, 81

H

Highly adaptive project life cycles, 26
Highly adaptive software development, 37–38
Highly predictive project life cycles, 26
Histograms, 158–159
Historical productivity data, 60
Historical velocity, 184
Human resource management plan, 164–165

I

Ideal time, 128
Identify Risks, 193, 196–199
   inputs, 196–198
   outputs, 199
   tools and techniques, 198–199
Identify Stakeholders, 229, 230, 231–233
   inputs, 231
   outputs, 233
   tools and techniques, 231
IEEE Computer Society, 3
IEEE Software Engineering Code of Ethics and Professional Practice, 3
IEEE Standard 828, 158
IEEE Standard 829, 151
IEEE Standard 830, 70, 141
IEEE Standard 1008, 151
IEEE Standard 1012, 151
IEEE Standard 1044, 148
IEEE Standard 1362, 70
IEEE Std 1028 - Software Reviews and Audits, 139
Incremental life cycles, 30–32
Incremental product development, 30–32
Incremental product planning, 111
Independent quality audits, 141
Independent verification and validation (IV&V), 98
Information dissemination, 54
Information radiators, 54, 183, 185–186, 237
Information Technology Infrastructure Library (ITIL), 122

Initiating Process Group, 41, 42–43
Inspection, 81, 157
Integrated change control, 46, 58–60
Integration processes, 49
Integration testing, 131, 157
Internal iteration cycles, 35, 36
Internal stakeholders, 23
Interviews, requirements collection, 69
Introspection, 171
ISO Guide 73:2009, 191
ISO/IEC 20000, 122
ISO/IEC 25000, 141, 142
ISO/IEC 27000, 122
ISO/IEC/IEEE Standard 1028, 114
ISO/IEC/IEEE Standard 12207, 21, 27, 92, 114
ISO/IEC/IEEE Standard 15026, 144
ISO/IEC/IEEE Standard 16085, 191, 213
ISO/IEC/IEEE Standard 16326, 21
ISO/IEC/IEEE Standard 24765, 2
Iteration backlog, 35
Iteration cycles, 27
   LOE across, 42
   Process Groups and, 40
   refactoring in, 36
   role switching in, 174
   scope control, 84
Iteration feature set, 35
Iteration plans, 179, 190, 235
Iterative-incremental product development, 32
Iterative life cycles, 30–32
   reprioritization reviews in, 116
   scope in, 73
Iterative scheduling with backlog, 88
ITIL. *See* Information Technology Infrastructure Library
IT projects, 4
IT service transition, 4
IV&V. *See* Independent verification and validation

K

Key performance indicators (KPI), 210
Knowledge Areas, role of, 44
Knowledge-sharing experiences, 20
KPI. *See* Key performance indicators